I0127012

THE MIDLAND SEPTS AND THE PALE

AN ACCOUNT OF THE EARLY SEPTS AND LATER SETTLERS OF THE KING'S COUNTY AND OF LIFE IN THE ENGLISH PALE

F. R. Montgomery Hitchcock, M.A.

Author of "Clement of Alexandria," "Mystery of the Cross," "Suggestions for Bible Study," "Celtic Types of Life and Art," Etc.

HERITAGE BOOKS
2012

HERITAGE BOOKS

AN IMPRINT OF HERITAGE BOOKS, INC.

Books, CDs, and more—Worldwide

For our listing of thousands of titles see our website
at
www.HeritageBooks.com

A Facsimile Reprint
Published 2012 by
HERITAGE BOOKS, INC.
Publishing Division
100 Railroad Ave. #104
Westminster, Maryland 21157

Originally published Dublin 1908

— Publisher's Notice —
In reprints such as this, it is often not possible to remove blemishes from
the original. We feel the contents of this book warrant its reissue despite
these blemishes and hope you will agree and read it with pleasure.

International Standard Book Numbers
Paperbound: 978-0-7884-0901-1
Clothbound: 978-0-7884-9191-7

UXORI BENIGNAE ET BEATAE.

— : o : —

Rapta sinu subito niteas per saecula caeli,
Pars animi major, rerum carissima, conjux.
Mox Deus orbatos iterum conjunget amantes ;
Et laeti mecum pueri duo limina mortis,
Delicias nostras visum, transibimus una.
Tempora te solam nostrae coluere juventae ;
Fulgebit facies ridens mihi sancta relicto
Vivus amor donec laxabit vincula leti.
Interea votum accipias a me mea sponsa libellum.
Gratia mollis enim vultus inspirat amantem,
Mensque benigna trahit, labentem et dextera tollit.
Aegros egregio solata venusta lepore es :
Natis mater eras, mulier gratissima sponso.
Coelicolûm jam adscripta choris fungere labore,
In gremio Christi, semper dilecta, quiescens.
Christus enim servat, servum revocatque Redemptor.
Usque novissima vox mea pectora personat illa.

PREFACE.

THE favourable reception of "Celtic Types of Life and Art" has emboldened the writer to attempt another book on Irish life. This second venture deals principally with the history of the original Irish septs and the later English settlers of the King's County, giving contemporaneous glimpses of the unhappy progress of life in the district known as "The Pale." It will be seen that the story of the settlers makes even greater demands upon the sympathy of the historian than that of the Irish septs of O'Carroll and O'Connor ; and that, while almost every English official propounded his scheme for the settlement of the country, the poet Spenser, for a time private secretary of the Deputy, Lord Grey, fell most completely under the spell of the land, not only writing his "View of the Present State of Ireland," but also wedding an Irish maid and composing the immortal "Faerie Queen" on Irish soil.

Subjects of controversy in religion and politics have again been avoided because of the conviction that there is a common platform on which all Irishmen, however opposed in these matters, may meet to consider the improvement of their country, the promotion of its industry, and the preservation of the annals of its past.

Sources and authorities of importance are given in every instance. In the second chapter a suggestion of the late Mr. T. L. Cooke has been worked out.

The writer expresses his obligations to the publishers, who have spared no expense to make the book a success; to the Rev. J. E. H. Murphy, Professor of Irish in Trinity College, the Rev. M. E. O'Malley, and Mr. E. Fournier D'Albe, B.Sc., his brother-in-law, who have given valuable assistance in the spelling of Irish names; and to his friend, Mr. Thomas Ulick Sadleir, B.L., who has contributed the important Appendix on the King's County families in the eighteenth century.

CONTENTS.

THE

MIDLAND SEPTS AND THE PALE.

INTRODUCTORY CHAPTER.

THE EARLY PEOPLES OF ERIN.

KEATING, in the preface of his History of Ireland,
complains of the manner in which the ancient Irish
have been misrepresented by foreign historians.
Strabo, for instance, declared that the Irish were
cannibals. Solinus asserted that there were no bees
in Ireland—a falsehood rebutted by another foreigner,
Camden, who stated that the multitude of bees is so
great that they are to be found not only in hives, but
also in the hollow places of the trees and ground.
Pomponius Mela represented the Irish as "ignorant
of every virtue." "That ignorant and malicious
writer," Giraldus Cambrensis, stated that the kingdom
paid tribute to King Arthur in A.D. 519, and added
insult to injury by describing the Irish as an inhos-
pitable race (gens inhospita), whereas Stanihurst
testifies to their hospitality in the sentence: "The
Irish are truly the most hospitable men, and you
cannot please them better than by visiting them
frequently and without invitation." Stanihurst himself receives the vials of Keating's wrath for his statement that "the meanest scullion that lives in the
English province would not give his daughter in
marriage to the most noble prince of the Irish"; and

for his uncomplimentary remarks to the Irish language, which he regretted was not expelled with the Irish natives from Fingall, Stanihurst was altogether ignorant of the mellifluous language, and, therefore, was unqualified, in Keating's opinion, to express his views on the subject. Stanihurst went still further, and although, as Keating remarks, he had no notion of music, harmony, or distinction of sound, had the audacity to pronounce the Irish "an unmusical nation." Keating wonders that this second Midas, on whose head Apollo, the God of song, would undoubtedly have fixed the ears of an ass, had not consulted Giraldus Cambrensis, that "inexhaustible fund of falsehood," as he elsewhere describes him, who states in his History: "I find the diligence of that nation praiseworthy in the use of musical instruments, with which they are better provided than any other nation." This testimony to the musical talent of the Ireland of the twelfth century is corroborated by the resemblance that has been discovered between the Irish melodies and the Norse, which must have been familiar to Ireland for some centuries at the time of Giraldus, and by the fame of the ancient Irish harpers. The present writer has heard people say that the Irish peasantry of the present age have no ear for music, and that part singing, which comes naturally to their Welsh brethren, is only learnt with great difficulty by the Celt on this side of the Channel. Be that as it may, there are few nations as susceptible to the charm of sweet sounds, or as subject to the sway of melody; while the Welsh Giraldus praised the Irish melodies of his age for their sweetness, swiftness, and "concordia discors." Then Spenser provokes

Keating's wrath by his audacious attempt to trace the pedigrees of the Irish gentry, and to assert that the MacMahons, who were lineally descended from Colla da Chrioch, son of Eochaidh Doimlén, son of Cairbre Lifeachair, Monarch of Ireland, were of English extraction, and descended from the house of Fitz Urse. Many, too, are the deficiencies of Meredith Hanmer, Doctor of Divinity, and the defects of his *Chronicle*, which commences with laudable precision "three hundred yeeres after the flood." For had he not the hardihood to challenge S. Patrick's right to be called the Apostle of Ireland, and to mention his predecessors Colmán, Declán, Ailbe, Ibar, and Ciarán, and to ascribe the discovery of S. Patrick's Purgatory to another Patrick, an abbot who lived in A.D. 850. But, worst of all, he ventured to deny the Irish origin of our island Hercules, Fionn MacCumhail, and to give him a Danish (Keating wrongly says "British") pedigree.

In a word, all these writers and others, Barclay and Moryson among them, were, according to Keating, utterly devoid of the qualifications required by an historian, and whether "from malice or ignorance" were unfit to essay the task. They seemed to follow the example of the beetle which selects the nastiest thing, rather than that of the bee which chooses the sweetest places to alight upon. They wilfully pass over all that was commendable and noble in Irish life and customs, and "dwell upon the manners of the lower and baser sort of people." Those of us who have read the histories of which Keating complains can not but feel that he had just cause of complaint; and that the worst types of Celtic life were described, while the best were overlooked, simply because the writers were " beetles " not " bees."

But here it to be observed that if the history of Ireland has been drowned by the cold water of its foes, it has been no less buried under the dry dust of its friends, for there can be nothing less stimulating to the eager student than the Irish annals, say those of the Four Masters.   Here a veritable mine of information lies buried beneath a pile of ancient dust, which, like the gravel dust of Europe, contain many treasures for those who can afford the time and means to dig and delve through layers of waste and worthless heaps before they strike the vein of ore.

On the other hand, no one could describe Keating as dull.   There are many entertaining pages in his work, and even if one takes exception to the length and doubtfulness of the pedigrees and legends he records, one cannot but admire his ingenuity.   Is it not refreshing to a tired imagination to be informed that hundreds of years before the Deluge, Ireland was visited by three daughters of Cain, with Seth, the son of Adam or MacAdam, the ancestor, doubtless, of the MacAdams, who gave their name to Cadamstown ? For, as the ancient poet sang :

> The three fair daughters of the cursed Cain,
> With Seth, the son of Adam, first beheld
> The Isle of Banba.

These distinguished dames, one of whom, Banba, gave her name to the island, were followed in remote ages by three strangers, Caffo, Laighne, and Luasat, precisely " twelve months before the Flood." But these unhappy " men of strength and fit for war," who were driven here by a storm, were unfortunately drowned in the Deluge at a place called Tuath Inbhir. But, according to "some records of the kingdom," which Keating mentions "out of respect," the first really historic personage who visited the island was Ceasar, the daughter of Bith, a niece of Noah, but whom the patriarch refused to receive into the Ark. She and some of her companions, whose names have been preserved in the Psalter of Cashel, with due con- sideration for future historians, landed in Connacht. There Bith, Ceasar's husband, died on Sliabh Beatha, now Slieve Beagh, on the borders of Tyrone, where his cairn is shown at Carnmór, near Clones, and Ceasar herself died of grief at Carn Ceasra in Connacht "six days before the rising of the Flood." Camden had, therefore, some ground for his assertion that "the island was not without reason called the ancient Ogygia by Plutarch, for they begin their histories from the most remote memory of antiquity, so that the antiquities of other nations are modern compared with theirs."

Noah's descendants in the order Japhet, Ham, and Shem seem to have been represented by the ancient inhabitants of Eire. Parthalón, a Scythian, with his comrades were of the posterity of Japhet, according to Dr. Meredith Hanmer and Keating. Parthalón, how- ever, who happened to be a parricide, "a boy who killed his father," was followed by the furies from Greece, and he, with all his followers, died of a plague, within the space of a week, at Benn-Eadair, or the Hill of Howth, having possessed the plain of Sean-mhagh- Ealta Edair (Shan-va-alta-edar), or the old plain of the flocks of Edar, which was also called Maghnealta, or Moynalty, the plain of flocks, which lay between

Howth and the Dublin Mountains, or may be the old name of Clontarf, as Professor Murphy suggests, the flocks being the sea-birds. On the Dublin hills near Tallaght there may be to-day sepulchral remains of Partholanus and his band; for Tallaght was known to the Four Masters as Taimhleacht-mhuintire-Phartha-lóin, or the plague-grave of Parthalon's people. In the time of Partholanus, according to Hanmer, " many of the cursed seed of Cham (Ham) arrived on this island with their captain Oceanus, the sonne of Cham, called of some Mena, of Moses Mitzraim." These were of great stature and strength, and after a time engaged in battle with the sons of Japhet, who annihilated them, but, neglecting the burial of the dead, died themselves of the plague which left its name to Tallaght. This was the end of Partholanus, and the country was desolate once more, " excepting a few silly soules scattered in remote places."

Then Nemedius, of Japhet's line, came with his three sons, and partitioned Ireland between them, and in his time, descendants of Shem appeared in the shape of "vagabond Africans." These were quite celebrated people in their way. They rejoiced in the name of Fomhoraigh, which Keating explains as sea-robbers, but which is anglicised into Fomorians. Piracy was their occupation, as it was of the Vikings of a later and more prosaic age. These sea-robbers seemed to have been great builders. Keating tells us that they built two royal seats, one called Cinneich at Ioubhniallain, and the other, Rath Ciombhaoith in Seimhne, for the Nemedians, who rewarded their architects by slaying them, and with Irish irony giving them a burial in *terra firma* at Doire Lighe, or the stone by the oak tree.

It would be of great advantage to us if we could locate these places. There are, however, many localities of the name Cinneich, the head or the hill of the horse, which may appear in Kinnetty as well as in Kineagh, in the south as well as in the north of Ireland. Ioubhniallain may stand for Uibh-Niallain (uibh, abl. case of Ua, grandson, generally written O), and would correspond, therefore, with Hy Niallain, an ancient tribe, who occupied the baronies of O'Neil-land in Armagh. The other place, Raith Ciombhaoith, may well be called after Cimbaoth, one of the famous trio of kings, who agreed to reign for seven years in alternate succession, and who had the good or bad fortune to marry Macha of the golden hair, daughter of Aedh-ruadh, the first of the three Kings, and foundress of Ard-macha or Armagh, and to escape, as far as we can tell, from the servitude to which that determined dame consigned the sons of Dithorba, the third monarch, of whom Tigernach writes. But this may be too venturesome an anticipation. It is, however, quite possible that Ptolemy, the geographer of the second century, refers to the place. For he mentions Isamnion Akron, or the Point of Seimhne (now Island Magee?), in which district the Rath of Cimbaoth was built. Nor is it improbable that one of these "royal seats" was further south. For we are informed by Keating that the first battle which Nemedius fought with the Fomorians after their coming was at Sliabh Bladhma, or the Slieve Bloom Mountains, in which district was the ancient Kinnetty, mentioned in the Felire of Aengus, which resembles

Kinneich, as well as O'Neill's town and O'Neill's well. Accordingly, it is highly probable that Nemedius, if he ever existed, established himself in two royal seats, from one of which he could control the north, and from the other, the south, west, and east of the country. The necessity of this is apparent when we notice how ubiquitous the Fomorians were, the first battle they fought being in the midlands at Sliabh Bladhma, the next in Connacht, the third in Dalriada in Antrim, and the fourth in Leinster. But at last these terrible sea-rovers, who had originally established themselves in an island off the Donegal coast, known as Tory Isle, not, however, from its political aspect, but from its torach, or tower-like, appearance, overwhelmed Nemedius and his people, and gave their name to the Giant's Causeway, which is called in Irish Clochan-na-bhFomharach (Clohan a vowragh) or the stepping-stones of the Fomorians.

After the Fomorians came other invaders, the Firbolgs and Tuatha-de-Danann. One division of the former people landed at Inver Domnainn, the river mouth of the Domnann or Firdomnainn, men of the deep pits, now called Muldowney, which means the whirlpool of the Domnann, and is probably the treacherous channel formed by the sea at Malahide. It is also interesting to note that one of these Firbolg princesses, Eadar, the wife of Gann, one of their five commanders, gave her name to the promontory now called Howth Head (Howth = Head in Danish, cf. German *Haupt*), but which was then styled Benn Eadair, the point of Edar. Ptolemy, the geographer of the second century, mentions a place, Edrou Heremos, or desert of Eder, opposite Eblana, ancient Dublin, which preserves the name of this lady. It is also said to be taken from a Tuatha-De-Danann chief, Eadar, son of Edgaeth. The Firbolgs, according to Keating, were the exiled Nemedians, who had sailed to Greece to escape the tyranny of the Fomorians, and there grew and multiplied until the Grecians rose to oppress them. They then set sail, and safely landed on the Irish shore.

The Firbolgs were divided into three tribes. Their first king was Slainge, and their last was Eochaidh, and for fifty-six years they reigned. Eochaidh, the sixth and last of these, was a good and wise monarch, who sought to restrain the violence of his subjects by making good laws. In his days " peace and plenty cheered the labouring swain." For we read that, " in his time the weather was temperate and healthy, the produce of the earth was not damaged by any immoderate rains, and plenty and prosperity prevailed throughout the whole island." How pleasant must have been the climate of Éire in those days, and how sadly it has altered for the worse ! This king is said to have wedded Taillte, daughter of Magmór, the king of Spain, in whose honour the assembly of Tailltean was instituted by Lewy of the long hand, one of the Tuatha-de-Danann kings. Taillte is said to be buried at Tailte (gen. Tailltenn), now Teltown, in Meath. As for Eochaidh himself, he perished in battle with the three sons of Neimhidh, son of Badhraoi, at Magh Tuiridh, the plain of the tower, to be identified doubtless with Moytura, not far from the interesting village of Cong, which, with the ruins of its noble abbey, stands on the cumhga or isthmus connecting Loughs Corrib and Mask in Galway. Badhraoi is a strange name, and may be connected with the old Irish *Badh-ruadh*, or God of Wind, who corresponded with the Gallic deity *Vintios*, and if so would be an instance of the manner in which pagan pantheons were filled with deified mortals. A short while previous to his death Eochaidh had been routed by the Tuatha-de-Danann under their king, Nuadha of the silver hand (Airgiod lamh). These people are said to have possessed wonderful skill in magical arts, by which they impressed the natives whom they subjugated, and by whom they were practically deified after they in their turn were vanquished by the fierce Milesians. A poem in the Book of Invasions describes by " what charms, what conjuration, what mighty magic " they won the land. One of their powers was to "raise a slaughter'd army from the earth, and make them breathe and fight again." Our chief interest in these cryptic people is centred in the four curious articles which they are said to have brought with them from Denmark, namely the Lia Fail, or stone of destiny, because a very ancient prophecy foretold that, at whatever place the stone should be preserved a person of the Scythian or Scottic race would have the sovereignty ; the sword of Lug (Luighaidh) the Long-handed, the spear of the same warrior, and the cauldron or girdle (coipe) of their deity Daghda. These settlers occupied the land for " a hundred and ninety-seven years," as an ancient poem, preserved in the Psalter of Cashel, states with remarkable precision. Their divinities were many and various, male and female. Keating mentions Badhbha, Macha, and Moriogan, and states that the three Danann princes, Macuill, Maceacht, and Mac Greine, who divided the land between them, were so called from the objects of their worship, Macuill adoring a log of hazel wood (cuill), Maceacht a ploughshare (ceacht), and MacGreine the sun (grian). It is more than likely, however, that these patronymics were given for other reasons. In a manuscript of the Seabright Collection, used by General Vallancey, if we can depend upon him, a list of the inferior Tuatha-de-Danann deities is given. One of these is Eochaid il-dathach. *i.e.*, Dagh-da. Il-dat-hach signifies "many-coloured." Daghda was one of the Danann kings. The point to which attention is here directed is the name Eochaid, which means horseman, and to which we shall return. Suffice it to say here that Eochaidh, or horseman, was the name borne by the last of the Firbolg kings, by princes of the Tuatha-de-Danann, and also by the kings of the Milesians.

The Milesians came to Ireland, according to the "faithful Cormac MacCuillenan in his Psalter of Cashel" (so Keating), about 1,300 years before the birth of Christ; but, according to that "idle writer" and "inexhaustible fund of falsehood," Giraldus Cambrensis, during the reign of Gorgundus, who lived not much more than 350 years before Christ. This is a difference of nearly 1,000 years, a comparatively short term considering the obscure ages of which we are treating.

The Milesians, or Goidels or Celts, came ostensibly to avenge the death of a distant relation, one Ith, commander of the Gadelians, "who was inhumanly slain in defiance of the established laws of nature and of nations" by the three reigning princes of the Tuatha-de-Danann. Ith is said to have discovered the island with an ancient telescope from the pharos of

Brigantia, or more probably to have become acquainted with it in his piratical raids, or through the political relations between the ancient Spaniards and Irish, which had been cemented on more than one occasion by marriage. At all events, Ith, " the son of Breógan, son of Bratna," " son of Magog, son of Japhet, son of Noah, son of Lamech" (Psalter of Cashel), and uncle of Milesius, encountered the three sons of Cearmad, son of Daghdha, kings of the Tuatha-de-Danann, who were quarrelling over some family jewels at a place called Oileach Neid, on the borders of Ulster, and in a charitable, we had almost said Christian, but that would have been a slight anachronism, spirit preached to them an eloquent sermon of peace and goodwill, and induced them to shake hands and be friends. Well had it been for Ith if he had not undertaken the rôle of peacemaker, for the three brothers united their forces against him, and slew him, for all his courage and eloquence, as he was returning to his ship, with a conscience void of offence and a small escort, in Magh Itha. Then Lughaidh, the son of Ith, carried back the dead body of Ith to Spain. The Book of Conquests states that Tor Breógain, the tower of Brigantia, was the place. After having exposed the slain hero's body on the sea shore, in the sympathetic presence of the family of Milesius and the sons of Breógan, the son related the story of his father's " taking-off." The Milesian warriors, standing round the speaker in a grim circle, moved by the sight of their sweet comrade's wounds, "poor, poor dumb mouths," and by the son's "power of speech," felt " the dint of pity." Tears trickled down their iron cheeks; and they expressed their feelings after the manner of their forefather, and vowed to sacrifice the blood of the sons of Cearmad " to the manes of their great-uncle," just as the Gauls of Caesar's time " sacrificed human beings as victims." Their Celtic blood was up, the mischief was afoot. One sympathises, however, with the interesting Tuatha-de-Danann princes wrangling over heirlooms, and losing their kingdom and their beautiful and virtuous princesses, Fodhla and Banba, and Eire, who fell in battle with the Goidil.

The Milesians were a wandering race, who eventually found a resting place in our little island. They are said to have been of Scythian blood and Japhet's noble line. They had, it is said, some intercourse with Moses, but no Irish chronicler gives them a Semitic origin, which fact tells somewhat against the British-Israel theory. From Magog, the son of Japhet, was descended the Scythian ruler, Feinius or Fursa, whose son, Niul, is said to have married Pharoah's daughter, the beautiful Scota. Their son, Gadelus, is the reputed ancestor of the Goidels or Gaels. According to the royal records of Tara, he was attacked and bitten, when a babe, by a serpent, but was healed by the wand of Moses, who is said to have foretold that the countries where Gadelus, or any of his race should live, would not be invested with any reptile or venomous beast. This is said to be the reason why the serpent was a favourite device of the Milesians, appearing on their banners and in their scroll work. The learning of Feinius, or Fursa and Niul, his son, was marvellous for their age. Niul, we are told in all seriousness, " erected schools and seminaries, and taught the sciences and the universal languages to the youth of Egypt." Unfortunately

for his people, Niul sympathised so greatly with
the down-trodden Hebrews, that he drew upon
his own race the vengeance of another Pharoah.
They, under the guidance of Sru, and not Gadelas, as
Hector Boetius and "such pretenders to history"
relate, sailed away in four ships to the Isle of Crete,
to escape the might of Egypt. From Crete they
removed to Scythia, thence to Gothland, thence to
Spain, back again to Egypt, back again to Gothland,
back again to Spain, and, finally, these unsettled, but
unconquerable colonists, after wanderings to which
those of "much-enduring" Ulysses and "pious"
Æneas were child's play, came to Ireland, where they
pitched their tents for aye. This is the record in the
chronicles of Ireland, and, as Keating says—although all
may not assent—unless we depend upon their authority,
it is impossible to arrive at any certainty regarding
the antiquities and the religious and political state of
the kingdom. It has been the custom to regard the
Celts as a branch of the great Aryan race, which had
its original home in the northern hills of India. But
some philologists, Prof. Anwyl among them, arguing
from the resemblance of Celtic forms of speech to the
Latin, hold that there must have been some common
centre of Aryan-Celtic speech in Europe, from which
the Indo-European languages could have radiated
eastwards and westwards, towards India, Persia,
Armenia, on the one side, and Greece, Gaul, and
Britain, Italy and Ireland on the other. This centre
is supposed to have been the Danube valley of the
modern Carinthia. But while the Aryan race impressed its language, social customs, and military ideas
upon the peoples it conquered, right, left, and centre,

it was not always successful in making the conquered races accept their religious views—whatever they may have been—or in preventing their retention of myths, legends, and national folk-lore. This is, probably, the reason why so many incongruous ideas are found in the Celtic religions.

The Milesians derive their name from Milesius, or Gallamh grandson of Breógan (Bryan ?), from whom the Brigantes of Spain, according to Keating, were descended. Milesius was like Moses in this, that he never set foot upon the promised land, dying before the expedition set forth to avenge the death of his uncle, Ith. However, his widow, Scota, an Egyptian princess, and his eight sons, Donn, Ir, Aireach Feabhruadh, Arranan, Colpa, Heber, Heremon, and Amergin took part in the invasion which the uncles of Milesius organised. That expedition was disastrous to many of these; for Scota perished, with five of her sons, before the country was eventually divided between Heber and Heremon. The grave of the heroic Scota, who fell at Slieve Mis, in Kerry, is said to be seen between Slieve Mis and the sea, and is by the Finglas stream in Glenscoheen, or Scota's grave. Bladh, a son of Breógan, was slain on the hills which are now called the Slieve Bloom (Sliabh Bladhma), an interesting connection with the modern King's County. Other Milesian warriors, Fuad and Cuailgne, gave their names respectively to the mountains of Slieve Fuad, the highest of the Fews Range in Armagh and the Cooley Mountains (Sliabh Cuailgne) near Dundalk. The brave Tuatha-de-Danann princes, whose magic proved ineffectual against the Gael, were slain, and their forces scattered at the decisive battle of Tailltenn. Then Heremon and Heber, sons of Milesius, the former in the north, and the latter in the south, reigned peacefully over their provinces, until the wife of Heber, coveting the three vales of Erin, sowed strife between the brothers, who, finally, settled their dispute on the plains of Geisiol—the modern Geashill—in Leinster, where valiant Heber fell. Heremon then succeeded to the throne, and he was followed by his three sons, after whom the sons of Heber Fionn seized the throne, which became a bone of contention between the descendants of Heremon and those of Heber Fionn, and passed now into the hands of one party, and anon into the hands of the other.

Geisioll, or Geashill, in the King's County, is in the ancient territory of Offaly. We read in Keating (p. 154) that Eithrial, King of Ireland, grandson of Heremon, in 2766 A.M., cut down a great wood, called Magh Geisile, at Iobh Failge, which is the same plain of Geashill in Offaly; and another at Magh Rath at Iobh Eachach. Is it possible to identify this latter place with the locality now known as Thomastown, but formerly as Rath, some three miles from Kinnetty? Iobh Eachach may stand for the O'Eachach, the descendants of the Eochaidh, who gave his name to the latter place.

CHAPTER II.

THE RACE OF THE HORSEMAN AND AN ANCIENT RELIC.

THE Introductory Chapter dealt lightly with the general history of the early peoples of Éire. In this we shall deal more particularly with the midlands of Ireland, the country around Kinnetty, and shall select the kings of the name Eochaidh, who were connected with the district. Prof. Connellan gives an interesting note on the name Eochaidh in his translation of the Four Masters (p. 41): "Eochaidh, pronounced Eochy or Eohy, anglicised Achy, and latinized Eachadius, Accadius, and Achaius, a name of many kings and chiefs, is derived from Each or Eoch, a steed, and therefore signifies a horseman or knight." O'Flaherty in his *Ogygia* gives the name as Echod or Etac. Donovan in the Book of Rights interprets Eochaidh as eques or horseman. O'Reilly in his Irish Dictionary gives ᵉoċᴀᵶ, Eochaidh, a man's name, with genitive ᵉᴀᵼᴀċ. In Colgan's Life of S. Nennius the same genitive is given. This being aspirated would be pronounced Eathach, and is probably the latter portion of the name Kinnetty. We shall now see that quite a number of kings of the name Eochaid were connected in some way with the districts around Kinnetty.

The first of these was Eochaidh Eadgothach (2866 A.M.), or as O'Halloran explains it, Eochaidh "of many colours." If that be correct it would be this Eochaidh and not his predecessor Tighernmhas

B

who established the law of colours by which the colour
of one's coat or dress was regulated, a slave being
allowed but one colour, a soldier two, an officer three,
a gentleman who could entertain, four, a nobleman
five, the bards, historians and royal family six. Another
derivation of the name would connect it with singeing.
This would recall the fact that it was an Eochaidh
who is alleged to have introduced the custom of driving
horses and cattle between the fires of Beal or the sun,
on the day of Beltaine (ʟᴀ ʙᴇᴀʟ-ᴄɪne), which, according to Cormac's Glossary, means the two fires which
used to be made by the lawgivers or Druids with long
incantations, when they drove the cattle between them
to guard against the diseases of each year.   This day
is said to have been the first day of summer, the first
of May.   O'Donovan's Almanac (Celtic Society) for
May, 1848, gives " May-Day, 1, Monday, La Beall-
taine, SS. Philip and James, S. Mochœmius, Abbot of
Terryglass.   There is a Bell hill in Clareen, near
Kinnetty, where S. Kiaran is said to have rung his
bell, but which is more likely to be connected with the
ancient fires of Beal-taine kindled originally in honour
of the Sun-god, but kept burning to the glory of the true
God by S. Kiaran, who, according to Colgan, " arranged
that the paschal fire kindled in his monastery should
not be extinguished."   Mr. Cooke, a writer of 1850,
stated that " this fire still continues to be ignited with
sparks from flint on every Easter Saturday."   The
next Eochaidh was Eochaidh Faobharghlas, because of
his green flashing brand. He is said to have been an
early ancestor of the O'Carrolls, princes of Ely, in the
present King's County, being descended from Heber
Fionn.   He was a great destroyer of woods, having

cut down seven forests, one known as Magh Smear-thuin—with which compare the Irish word Sméaróit, a burning coal—which Keating locates in I've Failge (Offaly) also in the King's County. The next Eochaidh, called Mumho, was grandson of the last named, and, according to Keating, began to reign A.M. 2954 (B.C. 1050). He is said to have wrested the throne from Fiachadh Labhruine, whom he defeated at Beal-gadain, a place which may be identified with the present Ballygaddy, often known as the "Three Sisters," where three roads meet between Birr and Leap Castle. He is also said to have fought a battle at Claire, Clara or Moyclare, near Ferbane in the same county. The Four Masters tell us that this Eochaidh was "of Munster." It is probably after him that Munster or Mumhan-ster is called. In those days the district of Ormonde which embraces the southern portion of King's County belonged to Munster, being as its name implies East Mumha or Munster. There are two places near Kinnetty which may be connected with this king, Munnu or Money near Frankford, in the district of Fearcall, and Lismoney, a hill near Knock-na-man, which is derived from Lios or lis, a fortified residence, and may mean the fort of Mumha or Mumho. This is as probable as the other explanation, the fort of the brake (Muine), which, suggested the name of Moneyguyneen—the rabbit's brake—now the residence of Mr. Assheton Biddulph, the Master of the King's County Hunt. It is said that a prince of the name Eochaidh lived at a place called Raheenevil (or the fort of the burning coal, eaḃall) near Frankford, Birr. The next Eochaidh was celebrated as Ollamh Fodhla, or learned doctor.

The Four Masters and the Book of Clonmacnoise give Eochaidh as the name of this Ollamh Fodhla, the Irish Confucius. This Eochaidh wore a girdle and is said to have loosed it when about to speak at the assemblies. He made good laws, such as (1) Let no man slay his fellow; (2) Let not man take of the belongings of another man's property; (3) Let not the lips utter what the mind knoweth to be false; (4) Man be merciful; (5) Let man do ever as he would be done by. When his son Fionn was going to Munster our Irish lawgiver said to him : " When mirth and joy prevail, gravity and wisdom are out of time. In Muma all is sport and dance and song and music and the chase and drink. Whilst thou abidest be as Muma in all but the last." Even in these early days Munster was famous for the hard drinking and fearless riding of its sons. The son of this learned monarch was Eochaidh, king of Uladh (Ulidia = Ulster) and also Ard-rí or High King. He was specially skilful in the management and breeding of horses. The next Eochaidh was called Uairceas, from the small skiffs which he caused to be made, *uairceas* being the Irish for boat. This boat was doubtless similar to the corach or coracle used in the western portions of the country. This monarch was twentieth in descent from Eochaidh Faobharghlas, the ancestor of the O'Carrolls of Ely, and was slain by Eochaidh, called Fiadhmhuine the hunter, " because he took great pleasure in the chasing of deer and other wild beasts, which he frequently hunted in the woody and wild parts of the country;" *Fiad* means deer and *muine* signifies brake. This hunter of the line of Heremon was slain by Luighaidh Lamhdhearg or Lewy of the

Red Hand, of the line of Heber Fionn and son of Eochaidh Uaircheas, the boat-builder. He was succeeded by other Eochaidhs, the most important of whom was Eochaidh Foltleahan or the Broad Locks, who began his reign 254 B.C., and seems to have met his end in the district of Ely O'Carroll, of which princely line he was also ancestor. For he was slain by Fergus Fortamhaill (vigorous), a valiant and strong-bodied prince, who may have left his name to the Fortal cross roads between Kilcolman and Kinnetty. The next Eochaidh was Feidhlioch, who commenced to reign about B.C., 64, and who was the father of the celebrated Queen Maev (Meidhbh) or Mab of Connacht. The king and his counsellors determined that a royal seat should be made in Connacht, and Tinne, one of the princes of Connacht, having offered a site for the palace was rewarded with the hand of the princess. The ditch and rath were made, and a poet describes how the Rath Eochaidh became known as the Rath Cruachan, after Cruachan Crodhearg, the mother of the illustrious Mab. Rath Crochan is doubly interesting to us because of S. Patrick's visit to its fountain, where he had the interview with the daughters of the Ard-ri of Ireland, Ethne the Fair and Fedelm the Red. In the sepulchre of the kings close by this fortress Dathi, the brave Irish prince, who is said on good authority to have assisted the Romans in the Gallic campaign of 428 A.D., is buried according to the Irish poem of Torna-Éices——

Under thee is the King of the men of Fail (Ireland), Dathi son of Fiachra, the Good.
Croghan, you have hidden him from the Galls, from the Goidels.
Under thee is Dungalach the swift, who led the king (Dathi) beyond the seas.

This Eochaidh was a great prince, he restored the laws and encouraged the sciences.

The next Eochaidh (A.M. 3952. Keating ; *Ogygia* A.M. 3934, B.C. 70) was called *Aireamh (grave)* from having introduced the custom of burying the dead in graves, considering it neither decent nor secure to raise cairns of stones over their bodies. He was slain by Siodhmall (a fairy of the hill). The next Eochaidh was called Ainchean, a depraved person who caused the unhappy death of two fair princesses, the daughters of King Tuathal, and in consequence brought the terrible tax called Boroimhe Laighean, or tribute of Leinster upon his kingdom. The story is fully given in Keating's history. Suffice it to say :—

> Two princesses, the daughters of Tuathal,
> The fair Dairine and the lovely Fithir
> Fell by the deed of Eochaidh Ainchean.

S. Moling in after years obtained a remission of the taxes from Fianachta, by a verbal quibble, requesting a respite until a certain Monday but employing an idiom which meant Doomsday.

We now come to three celebrated kings, Cathaoir Mór, Conaire and Oilioll Olum. From Cathaoir Mór, the father of twenty sons, are descended the O'Connors of Offaly, the O'Dempseys of Clanmalire, and O'Dunnes through his eldest son, Ros of the Rings (Failge), all of whom are leading King's County clans. Conary had three sons by Sarah, daughter of Conn of the Hundred Battles, called the three Cairbres, Cairbre Rioghfhada, Cairbre Baschaoin and Cairbre Muisg. From the eldest of these, Carbery Riada,

called Reuda by Bede (Ecc. Hist. I, I.), sprang the
Dalriada colony of Scotland :—

> The noble tribe of the Dalriads
> Descended from the illustrious Conaire.

There were two districts of his name, one in Argyle,
the other in Antrim, to be distinguished from the
Dalaradia or the Pictish colony in the same territory.
From that ancient Irish colony in *Airer-Gaedhil*, Arrer
gale or Argyle, the "land of the stranger" came
the Stuart line of kings, from which our king is
descended. Sadhbh, the other daughter of Conn, was
wedded to Oilioll Olum, from whose second son,
Cormac Cas the valiant Dalgcais (more generally
known as the Dalcassian tribe), the O'Bryans, the
MacMahons and MacNamaras claim descent; and
from whose blind son Cian, the O'Carrolls of Ely
sprang. Their brother Eochaidh with seven other
brothers was slain in the battle of Magh Muchruime.
Conn of the hundred battles had a famous brother
Eochaidh Fionn who helped to reinstate Cuchorb, King
of Leinster, in his kingdom, and routed the Munstermen in Leix and Ossory. The Mumonians or Munstermen seems to have held possession of Ossory and Leix
at the time, but Eochaidh beat them at all points.
One of the battles was fought at Athtrodain, now
known as Athy, on the river Barrow. The Leinstermen followed up their advantage, and almost annihilated their foe. In gratitude for his services Cuchorb
made Eochaidh lord of the seven Fothortuaths, while
his general, Laoigseach (Leeshagh) was rewarded with
the district of the Queen's County, known as Laeighis
(Leesh) and anglicised into Leix, the ancient territory
of the O'Moores. About A.D. 250 we find an Eochaidh

Kinmarc King of Munster. ᵯᴀᴘcáɴ in Irish means a little horse; ᵯᴀᴘcᴀċ means horseman, while kin may represent cean, head, or kinel, tribe. The chief horseman or the tribe of the horseman would be a suitable name for an equestrian hero. Another Eochaidh worthy of note was king of Ireland from A.D. 358 to 365. He was known as Eochaidh Muigmedón or Moyvane, or the midland plain, and was the father of the celebrated Niall of the Nine Hostages, and ancestor of the Southern Hy Nialls, the princes of Meath and the O'Molloys of Fearcall, an ancient portion of King's County, coterminous with the parish of Eglish, and also of the Sliocht Geoilen, or tribe of Cullen, which gave its name to Drumcullen, one of the most ancient ecclesiastical localities in Ireland, just outside the village of Kinnetty. Eochaidh, son of Eana Cinsalach, king of Leinster, slew the great Niall, who raided Scotland, and is also said to have harried the Loire district of France. There was an Eochaidh in the sixth century styled Muinreamhair, or fat neck, also called Andoid, or the swift. The annals of Tigernach for the year 553 A.D. give the note:—" The death of Eochaidh, the son of king Conla, of Ulster, from whom the O'Eachi of Ulster sprang." Keating mentions an Eochaidh of Ulster, first king of the Dalnaruidhe. Under A.D. 550 Keating gives us Eochaidh, son of Daniel, as king of Ireland, whose cousin, Fiachadh, engaged in the bloody battle of Folla and Forthola against the inhabitants of the districts of Ely and Ossory, and obtained a complete victory, slaying numbers of the enemy. Forthola may be identified with Fortal in the neighbourhood of Kinnetty and in the district of Ely O'Carroll. Another Eochaidh, son of the Aongus, baptized by S. Patrick, reigned peaceably at Cashel. In O'Dugan's poem on "the kings of the race of Eibhear," there is this mention of him :—

> Noble Aongus his son Eochaidh rightly called,
> He thirty years succeeded ;
> Who patient being and prudently stoute,
> His life near Cashel ended.

In the translation of the Book of Rights (p. 226, Celtic Society's Edition), there is an account of S. Patrick raising a Danish chieftain of Dublin, one Eochaidh Balldhearg, or the Red. The record of this curious revival begins—

> The day at which Athcliath arrived
> Patrick of Macha of great revenues,
> On the same day cruel death had taken off
> The only son of valorous Ailpin,
> They brought to the descendant of the deacon
> The only son of the king of the Galls, the fierce Eochaidh,
> To the Apostle it was a reproach—
> " If thou shouldst bring a soul unto him,
> O cleric pure and powerful,
> I will submit to thee at Coill Cheanainn
> And the Galls of the green lands shall submit to thee.
> They went round him thrice right-hand-wise
> So that he rose up into life
> The comely hero, the noble Eochaidh.

We have thus seen that Eochaidh was a favourite name of the pagan Irish princes, many of whom such as Eochaid Faobharghlas, the ancestor of the O'Carrolls; Eochaidh Broadlocks, who was slain at Fortal; Eochaid Munho, who may have given his name to Lismoney and defeated his predecessor at Ballygaddy near Kinnetty; Eochaidh Muigmedón or Moyvane, who was the ancestor of the O'Molloys; Eochaid Fat Neck, from whom the O'Eachi sprang, and Eochaidh, the son of Aongus, who resided at Cashel, had various connexions with the midland

districts of Ireland, especially the vicinity of Kinnetty.
This would point us to a solution of the name
Kinnetty.

Dr. O'Donovan, in a note to a passage on the Four
Masters, says :—" Kinnitty (ceᴀn eıcıʒ) *i.e.*, the head
of Etech, so called according to a note in the Felire
of Aengus at the 7th April, from Etech, an ancient
Irish heroine, whose head was interred there." There
appears to be some confusion here. Etech was associated with the neighbouring parish of Ettagh, and
may have some connexion with Kinnetty. But the
tradition may point to the burial of some ancient relic
in the place. It has been said that *Eathach* is the genitive of *Eochaidh*, horseman, and taking into account
the number of Eochaidhs connected with Kinnetty, we
may infer that they have given the locality its name.
This inference is strengthened by a find of a small
equestrian statue which was unearthed from an ancient
rath on the Castle Bernard estate known as " the
Moate." This discovery was made in 1850, and is
described by Mr. T. L. Cooke, of Birr. Some of the
labourers informed him that they were engaged in
some work on this rath when they came across several
large stones weatherbeaten as if they had been exposed
to the air before their interment. These were two or
three feet below the surface, and when all the stones
were laid bare, they presented the form of a cross,
which was not unknown to the pagan world. Where the
arms of the cross intersected the shaft this statue of a
male horse, without legs, measuring seventeen inches
from head to tail, was found. The bridle of the horse
serves also as a bit, like those described by Gerald of
Wales. The saddle has a high cantle and pommel,

the saddle cloths are well padded, and have invected edges. There is a stirrup for the right foot to give the rider support when striking, but none on the mount-ing side. The Irish used both saddle and bridle in ancient times, although this custom with other good customs dropped after the decline and fall of Ireland in mediaeval times. For we read in the Book of Rights (A.D. 800, p. 208)—

> A hundred cows to the brave Ui-Censealaigh,
> A hundred steeds by which power is added to the territory,
> Ten ships, ten bridles, ten saddles.

The rider is an interesting figure, thick-set, bull-necked, clean-shaven, with large and truculent features, clad in a large overcoat, of which there is no opening in front, and the folds of which are gathered in by a large girdle. A long, heavy sword, unlike the short Irish weapon, is visible underneath. A light-fitting cap covers his head. It was the custom of the Irish kings to wear a mantle over their sword when riding. In O'Connor's description of the meeting of Oilioll of Uladh and Oilioll the Ard-rí (B.C. 594) we are told that the Ard-rí dismounted, opened the clasp of his mantle, and laid it on the ground. He also loosed the belt of the sword and placed it on the mantle, saying—"These are of peace, let them be hung up in the tent of the king." The other king when he saw the Ard-rí stand-ing on the ground also came down from his horse, loosed the clasps of his mantle; threw it from him, and the sheath of his sword he flung away.

A remarkable thing about this horseman is the small cavity beneath his hands, which was clearly intended for some object now missing, which might possibly have been a model of the Lia Fail, to judge from the depth, clear cut and conical form of the cell. In Cormac's Glossary there are two lines ascribed to Guaire, king of Connaught, on the subject of Marcan, a horseman—

> In precious stones are hidden great wonders as in
> The stone of Marcan, son of Hugh, son of Marcene.

One of the Eochaidhs was also called Kenmarc, or Chief of the Horse. Another Eochaidh surnamed Gunnat, as an Irish manuscript cited by Dr. Petrie informs us, removed the Stone of the Hostages from Temur and carried it to Cruachan. He also describes the Lia Fail as an idol stone. Was this little horseman an idol or a statue? It is strange enough that this horseman has representations of the three magic things the Tuatha-de-Danann brought to Ireland, the sword of Lug, the girdle (coire = girdle as well as cauldron) of Daghda, "which would not fly away from him like a hidden stag," and the receptacle for the Lia Fail. It is no less strange that the whole vicinity of the Slieve Bloom is associated with the horse. Mr. Seward, in his *Topographia Hibernica*, described a large pyramid on these mountains known as Copall-ban, or white horse. The present writer has not been able to verify this statement; but he has been informed on good authority that there is the shape of a horse visible on the hills between Mountrath and Clonaslee, not, however, as prominent a land mark as the White Horse of Berkshire and its stumpy thorn bush around which the armies of Alfred and the Danes met with a shock. There is a well in Drumcullen known as the Horse Well (copap-eaċ). The Irish set great store on their horses. In the Leabhar-na-h-Uidhri we find one Midir of Brigleigh, which may be the same as Brig-Eile or Ely-O'Carroll challenging an Eochaidh to a game of chess, saying : " I shall have for thee fifty dark grey steeds if thou win the game." There were clans in the north and south called after Eochaidh, even the Hy-Eachach of the townland of Armagh in Down, the Hy-Eachaid of Kinelmeaky, Cork. There were also Kienachta in Londonderry, and Kienachta in Cork. The tribe of the Horseman would be a suitable name for an Irish tuath or district. This in Irish would be Kin-Eathach (cine-eᴀṫᴀċ). The image of the horseman also suggests as a possible derivation cᴀon-eᴀṫᴀċ, image of horseman, pronounced Kin-etta. Either of these derivations would agree with the pronunciation of the natives, Kinnetty. Could this horseman have been an idol ? We find many idols and idolatrous customs connected with horses in the ancient world. Herodotus (iv. 71) relates a curious custom of the Scythians, who honoured a dead king's memory by impaling fifty of his servants on fifty slaughtered steeds on the mountain side. The Roman Castor and his brother were mounted on white steeds. The Northern Woden was represented as riding on a white horse. This is possibly the reason why the white horse was placed on the arms of Hanover. The horse was worshipped by the ancient Arabs. The god Irru of Ceylon, corresponding with the sun, is mounted on a white horse, which was also one of the sacred emblems of ancient Gaul. In the Museum at Mayence is a bas relief of Epona, the goddess of horses, on horseback ; and a bronze image of a horse was found at Neuvy-en-Sullias, and is now in the Orleans Museum. The Celts of Ireland may have had a god Eochaidh corresponding with Epona of the Galli, who had many animal totems such as the boar (moch), the bear (artos), the bull (tarvos) and the ass (mullo). It is quite possible that idolatry or the worship of images—although none have actually been found—was practised by the early inhabitants of Ireland. Crom Cruadh was one of the most celebrated of these images. He was set up in the plain of Magh Slecht in Breffny, was worshipped by Tigernmhas, but was smitten by the crozier of S. Patrick, according to the *Vita Tertia*. Keating informs us of the three De Danann princes, Macuill, Maceacht, and Mac Greine, who worshipped respectively a log of wood (cuill), a ploughshare (ceacht), and the sun (grian), and also relates that Cormac Mac Art refused to worship "a log of wood fashioned by the workman's hand." Some peculiar things have been found and in strange places, which may be representations of the Celtic Goddess Ana or Earth Mother, who, "with her progeny of spirits, springs, rivers, mountains, forests, trees, and corn, appears to have supplied most of the grouped and individualised gods of the Celtic pantheon." (Prof. Anwyl, *Celtic Religion*, p. 28), Cormac's Glossary describes her as the mother of the Hibernian gods, because "she fed the gods well." There are two hills in Kerry which may be called after Ana, Da-chich-Danainne; also a hill called Chich-awn in the Slieve Bloom. Grotesque representations of the female have been found in the walls of the old church of Seirkieran, and also in the castle of Bally-finboy near Finnoe. The late Mr. Cooke stated that he had in his possession an image called by the peasantry "the witch," which originally stood in

Cloghan in the King's County, the old name of which was Cloghan-na-gcaora, the stone of the sheep, which represented an Hermaphrodite, one of the breasts being like the sun and the other a crescent like the moon. This image may have given its name to the neighbouring town of Ferbane, which may be composed of fear (man) and bean (woman). It is said that the Druids worshipped the Sun-god Apollo under the form of an Hermaphrodite. He was worshipped by the Celts under various forms, one of his names being Borvo, "the boiler," the god of hot springs, whence the name Bourbon. Another title was the Grannos, or Sun, as in Aquae Granni, the old name of Aix-la-Chapelle. Grian means sun in Irish. Now the customary offering to the sun was a horse among the ancient Persians. Xenophon gave a horse to the priest to be sacrificed to the sun, and Pausanias states that the Lacedæmonians sacrificed a horse on Mount Taygetus to the sun. It is said that the Irish, too, burnt a horse's head in the bonfires of the first of May, and that the peasantry about Croghan Hill in the King's County, distinctly visible from the Kinnetty mountains, were in the habit of sliding down the hill seated on a horse. We have also some indications that the sun was worshipped in the district around Kinnetty. Knock-na-man, the hill that was above the village, means the hill of the women. Mann also means God. Some kind of worship was doubtless offered within the remarkable circle on its summit. Clonbela, in the neighbouring parish of Drumcullen, means the meadow of Belus or the sun (cluαin-beαl). We have Bell-hill in Seirkieran, where the fires of Beltaine, on the first of May, were kindled. We have, in *Glendissaun*, a glen between

Forelacka Hill and Glen Regan, which, probably means the Glen of the shrubs, but in which there may be a reminiscence of the fires of Samhain (Sowan) of the first of November. And Coola-crease, near Cadamstown, may mean the retired place of the sun (crios). While it has been plausibly suggested that Lacaroe, the *red hill side* near Cadamstown, was the ancient Tlachtga which the Abbé Macgeoghegan stated was in the neighbouring parish, Clonlisk, and which was the site of the inauguration of the fires of Beal tinne. Lacaroe lies also on the ancient borders of Munster, which embraced Ormonde, and Meath which almost touches it. And we read (Keating, p. 233) that Tuathal erected the royal seat of Tlachtga " in the tract he divided from Munster and added to Meath." However, this is only conjecture ; for Tlachtga is believed by others to be the Hill of Ward near Athboy, but the fact remains that there is some connexion between the Celtic pantheon and these ancient hills. Lacaroe is in the parish of Letter luna, which may be connected with *luan* the moon, letter meaning hill-side. There are certain stone piles on the top of the different hills, such as those on Ard-na-h-Éireann and Botheraphuca, the road of the Sprite. The latter of these is called in Irish " Fear-brogac " (Far breague), which means a coarse man and is known as the Hardy man. This may be identified with Mercury, who was worshipped in Gaul under the form of Jovantucaros or lover of youth. It is possible that this equestrian image may have been originally an idol, although such idols have rarely if ever been found, representing some local Celtic or pre-Celtic divinity (for we find that the Milesians often assimilated cults they cared not to or could not obliterate), attached to the gens of the Kin-Eatach or tribe of the Horseman, just as the Gallic Essus was the patronymic God of the Essui. The early Christian settlers may have buried this image and its temple, and ascribed the origin of the name to the interment of the head of Etech, a Christian saint. Be this as it may, the visitor who makes his way through the Slieve Bloom must be awe-struck at times by the great sense of solitude and by the vastness and silence in which he moves, and which suggest the Presence of the Invisible at every step. For ought that can be proved to the contrary, this district is the cradle of the Irish people, the ancient home of the mysterious Tuatha-De-Danann, be they people or be they fairies. The latter indeed would have had many a suitable *Sidhe* or abode in the ancient mounds and knolls and magic circles of these rolling hills, in which the race of Eochaidh the Horseman once held dominion.

NOTE.—In the *Four Masters* Kinnetty is spelt in different ways. *e.g.* 850, Cind Eitiġ (gen.); 884, Cinn Ettiċ (gen. case); 903; Cindéittiġ (gen.); 1213, Cinneitiġ (gen.); 1397, Chinn Eitiġ (gen. not our Kinnetty). Cf. *Cind Fine*, or children of the family. The form given for year 884, Cinn Ettiċ, is most in harmony with the spelling and derivation suggested in these pages.

Also as regards the hardening of the aspirated consonants in Leinster place-names, cf. "Stoneybatter" and "Booterstown" (formerly "Butterstown") near Dublin. "Batter" or "butter" is the Irish bóċaṕ, pronounced boher, as in Boheraphuca. A prosthetic *n* is sometimes found, *e.g.*, the old name of Lough Neagh is spelt in the Book of Leinster both *Loch-nEthach* and *Loch-Echach*, the lake of Eochaidh or Eochy. The former supports the suggested explanation of Kinnetty.

CHAPTER III.

THE KING'S COUNTY AND THE SLIEVE BLOOM.

THE best way, perhaps, to realize what life in an Irish sept was like, would be to glance at the annals of some of the more prominent and pugnacious of the clans. Of these the O'Connors and the O'Carrolls may be selected as being the King's County clans. They are connected with some of the most stirring events in the history of the conquest of Ireland, and proved a constant source of annoyance to the English Government and of anxiety to the English settlers of the Pale.

The King's County occupies the midland districts of Ireland. Sir W. Petty, in his Survey Map (1657) marked the site of the old church of Birr as "umbilicus Hiberniae," the central point of Ireland. Archbishop Ussher mentions that in his life-time a peculiar mass of limestone in Birr was considered the centre of Ireland.[1] This rock stood near the present railway station at Seffin or Seefin, the seat of Fin (suidhe Finn) outside the town. Athlone is now regarded as the centre of Ireland. Giraldus Cambrensis in his "Topography of Ireland" (iii. 41), which he read with so much pleasure to himself if not to others, before admiring crowds in classic Oxford, also described the town of Birr as the middle point of Ireland, being situated in the very heart and centre of the country, and makes some interesting remarks on the colossal stones which are found in the country, which he described as *chorea*

---

[1] Elrington's Edition, v. 518.

gigantum, or the dancing places of the giants. It is matter of regret that this great stone of Seffin, which was supposed to mark the centre of Ireland, was removed from its ancient site by Mr. Thomas Steele, who had it conveyed to Clare in 1833.

The present King's County contained the larger portion of the ancient kingdom of Hy Failghe or Offaly, which also comprised certain districts in Kildare and the territory of the O'Dempseys and O'Dunnes in Queen's County. From olden times this district has been associated with the O'Connor sept. In 1170, soon after their landing in Ireland, the Normans penetrated into these parts. Hugh de Lacy, perhaps the greatest of the territorial barons, was slain in 1186 at Durrow in the northern barony of Ballycowan. At the time he was engaged in superintending the laying of the foundations of a frontier castle, for which he had seized portion of the lands of the ancient abbey, founded by S. Columba in 546. These lands belonged to an Irish chieftain called Fox, who sent his foster brother O'Meyey to watch for an opening against the ruthless invader and desecrator of Celtic sanctities.

One morning the baron was engaged at the operations, and to encourage the Irish men "who had prayed to be set on work for hyre," as Campion tells us, seized a pickaxe to show them how to work in the trench, but as he bent forward with the stroke O'Meyey, whose tool he had taken, seized his opportunity and struck down the unsuspecting baron with a blow of his light axe, and made good his escape to the wood of Kill clare or Coill-an-chlair, the Wood of the Plain, which is near Tullamore, and is interesting to philologists from the fact that *kil* here, like Kyle in Kyle-more, means wood not church. It is also probable that Fearcall means the man of the wood rather than the man of the churches, although the ecclesiastical name *Eglish* (ecclesia = church) suggests the latter. It was a strange coincidence that a Lord Norbury was attacked and decapitated by a woodman in the same place centuries after.

The whole district of Offaly was charged in the early days of the Norman settlement with twelve knights' fees as being part of Kildare, but when the English power declined in the following century the Irish clans who possessed it not only asserted their independence of the Anglo-Irish Government but imposed a heavy tax upon the English settlers of Meath and Kildare. O'Connor of Offaly at one time received annual pay- ments of £60 from Meath and £20 from Kildare. The colonists were thus compelled to buy off the hostility of the Irish as their forebears in Britain had been reduced to purchase peace from the Danes. But it was not from cowardice but from want of means and men that the English in Ireland were reduced to such measures. The terrible invasion of Bruce in 1314 and the wars of the Roses in which the Anglo- Irish took opposite sides, the Ormondes supporting the red rose of Lancaster and the Geraldines main- taining the white rose of York, had completely drained their resources and left them absolutely at the mercy of the " wild Irish our enemies " and the " Irish rebels," as Richard II. described them in his famous letter. In 1480 the whole force at the disposal of " the Castle " consisted of eighty mounted archers and forty lancers or mounted " spears," while the revenues reached the large sum of £600. Owing to the weakness of the Government the English settlers were compelled to form a league for their own protection under the name of " The Brotherhood of Saint George." This brotherhood, consisting of thirteen gentlemen, maintained a body of some 200 mounted archers, who were under the command of a captain annually elected, and who patrolled the borders of the four counties of the English Pale. This fraternity of arms was formed in 1473. The Irish enemies and rebels were not, however, to be denied, and often broke bounds in order to harry their hereditary foes. Accordingly, Sir Edward Poynings, who was sent over to Ireland by Henry VII. in 1494 with the twofold object of crushing the followers of Warbeck and of thrusting back " the wild Irish," was compelled to adopt other means of defence. In the Parliament of Drogheda (1494) chiefly noted for its provision that no parliament should in future be summoned in Ireland without the king's licence for its being held and the consent of the king and Privy Council to any bills it sought to introduce, an Act was passed enacting that the English settlers in the marches should build and keep in repair " a double ditch of six feet high above the ground." This ditch, according to the wording of the Act, ran : " From the water of An liffy to the mountain in Kildare, from the water of An Liffy to Trim and so forth to Meath and Uriel," as Louth was then called. Special care was taken to save the wall from trespass of man or beast. For any animal found injuring it in any way was to be confiscated and sold to repair the ditch, which was for " the great succour, comfort and defence of the county Dublin." This was at once a summary and satisfactory plan for keeping one's fences in order, unless indeed the sheriff's sales of those days realized as little as those of ours when boycott reduces business to a farce.

These incidents have been mentioned in order that the reader may form an idea of the straits to which the English settlement was reduced by the Irish clans who were no longer scattered remnants compelled to live in bog, mountain and forest, but formidable battalions elated with victory, and invincible but for their own lack of combination and esprit de nation or patriotism in the higher sense. In the course of these pages other facts will be mentioned which throw light on the unenviable plight of the settlers of the Pale, who were being slowly but surely crushed out of existence between the upper millstone in the shape of the English Parliament and officialism, and the nether millstone in the form of the Irish septs. Here it is sufficient to remark that much misery would have been saved both to the English Pale and the Irish enemies had the former been either suitably supported by the home government, or permitted to conciliate the surrounding septs as they desired.

King's County, on the septs of which we are to fix our attention, is an interesting district. In many places it is rendered decidedly picturesque in spite of its general flatness by the vast extent of bog and moorland, whose rich and brilliant colouring and ever varying tints of green and brown and gold, especially in the setting sun, form a picture not easily transferred to canvas. The writer will never forget the wonderful landscape and atmospheric effects as he rode along the bog road from Tullamore to Kinnetty one evening in

October. The moon was young and high in the west
while the western sky was crimson with the rays of
the setting sun, which suffused the very atmosphere
with a soft iridescent glow which was Turneresque in
the extreme. Each small sand hillock, which the
Irish call *mullach*, and of which there are a few, on
both sides of the *tochar* or causeway, seemed a veritable *monaincha* or islet in the bog, floating upon the
white watery mist into which the bicycle kept plunging
as into successive waves of the sea, but gradually these
islets vanished into vapour and gloom as the sun sank
beneath the horizon, leaving the darkness a thing to
be realized and felt almost as a living presence, visible,
palpable and most uncanny. As we leave the torach
we notice that these mullachs are but detached portions
of the great line of eskers or sand hills which is an
outstanding feature of the midlands, and is known as
the Esker Riada or "the Ridge." This Esker extends
from Dublin to Galway and recalls the time when
Ireland was either submerged or was in the grip of
the abiding glacier. It also reminds us of two worthies
of the olden times, Mogh Nuadhat or Owen More, King
of Munster, and Conn of the Hundred Battles, King
of Ireland, the former of whom defeated the latter
and divided the island with him, taking as his share
the south, or Leath Mogha, and leaving the north, or
Leath Chuinn, to Conn. The most prominent of these
mullachs is the long green ridge, verdant with trees
and shrubs, that rises like the back of a great whale
above the parish of Killeigh, or the church in the
field, with its ancient Celtic shrine, stone roofed and
nobly arched, from the summit of which a pleasant
vision of the country can be obtained, its ancient raths

and cemeteries of the dead. The scenery of the country is varied by the beautiful range of the Slieve Bloom hills, which forms a striking barrier for over twenty miles between the King's and the Queen's Counties. From Ard-na-h-Éireann, the Height of Erin, 1,733 feet, the greatest elevation of these hills, which in many places rise to the dignity of mountains, one may see eleven counties stretching away to the distant horizon, and catch fleeting glimpses of the sea beyond the hills of Clare. As one looks to the west, tier after tier of mountains rise to the view. A remarkable feature of the nearest range is the so-called Devil's Bit, the ancient Bearnán Eile or the little gap of Eile—Bearnan being Irish for a little gap — the O'Carrolls boundary line. Then as an extension of this range rise the Silvermines, with the melancholy traces of an abortive enterprise on their barren slopes. Beyond these are hills of Newport, denoted by the noble Keeper, or Slieve Kimalta, and between Castle-town Arra and Killaloe, which is surrounded by great dark round hills, the Arra hills rise to a respectable elevation, Towntinna among them gazing threateningly over the Leinster plains with the graves of the Leinstermen on its summit, commemorating the place where they took their last look at their native woods and died. Behind all these, with the broad Shannon and the waters of Lough Derg, tower the mountains of Clare, Killaloe and Scariff, where Bryan Boroimhe and the scattered remnants of his followers lived in the high hills like the wild goats and in the rocks like the conies until they found themselves strong enough to strike a decisive blow at Sulchoit for their homeland against the pagan invader. " For it was better and more righteous," they said, "to do battle for their inheritance than for land usurped by conquest and the sword" (Wars of the G. G., p. 69). And behind and above them all the mountains of Kerry, great rocky blocks, throw their gaunt shadows over the scene. These mountain ranges rise one behind the other like dark masses of deepening shade drawn above the sky-line, while the great billowy plain that rolls away beneath our feet presents a varied landscape of bog and wood, plantation and pasture, glen and vale, through which streams gleam like silver ribands, as they glide along their winding course to pay their tribute to the river. Here are quiet hamlets; there solitary homesteads set in brake and scrub, where foxes make their coverts. Gently rising hillocks capped with green thickets, Golden Grove being especially conspicuous for its striking cluster of fir, and Knockshegowna or the Fairies' Hill, a solitary eminence beyond Birr, with the silver Shannon, the noble boundary of the county, shimmering beyond all, form an enchanting view even when haze and mist blur the picture. Here the sportsman may beguile many a tedious hour, whipping the streams, or shooting the moors, or walking the hills, or riding to hounds. Here, too, the lover of nature may find many an object to interest his mind and many scenes to delight his soul and quicken his imagination. It is, indeed, strange that so few English artists visit the midlands of Éire, where the colouring is so rich and varied, the air so still and luminous, and the distance forms so effective a background. One might go far before one could find more charming scenery or breathe sweeter air than the Slieve Bloom has in store for the visitor to its winding glens, purple hills and tumbling streams. On their wind-swept but easily reached and rounded summits that rise above the woods and parks of the Castletown (Castle Bernard) demesne, one understands why the Roman poets Lucretius and Virgil described living as feeding on the breezes, for to breathe the balmy air is literally to live and emphatically to enjoy life. Here, too, we stand on ground prolific with Irish memories, for Bladh, who gave his name to these hills and whose flagstone is preserved in Lickbla, in Westmeath, was one of the uncles of Milesius; and this range of hills is immortalized by Spenser as the mother of the " Gentle Suir," the " Stubborn Nore," and the " Goodly Barrow "—

> These three fair sons which being thenceforth pour'd,
> In three great rivers ran and many countries scour'd.

Slieve Bloom or Sliabh Bladhma, the hill of Bladh reaches by no means the highest point in Éire, being at its greatest elevation but 1,740 feet above the sea level. O'Dugan, the poet, who sang—

> Sliabh Bladhma the Fair is over the head
> Of Ossory, above the heights of Eire,

was, therefore, a little out of his reckoning. But standing on the summit of Ard-na-h-Éireann with one foot in the King's and the other in the Queen's County, one looks down upon a hundred realms of ancient Éire, the rich pasture lands of Ely O'Carroll, Leix, Offaly, Fearcall, Ossory and other principalities. To the plains of Ossory at our feet there is an approach through a narrow gorge between two steep hills, known as the Gap of Glendine (glen of the race) or Gleann-doimhin, deep glen, which might easily be held

by a handful of determined men against a host. As we
gaze down upon these storied plains we cannot but recall
the attack that was made by its chieftain Donough Mac
Giolla Patrick or Gillpatrick upon the splendid regiment of the Dal-gCais tribe as they were returning to
their headquarters at Kincora, Killaloe, from the
battlefield of Clontarf, where they had displayed a
courage and devotion equal to that of the Spartan
band of Leonidas at the pass of Thermopylae when
the Persian hosts were pouring into Greece, whose
epitaph ran with Spartan brevity—

> Go tell the Spartans, thou who passest by,
> That here obedient to their laws we lie.

The story is told by the Irish chroniclers and historians and is undoubtedly true. The King of Ossory
had a grudge against Brian Boroimhe, who for all his
splendid qualities, was regarded as a usurper by many
of the Irish chieftains, and formed the design of
attacking the bodyguard of that monarch as they were
returning from the sands of Clontarf through his
country, without their veteran king, and hampered by
sick and wounded—a pitiful but plucky remnant.
Accordingly he sent a messenger to Donough, their
captain, as they lay encamped for the night at Athy,
demanding hostages for the good conduct of his troops
while passing through his lands or else threatening to
oppose the march. Amazed at this treachery, Donough
replied with true Dalcassian spirit that he was prepared
to meet Mac Giolla Patrick—a man for whom he had
a profound contempt—any day in a pitched battle.
And as the messenger kindly but injudiciously advised
him to submit Donough ordered him out of his presence, saying that he would meet his master and his

master's men if he had but one man to stand by him.
The Dal-gCais at once set themselves in battle array.
The regiment was divided into three companies. To
one Donough consigned the care of the sick and
wounded, and with the other two he was marching
forth, when the wounded soldiers started up and besought their general not to leave them, but to allow
them to take their usual place in the ranks. As many
of them were unable to stand, stakes were cut from the
trees and driven into the ground, and the wounded
soldiers were tied fast to these stakes, and each
stationed between two unwounded men for mutual
protection and encouragement, while their wounds
were temporarily stopped with moss. O'Halloran
writes : " Between seven and eight hundred wounded
men, pale, emaciated, and supported in this manner,
appeared mixed with the foremost of the troops ;
never was such another sight exhibited." The men
of Ossory, more noble or more prudent than their
prince, refused to fall upon men who were determined
to conquer or die, as Moore, the Irish poet, wrote—

> Forget not our wounded companions who stood
>   In the day of distress by our side ;
> While the moss of the valley grew red with their blood
>   They stirred not but conquered and died.

It is unpleasant to add that Gillpatrick, though
unable to meet the warrior tribe in a fair fight,
succeeded in cutting off a number of stragglers in
spite of Donough's unremitting and ubiquitous vigi-
lance. Another Gillpatrick showed more patriotic
zeal and courage—even he who sent the bold message
by a monk to King Henry VIII.—" Stand, my Lord
King. My Lord Gillpatrick sent me to you and
ordered me to say that if you will not punish Red

Peter he will make war against you." " Red Peter " was the Earl of Ormonde, the Deputy, who was molesting this Gillpatrick. Through these mountains, Hugh O'Neill, Earl of Tyrone, marched in 1600 after passing through Fearcall, which submitted to him. The Four Masters state that he also despatched three plundering parties into the lands of Ely O'Carroll, which are commanded by the Slieve Bloom. The O'Neill repeated his ravages the following year, when he and his allies, as the same authorities relate, " were expeditiously conveyed across the Shannon at Shannon Harbour; from thence they proceeded to Delvin Mac Coghlan to Fearcall, to the borders of Slieve Bloom and into Ikerrin." This time the O'Neill and his army were making their way to Kinsale to help the Spaniards under Don Juan del Aquila against the English forces, commanded by Mountjoy and Carew. That expedition ended in disaster. For the Irish under O'Donnell and Tyrone were routed, and the Spaniards, who had marched out to meet the English troops thinking them to be their allies, were compelled to surrender, and O'Neill marched northwards to surrender to Mountjoy in the beautiful church of Mellifont Abbey in 1603—two days after the death of the Queen. The O'Neill's Well on the road to Mount-rath has possibly older associations, as it did not lie on the line of O'Neill's march, and both it and O'Neill's town may be a souvenir of the Southern O'Neills who had settled centuries before in these parts.

On these hills there are several cairns, one of which stands on Ard-na-h-Éireann, another on a hill near Clonaslee, and the third is the Hardy Man of Bohera-phuca. And there is said to be another pyramid called

the Capall bán, or white horse, said to be associated
with the celebrations of La Belltaine, the first of May,
when fires were lighted in every territory of the kingdom in honour of the pagan god.   It is possible that
these pillar stones and piles had the same origin as
the Maypole.   But be that as it may these piles and
circles are memorials of the religious ideas of a mind
that was haunted by stone.   There are also some
specimens of the Irish mote, which is not a deep
trench but a high rath, one at Castle Bernard and
another at Drumcullen and others elsewhere, which
were probably the sites of the dwelling-places of the
Irish chiefs and nobles or members of the " flaith "
class, while a chain of forts are found on the Ossory
side of the Slieve Bloom, and another chain com-
mands the many tochars or causeways through the bog.

On the picturesque road to Mountrath hills roll
away to the right and left, leaving between them
beautiful glens and river valleys planted thick with fir
crowned by grassy slopes and here and there by dark
hills of peat.   On the right of the road from Kinnetty
Knocknaman rises with its fir trees standing like a
frill on its nearer slope, gapped here and there by the
storm of four years ago, and with its ancient ring on
its rounded brow.   The bare hill of Forelacka then
looms past, followed by the long, gently rising mountain
of Glendissaun, with its great druim or ridge of un-
reclaimable bogland.   As we glance back we catch
exquisite glimpses of the Shannon and the hills beyond,
and the plain shimmering in the light of sun and
sunlit clouds.   On the right are the Boro' hill, Glinsk,
and Letter, all grass-covered slopes reclaimed within
the past fifty years, and on which an occasional deer

may be sighted. The road gradually winds up over the hills, which seem so close in places that a stone could almost be thrown from one summit to another. Deep below lies a valley, through which a winding stream purls its gentle way over a sandy bed. Here the heron may be seen poised not ungracefully on one leg fishing, and at the sound of approaching man the imperturbable bird calmly spreads its broad wings, and in a few seconds has soared out of range. As the writer passed through these wind-swept solitudes, the afternoon sun lit up the hills in front, while the hills behind looked veritable masses of shadow, save where the sun, dazzling one's view, lit up the lone summit of Forelacka with a circle of bewildering brightness. The man who thinks he knows Irish scenery has something still in store for him if he has not yet seen the Irish sun gleaming on these great mountains of green and brown, amid the tears of Éire weeping, as one who would never weary of lamenting the departed glories of her ancient woods and hills, and sorrowing, as one who would not be comforted, because the present age with its sordid prose has brushed aside as a myth the weird and interesting people who worshipped Belus and Ana, the host of heaven and the powers of nature, in the mists and sunshine of their sympathetic glens and hills. Standing on the summit of Knocknaman we are within a magic circle of mountains, which recall the Welsh hills of Penmahnmawr, whose varying shades of brown and green and black on their scarred summits, steep sides or gentle slopes form a bewildering and dreamy vision as they rise above us or recede from us into the distance.

In the vastness and solitude of these hills "airy nothings," mist-like forms "white presences" might easily assume a "local habitation"; and in the midst of these deep-bosomed hills the soul of man can commune with its Maker in a prayerful silence broken ever and anon by the sighs of the wind or the soft cadences of the distant streams, or the call of the passing bird.   And nothing reminds of man save the ring forts which are everywhere in points of vantage on the hills or in the vales.   One of the largest of these is on the top of the Comber mountain ; it is surrounded by a double ditch and fosse, and is some 162 yards in diameter.   The average diameter of the forts which the writer has paced himself is about 53 yards.   Some interesting stones of conglomerate formation are to be found in these mountains behind Cadamstown.   Beyond the marshy slopes of Seskin we cross the Kilnaparson river, the boundary between the counties, and there on the side of the hill, all one great moor save the haggard of the herd and the field where we stand, are five conglomerate stones, which are simply masses of small pebble cemented and solidified doubtless by the action of a glacier—laid flat over deep holes where interments were evidently made centuries back, for the locality is known as the Giant's Grave.   One of the stones resembles a coffin in shape.   Another large stone is to be seen in a hollow in Ballykelly, Lacaroe, some 200 yards from the road, and has the quaint marks of the hoof of a great beast, and a huge hand, thumb and fingers, which may be a trace of an ancient moraine, and which created the impression among the people that it was cast there by a giant's hand, which grasped it so tightly as to leave its impression on its side. Similar stones known as the Bracket Stone are found on Borlacan, or the top (Baur) of the hill side (laca.) Standing on Borlacan we have an excellent view of the surrounding country, the steeples of the Churches of Tullamore, and the smoke of the steamers on the Shannon being distinctly visible. Thence we see an ancient fort on Magherabane or the white plain, facing another fort on Letter or the side of the hill. The finest of these forts, however, are in the vicinity of Leap Castle, one of the O'Carroll Castles, of which more will be said anon. There is a ruined castle at Cadamstown which belonged to the Malone family. Two of the most striking glens on the road to Mountrath and well known to sportsmen are the Black Stairs, where Glenregan joins Gorteen, and where the mountain stream tumbles down zig-zag as down a stairs from the dark and gloomy recesses of the hills ; and the Black Curragh, where Gorteen joins Letter. There is much slate and coal in the heart of these ancient hills, as there is excellent limestone on the road between Cadamstown and Clonaslee, which is bordered by a glen almost as beautiful as the Dargle ; but there is no capital, no railway, and no enterprise, and therefore it were idle to speculate on possibilities which may never be realized ; and yet a true patriot cannot but dream of Ireland becoming another Wales, and giving out of her deep-bosomed hills the mineral wealth which untold aeons have generated and innumerable centuries have stored within ; and attracting to her romantic mountains and fairy glens lovers of nature and disciples of sport from every clime.

There are other eminences that rise here and there

D

above the wide sweep of level moor bogland and
pastures. The Hill of Cloghan, a little distance from
Shannon Harbour, relieves the monotony of the flat
plain between the Brosna river and the Slieve Bloom,
while Croghan Hill, with its quaint top knot, a few
miles to the north of Philipstown, forms a conspicuous
landmark for miles. Near it is the famous Tóchar
Cruachan of Bri Eile, which is now known as Tyrrell's
Pass, and was the scene of many a victory and defeat
of the O'Connor of Offaly.

The county abounds in ruins of ancient churches
and monasteries. Those at Clonmacnoise, Durrow,
Killeigh, and Seirkieran, are the most remarkable.
But there are also ecclesiastical ruins of high antiquity
at Killyon (Killiadhuin) a religious establishment on
the road half-way between Kinnetty and Birr, founded
by S. Kieran for his mother Liadana ; Drumcullen,
Kilcolman and Lynally. The latter place is near
Tullamore, and preserves the word *lann*, church or
sacred land, which occurs so frequently in Welsh
names. It means the Church of Elo, so called from
Colman, a nephew of S. Columba, who settled here in
the wood of Ela (Fidh-Elo) saying : " My resurrection
shall be there, and I shall be called from that place,"
i.e. Colman-Elo. With regard to Dervorgilla's Church
at Clonmacnoise, with its classic pillars and its deli-
cately carved arches, completed in 1180, the late Miss
Margaret Stokes writes that "no work of purely
Celtic art, whether in the illumination of her sacred
writings, or in gold, or in bronze, or in stone, was
wrought by Irish hands after that century." There is
a noble grace about this church which was built by an
Irish queen whose story so closely resembles that of

Arthur's Guinevere, both in its pathos and its penitence, and in the ruin it brought upon her native land. The chancel of Rahan Church near Clara, the most enterprising locality in the South of Ireland, is of rugged masonry, and it possesses in its rose window an architectural feature, of which Dr. Petrie said, "it is not only the most curious of its kind in the British Isles, but also the most ancient." These churches— all that is left of them—are a testimony to the fact that Celtic art and architecture were developing gradually and gracefully on their own lines when they were suddenly and cruelly arrested in their course.

The county is skirted on three sides for many miles by the Shannon, Barrow and Boyne; but its own rivers, the Brosna, Silver River, and Camcor are small. The lakes are not extensive but picturesque. Of these Lough Pallas and Lough Anna are the largest. Lough Coura, which was once a considerable lake, has been drained within the last twenty years by Mr. Thomas Drought, of Whigsboro'. That lake is chiefly remarkable for its islets and island forts, on one of which are the ruins of an ancient castle and circular tower of great extent and strength called Le Porte Castle, near which an Irish canoe, old weapons, and several curious bronzes have been found. In the vicinity is Dowris, celebrated for the find of bronzes made there in 1825. And not far off is the plain of Moylena, where the sanguinary battle, Cath Muighelena, was fought in 192 A.D. between Conn of the Hundred Battles and Owen More of Munster, and another in 907 between Cormac, King and Archbishop of Cashel, and Flann Sionna, the Ard-ri, when the latter was defeated.

The county contains twelve baronies. Of these

Ballyboy, Ballybrit, Clonlisk, Eglish and Garrycastle form the Birr Parliamentary division; while the remaining seven, Geashill, Kilcoursey, Lower and Upper Philipstown, Warrenstown and Coolestown constitute the Tullamore division. Of these baronies the O'Connors of Offaly possessed Warrenstown and Coolestown with portion of Geashill and Philipstown. They were also lords of the baronies of East and West Offally in Kildare, and of Portnehinch and Tinnehinch in Queen's County. The district of Ely O'Carroll comprised Clonlisk and Ballybrit, with the baronies of Ikerrin and Elyogarty of County Tipperary. The O'Mulloys, princes of Fearcall, were rulers of Ballyboy, Eglish and part of Ballycommon, the other portion being held by the O'Dempseys, lords of Clanmalire. The MacCoglans, the chiefs of Delvin, divided with the O'Maddens of Siol Ammchada (Silancia) Garrycastle, the largest of the baronies and the most interesting, inasmuch as it can boast of the historic fair of Banagher and the famous abbey and churches of Clonmacnoise.

The hills and plains and vales of the county are thinly populated. The soil is light and the pasture moderate. There is little more than fragrant breezes on bog and mountain for the people to enjoy. While, generally speaking, they lack the arts as well as the means of living. The industrious may exist upon their small farms happily if frugally, while the idler must pass forth to pastures new. The population, which was 144,225 in 1831, has since fallen to 60,187, but mules and asses, for which the county has always been famous, are on the increase, according to the returns of the Agricultural Department.

CHAPTER IV.

The O'Connors and the Pale.

ACCORDING to the early historians of Ireland a great battle was fought on the Slieve Bloom hills between the Fomorians and Nemedians a thousand years before Christ, and at Geashill, Heremon and Heber Fionn, sons of Melesius, fought for the supremacy, and Heber fell, to leave his son, Conmaol, an avenger of his father's cause. For the scene of Heber's defeat witnessed the discomfiture of Heremon's army and the death of Palpa, his son.

The conflict between the brothers arose, as the ancient poets inform us, through a quarrel between their wives. For "they reigned in peace until the ambition of a woman's heart, the wife of Heber, urged them on to war." She desired to possess three vales which were said to be the most fruitful in the land, but one of these Heremon possessed and would not surrender. Whereupon Heber's wife, as the poet describes her, "raged passionately, and swore she would never sleep on Irish ground till she was mistress of the three vales." Then followed the battle of Geisioll, or Geashill, where Heber fell a sacrifice to the ambition of his wife, and Heremon reigned as king. As the poet says :—

> Three of the fruitful valleys of the isle,
> Druim Finginn, Druim Clasach and Druim Beathach,
> Occasioned the fierce battle of Geisiol,
> Where vailant Heber fell.

To descend from these lofty clouds of fancy to the lowly plains of fact, it is fairly certain that there was a personage called Cathaoir More (Cahirmore) monarch of Ireland, about A.D. 120. He was descended from the posterity of Heremon, and had thirty sons, according to the Irish poet, who were " most renowned in arms, most comely personages, and heroes all." But ten alone survived him. The eldest of these was Ros-Failge or Ros-of-the-Rings. From this Ros are descended the O'Connors of Offaly. History tells us little of Ros, save that his father addressed him as " my fierce Ros, my vehement Ros." These qualities of fierceness and vehemence have been duly transmitted and remarkably displayed by members of his sept. " They have exerted themselves as a posterity worthy of such ancestors," wrote Keating. " For they have shown themselves a valiant and generous tribe, free and hospitable, and true patriots when the cause of their country required their arms. They were so free of their blood in its defence that the family in process of time, were reduced to a small number, for the bravery of this illustrious house exposed them to the greatest dangers and difficulties and they would never fly or retreat, though oppressed by superior strength, but rather chose to sell their lives dearly upon the spot." That ancient document, the " Will of Cahirmore," translated in the Book of Rights, contains the information that Cahirmore bequeathed to his son, Ros-of-the-Rings, Leinster, ten swords, ten shields, ornamented with gold and silver and ten golden goblets.

The family of this Ros Faly were called Hy Faily or descendants of ·Faly to distinguish them from other families of O'Connor or O'Conchobar, and gave the name of Offaly to the districts occupied by their clan which contain extensive remains of previous civilizations in the shape of cairns, cromlechs, sepulchral mounds and fortified raths. In the fourteenth century we find the O'Connors ruling from the green hill of Cruachan, near Croghan and at Dangan, their chief fortress, now Philipstown, which they retained until the time of Mary and Philip. After the conversion of the Irish territory into shire land by Queen Mary—a deed performed with great cruelty—the O'Diomosaigh or O'Dempsey, Lord of Clanmalire, became the representative of the sept, holding strong castles at Geashill, Ballybrittas and Portnehinch until the Revolution of 1685. But almost from the time of the English Invasion in 1169, the Norman Welsh Fitzgeralds of Kildare, afterwards Dukes of Leinster, encroached upon the lands of the tribe and obtained the districts of the sept, that lay within the English Pale. These lands, known as "English Offaly" gave the title of Baron to the Fitzgeralds; while the Irish chieftains, the O'Connors Faily, were kings of the "Irish Offaly" in King's and Queen's County. The O'Connor is celebrated by the bard O'Heerin in the verses :—

> Let us westward proceed to Offaley;
> To which brave heroes make submission,
> Of their laws I make mention,
> Of their convention I make remembrance.

> The Lord of Offaley, a land of mirth,
> Not unknown to the poets,
> Is O'Conor, the mainstay of the fair plain,
> Who rules at the green mound of Cruachan.

There is the record of a battle fought about 1212 at

Killeigh, the church in the field, near Tullamore, between the English of Munster and Murtagh O'Connor.

Quantities of bones are still turned up when new foundations are laid in that neighbourhood. We read in Henry Marleburrough's *Chronicle* that "the Lord Theobald Verdon lost his men and horses going towards Ophali" in 1285; that in the year 1290 "was the chase and discomfiture of Ophaly and divers Englishmen were slaine;" that "Mac Coghlan slew O'Molaghlin," and that "William Bourgh was discomfited at Delvin (in the King's County) by Mac Coghlan." The same authority also states that in the year 1294, "the Castle of Kildare was taken, and by the English and Irish the whole countrie was wasted"; that Calvagh (Calvach O'Connor) "burnt all the rolles and tallyes of that countrie," and Richard Bourgh, Earl of Ulster, "was delivered out of the Castle of Leye (Leix) for his sons," *i.e.*, as hostages. And in 1305 he writes : "Jordan Comin slew Conther (Connor) de Ophaly"; and "Calvagh his brother was slaine in the court of Piers de Bermingham at Carricke and Balimor was burnt." Hanmer also gives us an occasional glimpse of this fighting clan. Writing of Richard Marshall, Earl of Pembroke, afterwards betrayed and murdered by his own countrymen, he describes him "in the year 1213, and the moneth of April, in a battell nigh Kildare, upon the great heath called the Curragh, fighting against the O'Connors." This is taken from Friar Clynn's Annals. Hanmer also relates, on the same authority, that Maurice FitzMaurice was not long after 1272 "betrayed by his own followers in Ophali, taken and imprisoned in the court of Piers de Bermingham, at Carricke, and Balimor was burnt."

Generally speaking, we do not hear much of the O'Connors of Offaly before the fourteenth century. Their great namesakes, the O'Connors of Connaught, were so great that their prestige eclipsed the smaller sept of Offaly. But we find them appearing on the scene when troubles began to gather round the Anglo-Norman settlers. The close of the thirteenth century marked the zenith of the Norman power in Ireland. From that time it began to wane. Many causes contributed to this decline. The dissensions among the Normans themselves, which had led to the shameful betrayal and murder of Richard Marshall, Earl of Pembroke in 1234; the weak and worthless character of Henry III. of England, of which the Celtic chieftains and Norman nobles alike took advantage, Hugh de Lacy going so far as to invite the King of Norway in 1224 to come to his assistance, as we learn from a letter of Queen Joanna of Scotland; and the want of some central authority in the land capable of managing its affairs and controlling its turbulent spirits. In consequence of this state of anarchy and disorder the Norman settlers did that which seemed good in their own eyes. Many of them made friends with the natives, adopted Irish customs and Irish dress; employed the Irish as domestic servants and soldiers; and sided with the native chieftains in their quarrel with the Norman Government. They became, as the saying is, "more Irish than the Irish themselves." They grew their hair long, cultivated moustachios, rode bareback, spoke the Irish language and lived according to the Brehon law.

All this was most offensive to their English brethren, and feelings of bitterness estranged the Anglo-Irish from the English-born. The latter were nick-named "English hobbies" and the others "Irish dogs." As these conflicts and differences were a constant source of weakness to the English community several laws were passed making the use of the English language, English law, saddle and bow, compulsory in the English districts. The saddle was made compulsory in order to prevent the English knights and cavalry forgetting the orthodox use of the lance. For their adoption of the Irish custom of riding made them unfit to appear in a tournament where their play would be as ridiculous as that of Shakespeare's "puny tilter that spurs his horse but on one side" and "breaks his staff like a noble goose." For the Irish either grasped their lances in the middle or hurled them like javelins, which was regarded as an un-knightly proceeding by those who were accustomed to ride full tilt with lances at rest straight at their foes. In 1295 a statute was passed condemning the use of the native garb, the moustache, and the "culan" by the English residents, and by the Statute of Kilkenny (1367) Irish games were forbidden. The wording of the Act was to the effect that "the commons of the said land of Ireland, who are in the different marches at war, do not henceforth *use the plays which men call hurlings*, with great sticks upon the ground, from which evils and maims have arisen, to the weakening of the defence of the said land and other plays which men call quoiting; but that they do apply and accustom themselves *to use and draw bows and throw lances and other gentlemanlike games.*" The real reason, however, was not consideration for the limbs of the athletes, but anxiety to prevent the deterioration of the settler. These prohibitive enactments reveal the weakness of the Norman garrison in Ireland. They had failed to maintain their authority over their own people, who in isolated places had been compelled by motives of policy to throw in their lot with the majority, and had donned the " saffron," married Irish girls, given out their children to nurse and educate with the families of their retainers, dismissed the expensive English guards and filled their castles with cheap Irish kerne and gallowglasses or quartered them for pay, food and fodder (coyne and livery) according to the Irish custom upon their tenants, who were humbled by their insolence and ruined by their demands.

Another weak spot in the armour of the Pale was the practice of absenteeism, which has been for many centuries one of the drawbacks to our national prosperity. Many of the Norman heiresses in Ireland had married English nobles, who preferred a life of peace at home to a life of broils and battles on the borders of the Pale, and accordingly left the estates their wives brought them to take care of themselves, and abandoned the tenants of these lands to the tender mercies of the surrounding septs who harried their homesteads and lifted their cattle with impunity. A statute was accordingly passed (1295) in the reign of that great law-maker, Edward I., and in the first English Parliament to which the three estates—clergy, barons, and commons—were only summoned to constrain the lord marchers who had left their tenants on the frontiers exposed to the raids of the Irish septs to return to protect them, and to compel the absentee landlords in England to assign a portion of their Irish revenues to the upkeep of a permanent armed force for the protection of the colonists.

In certain places the barons undoubtedly held their own, and protected by their castles and supported by their retainers kept the neighbouring tribes in fear and trembling; but their numbers and resources were being constantly drained by the demands of the English kings who never forgot the English settlement in Ireland when meditating a campaign in France, or Wales, or Scotland. For instance, a writ was issued in 1254 with regard to the army of Christians and Saracens who were hastening to the invasion " of the king's dominions in Gascoine, and who would thereby obtain an entry into England and Ireland; for this reason he is desired to come with all his friends to the king in Gascoigne, so that they be at Waterford against Easter, ready to embark with horses, arms and soldiers." And in 1295, when Edward I. was simultaneously menaced by the King of France, by Balliol's revolt in the north, and the Welsh rebellion in the west, he demanded a number of horsemen and 10,000 foot to be fully accoutred and sent for service to England. So when Edward Bruce landed at Carrickfergus in 1315 with 6,000 men and the bravest knights of Scotland, including Randolph of Moray, Menteith, and Lord Allan Steward, he had little difficulty in defeating the remaining colonists of Ulster, under the Red Earl (De Burgho) on the banks of the Bann, the forces of the Deputy De Boutiller at Ardscull, in Kildare, and the army of De Mortimer at Kells. It is to be noted that Edward Bruce came

on the invitation of certain native princes, the O'Neills
among them, who had befriended his brother, King
Robert, during his exile in the isles off the north of
Ireland and Scotland, and that these princes sent a
letter to Pope John XXII., in which they set forth
the Irish grievances at large, traced them all to Pope
Adrian's gift of Ireland to Henry II., and besought
the Pope to approve of their choice of Edward Bruce
as their champion. But the Pope preferred the
friendship of England to the devotion of Ireland and
replied with a sentence of excommunication against
all who should help the Bruce. And had the Bruce
restrained his soldiers from their merciless devastation
of the country and their wholesale destruction of towns,
castles, and even churches, from Carrickfergus to
Castle Connell he would have retained the allegiance
of his Irish friends and have won the crown of Ireland.
The accounts of his raid are sad reading. Spenser in his
View of the State of Ireland, informs us that Bruce
destroyed Belfast, Greencastle, Kells, Belturbet, Castletown, Newtown, and many other towns, and that "he
rooted out the noble families of the Audlies, Talbots,
Tuchets, Chamberlaines, Maundevils, and the Savages
out of Ardes." Friar Clyn and Campion give
equally pathetic descriptions of the havoc wrought in
Ireland, and the mischief done to the English Pale by
"Edward Bruise" who spoiled Cashel and "where-
soever he lighted upon the Butler's lands, those hee
burned and destroyed unmercifully." The latter
historian describes the soldiers of Bruce as "surfeited
with flesh and aquavitæ all the Lent long." They
"prolled and pilled insatiably without neede and
without regard of poore people, whose only provision

they devoured." " While," he says, " the people of
Ulster, now living in slavery under Le Bruise, starved
for hunger, when they had first experienced many
lamentable shifts, as in snatching the dead bodyes
out of their graves, in whose skulls they boyled the
same flesh and fed thereof." And to add to the unhappiness of the people Sir Roger Mortimer, the
Lord Justice, went away " indebted to the citizens of
Divelin for his viands a thousand poundes, whereof he
payde not one smulkin." But the end came to the
hopes and life of the Bruce in 1318, when he was
defeated and slain with all his officers at Faughard,
near Dundalk, by Sir John Bermingham. Campion
gives the names of Bermingham's officers : " Tute,
Verdon, Tripton, Sutton, Cusacke, and Maupas," and
notes some interesting incidents in the battle. The
Primate of Armagh accompanied the soldiers in person
and blessed their enterprise, " assoyling them all ere
ever they began to encounter." Verily the English
had learned a lesson from the conduct of the Scots the
night before their great victory of Bannockburn, which
the Scots themselves on this occasion seem to have
forgotten. And Maupas, who had pressed into the
throng to meet Bruce was " found in the search,
dead, covering the dead body of Bruise." Bermingham
thus dissolved the Scottish kingdom in Ireland, and
sending the head of Bruce to the king received the
earldom of Louth and the Barony of Ardee and
Athenry as his reward for this important service to
the State. In connection with this same invasion it
is to be noted that Edward Bruce's success was
largely due to the fact that the Anglo-Normans and
the native Celts had just before met each other in two

terrible battles at Athenry and Dysart O'Dea, and like
the Kilkenny Cats left nothing of each other behind
but the proverbial "tails," which were altogether
powerless to withstand the onset of Scotland's chivalry.
Richard de Bermingham had almost annihilated the
O'Connors of Connaught at the Battle of Athenry
(1315) of which Campion gives an interesting account.
He tells us the already familiar story of the Hussy of
Galtrim, whose family for centuries had disputed with
the O'Carrolls the lordship of Birr. According to
Campion, Sir Richard Bermingham had a young
squire called John Hussy who was sent by his master
to scan the dead, of whom eleven thousand lay around
the walls of the city, in order to see if O'Kelly, his
mortal enemy, was among the slain. While Hussy
and his attendant were engaged in turning over the
bodies he was observed by O'Kelly, who, "well
acquainted with the valiantness and truth of Hussee,
sore longed to traine him from his Captaine." Accordingly, the O'Kelly suddenly confronted Hussy, and
said, "Hussee thou seest I am at all points armed
and have my esquire, a manly man, beside me; thou
art thin and thy page, a youngling, so that if I loved
thee not for thine owne sake, I might betray thee for
my master's. But come and serve me at my request
and I promise thee by S. Patricke's Staffe to make
thee a lord in Connaught, of more ground than thy
master hath in Ireland." This munificent offer had
no effect upon Hussy, and then his own man, "a stout
lubber," rebuked him for not listening to O'Kelly, and
sided against him. "Then," writes the historian,
"had Hussy three enemies; and first he turned to
his own knave, and him he slew. Next he raught to

O'Kellye's squire a great rappe under the pit of his eare, which overthrew him. Thirdly, he bestirred himself so nimbly that ere any helpe could be hoped for, he had also slain O'Kelly, and perceiving breath in the Squire, he drawed him up againe and forced him upon a truncheon to beare his lord's head into the high towne, which he presented to Bermingham, and the circumstances declared, he dubbed Hussee knight and then advanced to many preferments, whose family became afterwards Barons of Galtrime."

This was an incident in one of the two suicidal battles that laid Ireland at the feet of the new invader. The other fights that weakened the Irish and Anglo-Normans took place in the South of Leinster, where the O'Carroll of Ely defeated the Norman settlers, and in the North of Munster, where the O'Briens gave an overwhelming defeat to Richard de Clare at Dysart O'Dea.

But that Scottish raid spelt ruin to the English tenants on the baronial estates, as well as to the Irish tribesmen. And if the Irish Annals of Clonmacnoise break forth into song over the death of Edward Bruce who was slain, " to the great joy and comfort of the whole kingdom in general, for there was not a better deed that redounded more to the good of the kingdom since the creation of the world, and since the banishment of the Finè Fomores out of this land, done in Ireland than the killing of Edward Bruce," what must have been the feelings of the English yeoman over whose ploughed fields, haggards, and farms, that desolating stream of lava had poured for three and a-half years, leaving him a ruined man by the roadside, to return a pauper to the shores of England, or to

sink to the condition of the tribal Irish, and to live as
the kerne, plundering others as others had plundered
him. The latter was, indeed, the fate of many a gallant
yeoman and of many a noble knight After the Scottish
invasion the English settlers abandoned and betrayed
by their own countrymen on the other side of the
water sank into a disorganised, hopeless community;
while the spirits of the Irish who had perhaps suffered
considerably less from the invasion and the famine
that ensued rose in a corresponding degree. The
dispossessed tribes recovered the lands devastated by
Bruce and deserted by the settlers. The septs of
Desmond rose to a man. No check was offered to
their advance by English Government, deputy, or
settler. Out of the mountain fastnesses of the
Slieve Bloom the O'Connors and O'Moores swooped
like birds of prey upon the plains of Leix and
Offaly. Friar Clyn gives an interesting account
of one of these raiders, Leysert O'Moore. He
writes :—

"In the year 1342 died Leysert O'Moore, a man
influential, rich and wealthy, and respected in his
tribe. By force he ejected almost all the English
from his lands and inheritance, for in one night he
burned eight English castles and destroyed the noble
castle of Dunamase, the property of Lord Roger de
Mortimer, and obtained for himself the lordship over
his country."

Had the English settlers but waited and presented
a firm front they would easily have held their own.
But while some were desirous of maintaining law and
order, others proved week-kneed and lukewarm. In
1323 the lords of the Parliament assembled in Dublin

undertook to arrest or cause to be arrested all felons and robbers of their family or surname. In 1327 the Viceroy was directed to take possession of the castles of the absentees and maintain them out of the revenues of the estates, while the Irish enemies and English rebels were ravaging the royal lands. In 1329 his own English tenantry in the County of Louth murdered John de Bermingham, the conqueror of Edward Bruce, with two hundred men of his family and household. And when summoned to answer for the crime before the king's court they treated the writ with contempt and remained unpunished. The events of that year (1329) are summed up in Cox's *Hibernia Anglicana* who ascribes the disasters of the English colony to their own dissensions. " When the Earl of Louth," he writes, " and many other of the Berminghams, Talbot of Malahide and an hundred and sixty Englishmen were murdered by their own countrymen, —the Savages, Gernons, etc., at Balibragan (Balbriggan) in Urgile (Uriel = Louth) ; and when the Barrys and Roches in Munster did as much for James Fitz-Robert Keatinge, the Lord Philip Hodnet and Hugh Condon, with an hundred and forty of their followers, what wonder is it if Macoghegan defeated the Lord Thomas Butler and others near Molingar to their loss of an hundred and forty of their men ? Or if Sir Simon Genevil lost seventy-six of his soldiers in Carbery, in the County of Kildare ; or if Brian O'Bryan ravaged over all the country and burnt the towns of Athassel and Tipperary ? "

The comment the historian makes upon this state of affairs is both acute and prophetic. " And yet," he says, "this common calamity could not unite the English, although their own experience taught them (and frequent instances have convinced the succeeding ages since) that the English never suffered any great loss or calamity in Ireland, but by civil dissensions and disagreement among themselves."

While the Irish septs of Connaught were seizing the royal castles of Athlone, Roscommon and Randoun, the O'Byrnes, O'Tooles, and MacMurroughs were raiding the lands of the settlers and driving off the cattle in Wicklow and Kildare; the O'Connors and O'Moores were harrying Offaly and Leix; the MacGeoghegan's and O'Melaghlins were devastating Meath, and the great sept of the O'Neills, the Clan Aedha Buidhe (Clan-na-boy) or tribe of Hugh the Red were sweeping over the eastern counties of Ulster which had been just reduced to a desert by Edward Bruce, and were establishing a principality of their own in the north, an event occurred which seemed to be the death-blow of the English settlement. This was the assassination of William de Burgh, the "Brown Earl," the successor of the Red Earl, in 1333, by Richard de Manneville at Carrickfergus. By English law the vast estates of the dead earl in Ulster and Connaught, which were the backbone of the English settlement, passed to his infant daughter, who was brought by her mother to England, where she afterwards became the wife of Lionel, Duke of Clarence. But William and Edmund Burke, junior members of the great house of De Burgh, sons of Sir William, the Viceroy in 1308, felt the absurdity of doing homage for their possessions to a young girl, at a time when every feudal baron held his lands and governed his vassals as much by force of arms as by right in law; and well aware of the inability of the heiress of the Brown Earl to support or defend them, as she on her part was duly bound to do, took the bold step of repudiating her authority. This step, however, was a breach of the feudal system, and the English sovereign was bound to take cognizance of it. Accordingly, the two Burkes found themselves compelled to renounce their allegiance to the English Crown. And feeling themselves more powerful when united with the Irish septs, stripped themselves of their Norman coats of mail and arrayed themselves in the saffron robes of the Irish chieftain on the banks of the Shannon, in full view of the garrison of Athlone. They, thereupon, assumed the names of McWilliam Uachtar (the "Nether") and McWilliam Iochtar (the "Further); and, dividing the country between them, one took Galway, and became the ancestor of the Clanrickarde house, and the other took Mayo, and from him the Mayo family is descended. They also adopted the Irish language, laws and customs. Their example was followed hy many other nobles. Bermingham, of Athenry, styled himself McYorris; Nangle became McCostelo; Fitzurse, McMahon; D'Exester, McJordan; the Baron of Dunboyne, McPheris; and the White Knight, McGibbon.

But Edward III. cared for none of these things. He was engaged at the time in putting forward an absurd claim to the throne of France, and his only desire was to obtain the wherewithal to make good that claim. With this object in view he began a systematic oppression of the much tried English colony, which appears through all the chequered annals of the history of English rule in the character of the much-enduring Ulysses. In 1341 the king issued a writ to the justiciary of Ireland to resume all royal grants of lands until he was " made certain of the merits of the grantees, the causes and conditions of the grants." The purpose of the writ to force the grantees to compound by payment of fines was clear to all concerned. And this flagrant act of dishonesty roused the whole colony who were already provoked by the king's gratuitous exclusion of Irish-born subjects from " the sweets of office," so that, as Campion observes, "the realm was ever upon point to give over and rebel." Other acts of injustice committed by his own English-born officials, Sir Anthony Lucy and Sir Ralph Ufford who had seized Desmond's estates, and was justly unpopular for his general character and conduct, brought matters to a head. The great Earls of Desmond and Kildare refused to attend the Parliament in Dublin (1341) and convened a meeting in Kildare, from which a memorial was despatched to the king, setting forth the grievances of the English settlement in Ireland, the state of destitution to which they had been reduced by the raids of the Irish enemy on the one side and on the other by the " embezzlement and extortions practised by English-born officials, who defrauded the constables of the royal castles ; entrusted their custody to incompetent warders, or to those who employed deputies, merely to extort fees ; charged the Crown for goods and valuables taken for its use, but for which they never paid ; entered into their accounts salaries to governors of castles which were either demolished, in the hands of their enemy, or had never existed, and exacted money from the king's subjects on various pretences." [1]

The Earl of Desmond, who had been allowed to escape from his imprisonment in Dublin, where he had been arrested by order of the rapacious Ufford, whose lady is described as "a miserable sott who led him to extortion and bribery;" also put down on the paper the pertinent question—"How an officer of the king that entred very poore might in one yeare grow to more excessive wealth than men of great patrimony in many yeares?"

Edward was forced to give way to such a memorial especially when supported by an appeal to *Magna Charta* and a resolute nobility who had been provoked beyond endurance by Ufford's insolence and tyranny. For in 1346 we find him conferring knighthood on the Earl of Kildare, another victim of Ufford's jealousy and greed, for his services at the siege of Calais, and making the Earl of Desmond, some of whose estates Ufford had seized, Lord Justice. It is surprising that Edward, with all his cruelty, was able to obtain a splendid Irish contingent for his foreign wars which eventually brought greater loss than lustre to England. It seemed, moreover, a sort of poetic justice to find the victims of Ufford's impositions thus honoured shortly after the death of their tormentor had been publicly solemnized with bonfires and other expressions of rejoicing in the land.

But Edward's hold on Ireland was growing weaker

---

[1] Richey, *Short History*, p. 225.

yearly. The Irish had grown excessively turbulent
since the invasion of Bruce had shown them the
weakness of the Anglo-Norman power. During 1330
there had been a great rising in Leinster, and "so
outragious were the Leinster Irish that in one church
they burned eighty innocent soules, asking no more
but the life of their priest then at Masse, whom they,
notwithstanding, sticked with their javelins, spurned
the Blessed Sacrament, and wasted all with fire."[1]
His justiciary was compelled to bribe some of the
Irish septs, the O'Tooles and others to defend the
frontiers of the Pale, and to offer reward for the capture and assassination of the more refractory chieftains.
The Irish insurgents, however, had not matters all
their own way in every part of the country, for we
read of men like Sir Robert Savage in Ulster fortifying
his manor house, and his son, Sir Henry, who led his
men against the Irish and defeated them. This Sir
Henry seems to have had a touch of humour, for,
having prepared a supper of wine, aqua vitae, and
venison, beef and fowl for his men on their return, he
was advised by his officers to poison the food, lest the
enemy should defeat them and secure the supper.
"Tush," he answered, "ye are too full of envy. If
it please God to set other good fellows in our stead,
what hurt shall it be for us to leave them some
meate for their suppers; let them hardly win it and
wear it." The gallant knight returned with his men
to enjoy his own supper.

Nor is it to be inferred from the charges that were
made against the English Lords Justices that they

[1] Campion, *History of Ireland*, p. 129.

were all bad and dishonest. For Sir Thomas Rokeby, who held office in 1353 was the impersonation of rugged honesty and sterling worth. When rebuked for allowing himself to be served with wooden cups, he answered: " These homely cuppes and dishes pay truly for what they containe. I had rather drinke out of wood and pay gold and silver than drinke out of gold and make wooden payment." This was of course an allusion to the almost proverbial dishonesty of the Lord Deputies.

CHAPTER V.

THE RISE OF THE O'CONNORS AND RICHARD II.'S EXPEDITION.

IN the foregoing chapter an account was given of the condition of the English Colony called the Pale, which may help the readers of this little work to form a general idea of the state of Ireland in the fourteenth century, when the O'Connors Faly rose into prominence. Of the great possessions in the hands of the English settlers and territorial barons at the beginning of that century but little remained at the end. Some of the causes, internal and external, that brought about this condition of things have already been set forth. But one has not yet received the attention it deserves. The tribes are beginning to act more unitedly, and to trust one another, and though still far from that Home Reunion, which is as vital to the existence of states as of churches, were taught by the "degenerate" English, who had cast in their lot among them, that they should, at least for the time being, bury the hatchet between themselves until they had swept the Colony into the sea.

A tremendous effort, or rather series of efforts, was accordingly made at various points of the Colony's possessions, and the English subjects and officials, unable to resist the overwhelming tide, were driven back upon their lines. Ulster was regained; Connaught was in revolt; parts of Leinster and

Meath alone remained faithful to England, and were compelled to purchase peace at a great price. It was at this time that Richard II. made his great expedition to Ireland, which commenced auspiciously for the Colony, but ended most disastrously (1394).

We shall now see what the Irish septs have been doing in the meanwhile. That they lacked neither wit nor courage, the following record shows. *The Four Masters* relate that one Donogh O'Gillpatrick was killed by the English in 1249. " This Donogh," they write, " was one of the three Irishmen who committed the greatest number of depredations on the English ; and these three were Conor O'Melaghlin, Conor MacCoghlan of the Castles, and the before-mentioned Donogh, who was in the habit of re-connoitring the market towns (of the English) by visiting them in the different characters of a beggar, a carpenter, a turner, an artist, or a pedlar, as recorded in the following verse :—

> He is now a carpenter, or a turner,
> Now a man of books or learned poet,
> In good wines and hides, a dealer sometimes ;
> Everything by turns as suits his purpose.

These O'Melaghlins and MacCoghlans had wrested half the County of Meath from the settlers at the end of the century, but were just as often engaged in fighting each other as in raiding the English lands. For the same authority tells us that in 1290, forty-one years after the death of this celebrated Irish comedian, Donogh O'Gillpatrick, whose histrionic performances proved a little more expensive to the English than those of his countryman, the late John Lawrence Toole, prince of good fellows, " Carbry O'Melaghlin,

King of Meath, the most valiant young warrior in
Ireland in his time, was slain by MacCoglan."

The year 1305 was, according to all accounts, a
disastrous one for the clan of the O'Connors. We
have already mentioned the fact that their neighbours,
the O'Dempseys, afterwards became their representatives. The sept of the O'Dempseys, or O'Diomsaigh,
dominated the district known as Clanmalire, which
embraced portions of the baronies of Geashill, Philipstown, and Ballycowan in the King's County, and
portions of the neighbouring counties of Kildare and
Queen's County. Of this tribe the poet O'Heerin
wrote—

> Clanmaliere is above all tribes,
> Noble is the source of their pedigree,
> The smooth plains of the land they have defended,
> The country is the inheritance of the O'Dempsey.

The present town of Tullamore is in the district of
this ancient tribe, which fought with conspicuous
success against the forces of Strongbow in 1173.
Morice Regan, the faithful scribe and follower of
Dermot McMurrough, relates in his Norman-French
poem, in which he gave an interesting, if somewhat
embellished, narrative of the English invasion, that
the O'Dempseys made an attack upon the English, in
which Robert de Quincy, the Standard Bearer of
Leinster, and son-in-law of Strongbow, was slain.
The principal fortress of this tribe was at Geashill,
near where Lord Digby's handsome residence now
stands. And as far back as 1305 we hear of the sept
of O'Dempsey defeating the sept of the O'Connors,
with great slaughter, near this castle. But the
O'Connors returned to the charge the following year,

and destroyed the Castle of Geashill, and swept on to Lea, in which parish Portarlington is now, and where the remains of a massive round tower and other fortifications on the banks of the Barrow, and several Irish raths in the vicinity, testify to the military prestige of the place, and, perhaps, to the operations of the O'Connor sept in 1305.

The ancient castle of Carbury in County Kildare is also connected with the fortunes and misfortunes of this fighting clan. Those bleak skeletons of wall and battlement, through which the winds murmur in weird cadences, standing in lonely grandeur on an isolated hill, form a conspicuous landmark, which reminds us of the new age of the prowess and perfidy of the Norman knights. To this massive keep Sir Pierce Bermingham invited the O'Connor Faly, with a number of his chiefs, to a banquet one ill-starred day in the year of grace 1305. Thirty chieftains attended the feast, and at night, when men had well drunken and suspicions were allayed, armed men arose and fell upon the Celts, and the night winds moaned in sympathy with their shrieks as they were done to death. Among those who fell that night were the O'Connor, his brother Maelmordha, and his heir, the Calvach O'Connor.

Sixteen years have passed, and the O'Connors have somewhat recovered their strength ; but they have not forgotten the Berminghams, their Norman neighbours, and burning to wipe out that deed of shame and barbarity, muster their forces and hurry to attack the Berminghams who were in great force at Monasteroris in 1321. This place, on the borders of the King's County, formerly Castropetre, was afterwards

known as Monasteroris, from the monastery founded
here for Conventual Franciscans in 1325 by Sir John
de Berminghan, Earl of Louth, who rejoiced in the
Irish name of Mac Feoris. But Monasteroris was a
place of bad omen for the O'Connors on this occasion,
as they were defeated by Andrew Bermingham and
the English of Meath. A generation passes away and
in 1348, as these unhappy memories were fading from
the minds of the O'Connors, a representative of their foe-
man's house was expelled from Connaught by Edmond
Burke, and forced to throw himself upon the mercy of
the O'Connor Faly. He found what seems never to
have been refused to friend or foe—refuge and hospitality. The politics of the Berminghams and of many
of the Norman barons had, however, changed in the
meantime. Several causes led to this. In 1329, Jean
de Bermingham, who had defeated Edward Bruce, was
murdered with all his kindred, some two hundred
souls, by the English settlers in Louth. Then in
1331, Sir William Bermingham and his son, summoned
to a parliament at Kilkenny, did not consider it safe
to appear ; but shortly afterwards was arrested by Sir
Anthony Lacy, Lord Justice, while sick in bed at
Clonmel, and accused of aiding the Irish rebels. The
father was hanged in Dublin on the 11th of July, to
the grief of many who esteemed him a noble and valiant
knight ; but his son Walter was released the following
year by John Darcy, a Lord Justice. The Earl of
Desmond was also arrested at Limerick, and sent over
to the king ; Walter Burgh and two of his brothers
were seized in Connaught and Henry Mandevil was
sent as a prisoner to Dublin, so that many of the most
loyal subjects of the Crown were turned into deadly

foes by repeated acts of oppression and injustice on the part of the deputies and lords justices.

It would seem that the fighting clan had now begun to give trouble to the English settlers in Meath by harrying and plundering their lands and cattle. One day, in the year 1385, Murrogh O'Connor, the Lord of Offaly, had led his kerne and gallowglasses across the borders of his territory and after spoiling the English, were returning with much booty. But the men of Meath were not long in assembling, and under the leadership of Nugent and others followed hard after their wild and stalwart foemen, who were able, as Froissart says, to overtake and pull a horseman off his horse, but who were now retiring leisurely with their plunder. In the level but boggy country around the hill of Croghan they were overtaken and compelled to give battle to their pursuers. Though superior in strength and agility, the badly armed kerne were no match at close quarters for the mailed and helmeted Normans, and many of them fell. Still retreating, and fighting as they retreated, they hoped to put the bog between them and their foes. But there was naught but disaster for the fighting clan that day. Behind them were the English cavalry, around them an impassable bog, and before them a narrow causeway or tochar, across which the road to safety lay. And in their efforts to cross, numbers of them were slain by the enemy or smothered in the bog. This was the battle of Tochar Cruachan Bri Eile, in which many of the English nobility, Nugent, Chambers and others, and their common soldiers entered " the vasty hall of Death " in company with the slain warriors of the Kinel Fiacha and O'Connor Sept.

The year 1394 is the beginning of a new era in the story of Ireland under English rule. For in that year Richard II. landed at Waterford, with 30,000 foot and 4,000 horse, and, proceeding by slow marches along the coast, eventually reached Dublin Castle, where he summoned the Irish chieftains to meet him. The chiefs, awed by the overwhelming display of force, and induced by the hope of favourable terms, attended to the number of seventy-five. Among these were the O'Neills of the North, the McMurroughs, and the O'Connors. It is clear that Richard had seen the necessity of reforming the English mode of governing Ireland, and especially of removing the grievances and injustices under which the Anglo-Irish groaned. Their lot had not been improved by the Statute of Kilkenny, although some of its sections were "more honoured in the breach than in the observance." Constant licences and exemptions were granted by the Crown to the Irish to the detriment of the settler. It may be observed in this connexion that the English Government has always been represented as treating the Celtic population with the direst cruelty. It is true that if the letter of the law were strictly observed the native Irish would be severely handicapped. But there were many modes of evasion of which the Irish were not slow to avail themselves. For example, the Irish where out of the King's peace were excluded from the protection of the King's Court. But an exception was made in the case of the "Five Bloods," the royal races of O'Neill of Ulster, O'Melaghlin of Meath, O'Connor of Connaught, O'Brien of Munster, and McMurrough of Leinster, who were styled "men of the King." This exception practically covered the whole island, as under it almost any Irishmen could claim the protection of the court. For instance, in 1355 one Simon Neal brought an action of trespass against William Newlagh for breaking his close at Clondalkin. The defence was that Neal was not one of the " Five Bloods." But the plaintiff argued that he was of the blood of the O'Neills of Ulster. One might well ask who could prove, or who could disprove, or who could decide that point. We also find cases where Englishmen charged with murder put forward in defence the plea that the murdered man was "a mere Irishman," *i.e.*, not one of the " Five Bloods," and where such a plea was not allowed. And we may be sure that the English officials of these days would not be capable of resisting a *douceur* from an Irish "enemy," for professional swindlers are loyal to no person or party, and Mr. Gilbert, in his History of the Viceroys of Ireland, gives us this description of those officials : " Many of the judges and chief legal officers of the Colony were illiterate and ignorant of law, obtained their appointments by purchase, and leased them to deputies, who promoted and encouraged litigation, with the object of accumulating fees. Ecclesiastics, lords, and gentlemen were not unfrequently cast into gaol by officers of the Crown on unfounded charges, without indictment or process, and detained in durance till compelled by rigorous treatment to purchase their liberation." It was not, therefore, more difficult for the Irish to evade the law then than now. In fact, they enjoyed a happy immunity and independence of a sort. For, though legally without the pale of the law, they were not disregarded politically ; and, according to the humour or purpose of the King and his Council, were bribed and petted, or whipped and scolded, much in the same way as naughty children are treated by nervous parents.

Richard II., however, came over with the very best intentions of training and restraining his turbulent sons. His policy was to conciliate the Anglo-Irish, and to compel the Irish enemies to acknowledge his authority. But the ready submission of the hostile chiefs both flattered and deceived him. He entertained them with a refined magnificence, for Richard II. loved art as much as grandeur, and left nothing undone to attract and impress. The Irish chiefs had, indeed, been accustomed to the royal receptions of the English monarchs, which Henry II. had inaugurated on a grand scale, as Hanmer describes in his chronicle :—" Christmas drew on, which the King kept in Dublin, where he feasted all the provincial princes, and gave them rich and beautiful gifts. They repaired thither out of all parts of the land,—and wonderful it was to the simple people to behold the majesty of so puissant a prince; the pastime, the sport, and the mirth and the continual music ; the masking, mumming and strange shows ; the gold, the silver and the plate ; the precious ornaments ; the dainty dishes furnished with all sorts of fish and flesh, the wines, the spices, the delicate and sumptuous banquets; the orderly service, the comely march and seemly array of all the officers ; the gentlemen, the esquires, the knights, and lords in their rich attire; the running at tilt in complete harness, with barbed horses, where the staves shivered and flew in splinters ; the plain, honest people admired and no marvel." The same round of entertainments again took place, which were again attended by the

F

Irish princes and chieftains, and again they tendered their homage, which the king graciously accepted. But Sir John Davis shrewdly remarked that " the Irish lords knowing this to be a sure policy to dissolve the forces which they were not able to resist," followed the same " trick and imposture " which their ancestors had put upon Henry II. and John. He thus describes this well-acted homage:—" The men of Leinster, namely, Mac Murrough, O'Byrne, O'Moore, O'Murrough, O'Nolan and the chief the Kinshelages, in an humble and solemn manner, did their homages and made their oaths of fidelity to the Earl Marshall, laying aside their girdles, their skeins, and their caps, and falling down at his feet upon their knees, which, when they performed, the Earl gave each of them *osculum pacis* (the kiss of peace)."

They then bound themselves and their swordsmen to be loyal dependents, and the Wicklow chiefs, in return for pensions—Arthur MacMurrough, chief of the Kavanaghs, receiving eighty marks per annum—agree to evacuate their lands, upon which the King intended to plant a new colony. When all the indentures had been signed, and all the submissions had been tendered, the king departed, " with much honour, but small profit," to his own country, appointing Roger Mortimer, the heir apparent of England, as his lieutenant. The old chroniclers relate some interesting incidents connected with the expedition of Richard. When in Dublin he offered to confer knighthood on the four principal chieftains, O'Neill, O'Connor, O'Brien, and MacMurrough ; but these princes declined the dignity, stating that every Irish prince was knighted at seven years of age, after having broken a

number of slender lances against a fixed shield. But
when the honour was explained to the noblemen they
accepted it, and it was conferred upon them in the
Cathedral, doubtless of S. Patrick. The king then
put them in the charge of one Henry Castide, who, as
Froissart relates, had no little trouble in schooling the
four noblemen, and teaching them to live and dress,
eat and drink and behave like Englishmen. They laid
aside their great mantles, and donned silken robes;
they used stirrups and saddles on horseback, and at
table they adopted English manners, but reluctantly.
Castide's experiences were varied by an adventure in
which he was taken prisoner by an Irish gentleman
" Brian Costeret, a very handsome man," who leaped
on the back of his runaway horse and took him as
prisoner to his house " which was strong and in a town
(*civitas* or lis) surrounded with wood, palisade and
stagnant water."

But " Caesar's thrasonical brag—I came, saw, and
overcame," did not apply to this magnificently conceived expedition. The Irish chieftains by well affected
humility, by bending and bowing had weakened the
storm and broken the army that had been gathered to
break them. But no sooner had the king and his
army withdrawn from the shores of the green isle and
his Deputy had proceeded to carry out the plantation
of Wicklow, than Art MacMurrough, who had been
suspected and imprisoned and then released, and em-
bittered, attacked the forces of the Pale. Carlow was
captured and the royal troops were defeated at Kells, and
Roger Mortimer, the Earl of March, and heir-apparent
of the English throne fell in the engagement
(1395).

Emboldened by this success, in which the O'Connors of Offaly, the O'Moores and O'Dempseys had taken part, the O'Connor Faly returned to his own country and made preparations to avenge the defeat he had suffered at the pass of the bog.   Receiving information that a strong force of the English were marching to plunder his country and the seat of his ancestors, he took a wide detour, and by forced marches was able to attack them in the rear, and clinging closely to their flanks eventually made their forces converge towards the very causeway that had been so fatal to his own clan some years before.   In the battle that ensued, the invaders were defeated with the loss of many men and horses, and the Tochar Cruachan (Croghan) again devoured more people than the sword destroyed.

Three years afterwards (1398), the Calvach, or eldest son of the O'Connor, succeeded in inflicting a smart defeat on the Earl of Kildare, the hereditary foe of his people, but with the fall of whose house in the days of Silken Thomas (1535) the O'Connors were involved.   The Earl, the ancestor of the famous Lord Deputy of Henry VIII., of whom we shall hear more anon, was taken prisoner, and handed up to Murrough O'Connor.   In 1406 Murrough O'Connor, " Lord of Offaly," who seems to have been a skilful general, defeated the English at Geashill, both parties having marched " to the upper part of Geashill."   " It was on this expedition," wrote the Four Masters, " that the chief holy relic of Connaught, called Buacach Phatraig, the mitre of S. Patrick, which was kept at Elphin, was taken from the English."   In the same year Meiler Bermingham slew Cathal O'Connor. In 1411 the same historians inform us that " the

Sheriff of Meath was taken prisoner by O'Conor Faily, and he exacted a great sum for his liberation." We read frequently in the annals of our country of doings in which sheriffs figure, sometimes gloriously, sometimes ingloriously. It seems to be part of the unwritten code of honour, part of the *noblesse oblige* of the Celt, to resist a sheriff. It is not suggested for one moment that the Irishman is not as anxious as the native of any other country to meet his creditors and to pay his debts, but the prospect of a brush with the law, to which they know they must yield in the end, has an exhilarating influence upon their nerves, which only an Irishman can understand. Much of the banter and bluster that accompany sheriff's sales is not to be taken *au grand sérieux*. Presence of mind and ready wit, or the saving grace of humour, is often more effectual than artillery on such occasions. It does not appear, however, that this particular sheriff had instituted any legal proceedings against, or had any process to serve upon, the said " O'Conor Faily," as Meath was his jurisdiction. But, like many another good fellow, Robin Hood of Sherwood Forest among them, O'Connor could not resist the temptation of bagging a sheriff—a temptation which had the additional relish in his case from the fact that the said sheriff was an English official, and one who could, in all fairness, be made to disgorge some of the exorbitant fees and fines he had squeezed out of the downtrodden English of the Pale. The capture of the sheriff seems to have given a sort of fillip to the rising spirits of the O'Connor. For three years afterwards (1414), with the help of

MacGeoghegan, he succeeded in inflicting a severe defeat on the English, as one may infer from the fact that one great baron, he of Skrein, was killed, and another, the Baron of Slane, was taken prisoner. This conflict took place at Killucan, near Mullingar.

But in 1421 the end came to Murrough O'Connor, who had taken the sheriff, and who, as the *Four Masters* have it, "had defeated the English and Irish who opposed them in many battles." The great chief died "after having gained the victory over the world and the devil," and was gathered to his fathers, and they buried him in the Monastery of Killachaid, or Killoughy, the church of the field, which had been founded, by a predecessor of the O'Connor sept, for friars. Its full name was Kill-achaidh-dromfada, or church of the field of the long ridge. This is in the barony of Ballyboy, while another church, Killeigh, with the same derivation, is in the barony of Geashill, founded by S. Sincheall (548), who is said to have lived to the age of 130, and is invoked in the Litany of St. Aengus, along with "1,500 monks, twelve pilgrims, and twelve bishops, and S. Sinchellus the younger, a presbyter, who rest in Killachaidh-dromfoda in the region of Offaly." There are the ruins of a fine Franciscan abbey at Killeigh, where it is probable that Murtagh O'Connor, after his victory over MacGilpatrick and the English of Leix, retired when he found himself attacked by an incurable disease, and "died in a month after he became a friar, and after a well-spent life," as the *Four Masters* say, having appointed Dermot O'Connor as his successor. And as we stand among the ruins of that pile we cannot but

feel that we are in the presence of valiant dead, who
might have been great.

> Here of old fought Erin's warriors,
>   Here they laid their sacred dead,
> Waiting till the trump shall wake them,
>   From the ridge that crowns their bed.

The spot is peaceful, though not neglected, and
offered a quiet resting-place to one who was weary of
" broils and battles."

It may surprise many to learn that the badly-armed
Irish kerne were able to make such headway against
the mail-clad forces with which they contended. But
the heavily-armed English cavalry and war-horses
which fell like a thunderbolt upon the splendid chivalry
of France at Crecy and Poitiers were useless in the bogs
and woods and mountain fastnesses of Ireland, just as
the heavy Norman brigades of William II. failed to
operate with success in the mountain fastnesses and
ravines of Wales. In such a country heavy armour
was an impediment, and English horses, which were
heavier and slower than the Irish, an encumbrance.
Here no level plains gave the much-desired opportunity
for the cavalry charge ; and the dense woods and scrub
made the close formation of infantry impossible, and
obstructed the aim and volley-firing of the archers, and
thus put out of action the most effective arm of the
service in those days. The lightly-clad and more lightly-
armed Irish soldier, fighting in his own native bog, or
heath, or wood, and knowing every pass and turn of the
country, accustomed to act and scout independently,
and possessing the sagacity and courage of a Red
Indian, and generally mounted on a swift horse, was
often more than a match for his heavily-armed

opponent who had been trained to fight in serried masses, and had no previous experience in guerilla warfare, which requires speed and cunning more than strength and courage. But the English were slow to profit by the lessons their frequent defeats might have taught them. The knights trusted in their armour and their lances, and would not alter their style of fighting for an enemy they could have mown down if they had met them in the plains of France or England, but who, unfortunately for them, happened to be located in the midst of a rough and rugged country, reeking with inaccessible swamps and bristling with impenetrable woods.

Hence the discomfiture and practical defeat of the magnificent army corps which Richard II. brought with him in 1399 to avenge the death of the Earl of March. Having landed at Waterford and marched to Kilkenny, the foolish monarch led his forces into the almost unapproachable country of the MacMurroughs. There the archers were useless in the woods, the cavalry were impeded by the bogs, and the infantry were discouraged by having to cut their way through the dense thickets. In the meantime the MacMurrough, too wary to risk an engagement, was constantly retreating and drawing his foes deeper into the woods of Carlow. Then supplies began to fail. And when hunger, the greatest enemy the soldier has to face, began to enfeeble their spirits and bodies, roving kerne and gallowglasses appeared in unexpected quarters, and having wrought havoc among the stragglers, speedily decamped. And as the horsemen rode past, the kerne would dash out from their ambush, and cut the reins with their pikes, hamstring the horses, and stab the riders with their sharp skeans. There was nothing for it but retreat. Pursued and harassed by the now triumphant enemy, the disheartened chivalry of England at last won the shore, and were gladdened by the sight of their transport ships in the offing. So this gallantly-equipped army, which might have made history on the fields of Europe, had all but gone down before the wild woodmen and hillsmen of Wexford, Carlow, and Kilkenny. Richard, however, had the sense to alter his tactics, and was engaged in despatching flying columns through the country, the only practical mode of campaign, when the fatal news arrived of the landing of Bolingbroke at Ravenspur. And he hastened back to England and to death, leaving the Irish septs to work out their own salvation.

CHAPTER VI.

IRELAND UNDER THE LANCASTRIAN KINGS.

DURING the reign of Henry IV. his gallant son, Lord Thomas of Lancaster, was Lieutenant of Ireland, but only stayed here some seven months, during which time he was wounded in an encounter with the O'Byrnes of the Dublin hills, a mile from Dublin. In the reign of Henry V., whose whole attention was given to France, Lord Furnival, the Lieutenant, went round the Pale receiving submission from the Byrnes, Tooles and Kavanaghs in the South, and passing on to the Moores, O'Connors, and O'Farrels in the West, and concluding with the O'Reillys, MacMahons, O'Neills, and O'Hanlons in the North. A record of his services was sent as a memorial to Henry V., then in France, by the grateful lords and gentlemen of the Pale, which Sir John Davis says he saw recorded in the White Book of the Exchequer at Dublin. But he was able to effect little permanent work owing to the small pay and worse discipline of his troops.

From this date the O'Connors became formidable foes of the English and such of their own countrymen who ventured to oppose their designs. Their forays became bolder and more extensive. Up to the very walls of Dublin they came, and Cahir O'Connor succeeded in improving upon the exploit of Murrough O'Connor, who took captive the Sheriff of Meath, by carrying off no less a personage than the Lord Deputy of Ireland in 1439. The account in the *Four Masters* is that "the King of England's Viceroy arrived in Ireland, and was taken prisoner by Cahir, the son of O'Conor Faily, and after he had remained some time in confinement, he was ransomed by the English in Dublin, who delivered the son of Plunket in his stead to Cahir." Sir Christopher Plunket was a former Deputy (1432). But it is not certain who the notable prisoner of Cahir O'Connor was. He can not have been the Lord Wells who was appointed Lord Lieutenant in 1438, for he never came over. But it was probably Richard Talbot who was then in Ireland. The distinguished prisoner was detained in the castle at Killucan on the borders of the county.

The capture of the King's chief officer in Ireland shows to what a low ebb the fortunes of the English Colony which was now reduced to the county of Dublin with parts of Meath, Louth, and Kildare, had fallen. The towns of ths sea coast were completely isolated, and owing to the disturbed nature of the country it was impossible for the great lords to attend the Parliament while the remaining colonists were compelled to pay tribute and "black rent" to the surrounding Irish chieftains. The fact was that the English nobles who tried to govern England and Ireland in the reign of the pious but weak-minded Henry VI. were unable to cope with the difficulties of the French campaign and the Irish rebels owing to their own divisions which eventually culminated in the great schism between the houses of York and Lancaster. This civil war was hailed with delight by the native Irish as well as by the English colonists; and the two houses had no keener adherents than their Irish allies. The Butlers of Ormonde fought for the Red ; the Geraldines of Desmond and Kildare contended for the White Rose. But the Irish chiefs who fought for Richard of York must not be forgotten. Their presence at Wakefield Green serves to illustrate the weakness of the Celtic system. At the time when the English colonists of the Pale were at their last gasp, and a sudden and well-combined movement of the Irish septs would have swept them into the sea, the opportunity of liberating their country was allowed to pass while the Irish chieftains carried on their petty feuds with one another, or allowed their sympathies to get the better of their reason.

The Irish statutes of the reigns of Henry VI. and Edward IV. fully reveal the feebleness of the Executive and the persecution to which the colonists of the Pale were subjected. For instance, in the 25th, Henry VI., Cap. 24 (1447) we read that as there was " no diversity in array between the English marchers and the Irish enemies," and that the latter under colour of being English marchers, or troops for the defence of the frontiers, entered into the Pale, robbing and murdering the common people by night, it was ordered that an Englishman shall have "no beard above his mouth, that is to say, that he shall have no hairs upon his upper lip." For the moustache was a favourite appendage of the Irishman. Although some such regulation was necessary in order that the Irish highwayman masquerading as a loyal trooper might be more easily detected, it was hard on the English settlers to be ordered to remove these hirsute embellishments, if they chose to wear them, under pain of being seized, as Irish rebels and held to ransom as Irish enemies. Were the Privy Council of 1908 to issue such an order it might create as much stir in the country as the Old Age Pensions Act.

From the same statute we learn that the lieutenants and justices of the land received divers Irish as liegemen and retainers doubtless because they were more easily hired and kept than English soldiers, and that these people, instead of acting loyally, " do rob, burn, and destroy the King's liegemen." For this the poor colonists had little or no redress. They were afraid even of defending themselves and their property against the Irish—who are not to be blamed—"for fear, as the statute says, " to be impeached," that means, to be brought to trial before the judges. What greater proof of the unjust conduct of the English officials of those days could be desired ?

A statute of 1450 tells us how the marchers of the different countries maintained their horsemen and footmen, Irish as well as English. " They do coyne them upon the poor husbands (husbandmen) and tenants of the land of Ireland and oppress and destroy them." The expression " coyne and livery " is frequently met in the Statute Book, and will be referred to in another place. Suffice it to say here that coyne and livery meant the food for themselves and their horses which the soldiers billeted upon the unfortunate farmer seized. It is certain that coyne has nothing to do with the English *coin*, but means man's meat, while livery means horse-meat and stabling, the accommodation that was *delivered* to a traveller. This, however, was a case of " stand and deliver." Spenser informs us that " a servant's livery is so called from his being required to deliver it up when dismissed from his master's service." An expression

in vogue in his day " the livery is served up all right,"
meaning that the carousal was kept up all night may
throw light on some of the customs connected with
the exaction of " coyne and livery."   For the gallant
officers in charge of the English frontiers, and
entrusted with the defence of the English Pale, were
not content with merely billeting their Irish kerne
and gallowglasses as well as their own troops upon the
English " husbands " and tenants.   The same statute,
28 Henry VI., describes other doings which were even
more intolerable.   For " the captains of the said
marchours " brought all their people, their wives and
their pages, and "the King's Irish enemies, both
men and women, and English rebels, with their horsemen and footmen," down upon their poor " husbands "
in time of war and peace.   And the " husband " was
compelled often to entertain one hundred of these
gentry, horse and foot, at night suppers called
"cuddies."   Hard times were those for the English
farmer in Ireland.   Hard, indeed, was it at harvest
time when the hay and the corn were being carted
home to be ricked and stacked in the haggard to find
a troop of the king's horse or of an Irish sept in
possession of the farmyard.   But harder still was it to
have the doors of his house—the Englishman's castle
—burst open in the witching hours of night by order
of the king's officer in charge of the district, to see
his victuals dragged forth from the larder and his wife
and children insulted and molested by a number of
strange men, rebels against the King and native
tribesmen, whose conduct, even if it did not exceed
wild hilarity, would be sufficient to cause any self-
respecting man to feel indignation.

Spenser, who must often have witnessed such scenes in which the soldiers dealt roughly with the poor men who were compelled to supply them with lodging and food, describes them with indignation, saying of the soldiers, "for they will not onely not content themselves with such victuals as their hostes, nor yet as the place perhaps affords, but they will have other meate provided for them, and *aqua vitae* sent for, yea and money besides laid at their trenchers, which if they want, then about the house they walk with the wretched poore man and his silly wife, who are glad to purchase their peace with anything."

But hardest of all was it to know that the men to whose keeping their lands and lives had been entrusted by the king and his deputy were in league with their enemies against them, and that "what tenant or husband will not be at their truce they do rob, spoil and kill."

The English Government in 1450, the year of Jack Cade's insurrection, actually went so far as to allow every loyal subject of the king to take or kill without impeachment any notorious thief caught in the act of "robbing and spoiling or breaking houses by night or by day." And in 1466, in consequence of the many highway robberies and murders that had been committed in the county of Meath upon "the faithful liege-people of the king" permission was granted to any person finding any thieves robbing *or going or coming to rob or steal,* to take and kill them and cut off their heads, which were to be brought to the "portreffe of the town of Trim," and to be put upon a spear upon the castle, and a reward was to be given to the slayer of the thief. By this statute the

English Government did not exhibit its cruelty but confessed its inability to protect the lives and property of the colonists, who were completely at the mercy of the roving bands of Irish kerne, and who had little chance of putting down the "Sheppards" and "Turpins" of those days unaided, much less of coping with the native chieftains on their native heath. It was in the same grim humour that a Chief Secretary of Ireland stated in the House that the victims of the recent cattle-scattering raids ought to protect their own property. Five years before the statute concerning the highwaymen of Meath, the O'Connor had marched with a thousand horsemen "all helmeted, fearless and undismayed," into the said county of Meath, burning and laying waste until at last "he received great presents from the English for granting them peace, as was always customary with those who held his place." A very small harvest of heads would the Portreffe of Trim have to show after such a thorough reaping by the Irish harvesters.

But such campaigns as these revealed at once the strength and the weakness of the Irish septs. The tribesmen of the various clans were devoted to their own tribe and chief. But they had not yet learned that the tribe was but a portion of a greater unit— the nation. Their patriotism was limited to the tribe and their loyalty to its chief. They carried on war more implacably with their own neighbours, their hereditary foes, than with the stranger, Dane, Norman, Saxon, or whatever he might be. There was no central authority which could coerce or combine the Irish chieftains, who ruled their own district by the sword. The country was divided among a number of petty kings and princes, whose dimensions rarely extended beyond the size of a modern barony, and who would have been invincible if united, but because they were simply a congeries of disorganized units were easily taken and dealt with in detail, but on the whole were difficult to conquer.

Nor were the English slow to take advantage of the quarrelsome and excitable nature of the Irish, of whom Sydney wrote—"They fight for their dinner, and many of them lose their heads before they be served with their supper." They often fostered discords and sowed dissension among the Irish tribes. The State Papers of Henry VIII. make this clear. The Archbishop of Dublin was sent to Waterford in 1520 to make peace between the Earl of Desmond and Sir Piers Butler, but while publicly exhorted to do this was privately directed to enfeeble and diminish the strength of the Irish enemy "as well as by getting captains from them as by putting division among them, so that they join not together." The story is also told of a Cromwellian officer who desired to reduce the Irish population in his district. Accordingly he gave a banquet and dispensed wine freely, and when the men had well drunk they found daggers placed near them with which they concluded their arguments. The story, no doubt, is apocryphal, but it may illustrate the point.

The English estimate of the Irish character and affection was not high. The Government in 1537 advised the keeping of a supply of ready money in Dublin as a remedy against rebellion, "because the nature of Irishmen is such that for money one shall have the war against the father and the father against the

G

child." [1] Some colour is given to this statement by the
Irish annals, which read in some places like a series
of Newgate Calendars rather than the history of a
civilized nation, and in others like the high-flown and
fulsome panegyrics of the orators of declining Greece.
There is little doubt that the annalists gloried in the
barbaric and bloody deeds of their heroes, rather than
in their services to the social and religious well-being
of their tribe. Professor A. C. Richey gives an
analysis of the Annals of the Four Masters, who were
principally concerned with the doings of the Ulster
and Connaught clans, from the year 1500 to 1534,
which illustrates this point. It runs :—" Battles,
plundering, etc., exclusive of those in which the
English Government was engaged, 116 ; Irish gentlemen of family killed in battle, 102 ; murdered, 168—
many of them with circumstances of great atrocity ;
and during this period, on the other hand, there is no
allusion to the enactment of any law, the founding of
any town, monastery or church, and all this is recorded
by the annalist without the slightest expression of
regret or astonishment and as if such were the
ordinary course of life in a Christian nation."

The *Book of Leinster*, a collection of similar records
of the deeds of the Leinstermen, makes one wonder
how Dermot Mac Murrough, who was taught by its
compiler in his youth, could have been other than he
was—cruel, revengeful and evil. This " Book "
eulogizes the violent deeds of the Leinster men against
the Connaught men, and at the end of every violent
tragedy, adds with exultation—" 'Twas the Leinstermen killed them," while the *Four Masters* describe

[1] A short History of the Irish People (Kane's Edition, p. 247.)

Mortogh O'Loghlin of the Northern O'Neills, who was King of Ireland and the ally of Dermot Mac Murrough in the latter's war with O'Rourke and Torlogh O'Connor of Connaught, as "the Monarch of all Ireland, the chief lamp of the valour, chivalry, hospitality, and prowess of the West of the world; a man who had never been defeated in battle till that time, and who had gained many battles." And yet this " Chief Lamp of the West" had broken an oath of peace sworn upon the staff of S. Patrick, the *Bachall Isa*, to certain chieftains, and when he had got them into his power blinded one, who is said to have been "the pillar of the prowess and hospitality of the Irish." And they eulogise Torlogh O'Connor, who broke the most solemn oaths without the slightest compunction, and in whose hands no man's life or lands were safe, and who had put out the eyes of his own son, Hugh, in 1136 as " the flood of the glory and splendour of Ireland, the Augustus of the West of Europe, a man full of charity and mercy, hospitality and chivalry."

There must have been, indeed, something rotten in the state of Ireland when such lives were regarded as standards of honour and rectitude, and such men were regarded as the "Chief Lamps of the West" and "the floods of the glory and splendour of Ireland." It is little wonder that under such conditions of life the native tribes were not improving, and although they had obtained many advantages in their border warfare with the downtrodden English colony, who were reduced to the condition of the scapegoats of the Home Government and the tributaries of the enemy, were unable to come to any permanent or satisfactory settlement with the invaders. When the chiefs of neighbouring clans could not arrange a *modus vivendi* with each other, they could hardly be expected to come to any amicable arrangement with the strangers, who only wished to live peaceably with all men and to be allowed to trade and prosper in the land.

Here we touch the solution of the problem, the lack of thrift and commercial spirit among the Irish. They scorned the one and they despised the other. It was foreign merchants, Norsemen, who came to the country after the removal of Turgesius, who founded Waterford, Limerick, and Dublin. And it was the Bristol merchants who made Dublin the leading city it was in the thirteenth and the fourteenth century.

A few words on the doings of our metropolis and the general state of Ireland in the period under consideration may not be an unsuitable conclusion to this chapter. The citizens of Dublin showed remarkable activity both by land and sea in the reign of Henry IV. In 1400 we read in Marleburrough's *Chronicle* that "the Constable of Dublin and divers others at Stranford (Strangford) in Ulster, fought at sea with the Scots, where many Englishmen were slaine and drowned." The year before, the trained bands of Dublin had invaded the O'Brien's country and "slue three-and-twenty of the Irish, and tooke fourscore men, women and children." And in 1402, on the fifth of the Ides of June, after the dedication of the Church of the Fryers Preachers in Dublin, and perhaps to signalise that occasion by a worthy feat, John Drake, the Mayor of Dublin, issued forth with the citizens and townsmen near to Bre, now known as Bray and meaning hill, and punished some of the wild

Wicklow tribes who had on Black Monday, in the year of grace 1209, massacred the Dublin citizens, their wives and children, as they were picnicing in the wood of the Cualanni, now known as Cullenswood, near Rathmines. John Drake and his valiant men "slue of the Irish four hundred, ninety-three, being all men of warre."

In 1405 we read in Marleburrough's *Chronicle* of a naval exploit of the Dublin sailors. This year which witnessed the capture of Prince James of Scotland on the high seas as he was on his way to France to learn "that tongue and eke courtesy," and who was brought to England to learn to love an English maiden, Lady Joan Beaufort, and to sing her praise in "The King's Quair," also beheld the Dublin ships putting into St. Ninian[1], where their crews "valiantly behaved themselves, and afterwards they entred Wales and there did much hurt to the Welch men and brought away the Shrine of St. Cubius, and placed it in the Church of the Holy Trinitie in Dublin."

In the same year 1405 there were serious risings in Leix, the country of the Moores and the O'Dempsey, who had been encouraged by the temporary successes of Art MacMurrough. But James, Earl of Ormonde, called the Chaste, quelled these disturbances. First of all, "in the red moore of Athye (the sun almost lodged in the west and miraculously standing still in his epicycle the space of three hours till the feat was accomplished, and no pit in that bogge annoying either horse or man on his part) he vanquished O'More and his terrible army." And soon afterwards

---

[1] Probably Whitorn in Wigtownshire, where S. Ninian preached the Gospel to the Picts in the fifth century.

he dispersed the formidable forces of Art. But James of Ormonde seems to have been a mild governor as well as a heaven-blest warrior. The O'Dempsey took advantage of his gentle rule and intruded into the castle of Leix, the property of the Earl of Kildare, from which he was expelled by the Deputy, who also "tamed the O'Briens, Burkes, MacBanons, Ogaghnraghte, MacMahons, all the captains of Thomond in three months." All this time the Lord Justice was materially assisted by the clergy of Dublin, who processed through the street twice every week with prayers for his success against "those disordered persons which now in every quarter, had degenerated to their old trade of life." Very solemn must those litanies have been. They remind us of the solemn *Miserere* of Bishop Mamertus of Vienne in Gaul (460) when the clergy walked in solemn procession through the streets chanting their litanies for deliverance from the plague. Verily the clergy of Dublin were as strong in prayer as they were stout in arms.

But our best governor died the same year, and was succeeded by Gerald, Earl of Kildare, 1405. Greatly encouraged, however, by their recent successes, the citizens of Dublin on *Corpus Christi* day, 1406, with the help of the country people, "manfully vanquished the Irish enemies and slue divers of them, and took two Ensignes, bringing with them to Dublin the heades of those whom they had slaine."

There seems to have been an unhappy mania for collecting dead men's skulls in those days. Instead of decently interring the remains of the ill-starred warriors they simply cut off their heads and carried them off triumphantly in almost the same way as a

Red Indian would scalp a fallen enemy, dead or alive, or a wolfhunter of those days would gather the heads of the wolves of which he had rid the land, and for which he claimed reward.

In the same year we read that the Prior of Conall with but 20 Englishmen vanquished two hundred Irish that were well armed, "slaying some of them and chasing others," in the Curragh of Kildare.

But all this time the Irish were giving great trouble to the settlers. Most pathetic is the application for assistance that was sent from the inhabitants of Cork, Youghal, and Kinsale, who were harassed by the Irish outlaws, who had become stronger than the Norman nobles of Munster owing to the dissensions of the latter, and of whom Lord Roche, Lord Courcy and Lord Barry alone remained. Nor was the Pale free for a day from the incursions of the raiders, who harried their borders, especially during the sessions of Parliament, "when," we read, "the Irish burned all that stood in their way." A strange instance of poetic justice is mentioned in Marleburrough's *Chronicle.* In 1408 he tells us that Hugh MacGilmore was slain at Cragfergus (Carrickfergus) within the Church of the Friars Minors, "which Church he had before destroyed and broken down the glasse-windows to have the iron barres through which his enemies the savages entered upon him." For one would opine that although the poet says :—

> Stone walls do not a prison make,
> Nor iron bars a cage,

that they would form a stouter protection than brittle glass against an armed host—unless half-naked and fearful of cutting their hands and feet. But the result was evidently regarded not as due to an error of judgment but as the consequence of a sacrilege, very much as the stout De Courcy of Ulster was thought to have brought a curse upon himself for having altered the Cathedral Church of the Holy Trinity in Down into " an Abbey of Black Monks from Chester, and dedicated the same to the honour of S. Patrick."

The same eternal feuds continued in spite of all the English could do, for the Celtic blood is irrepressible, so that the colonists once more turned their faces towards home, but were checked in 1438 by the statutes against absentees.

In 1449, a firm hand was laid upon the neck of the unmanageable Celt, and by kindness and firmness his spirit was tamed. But the same ruler—Richard Duke of York, in his letter to his brother the Earl of Shrewsbury—complained of Magoghigan (MacGeoghegan) and his turbulence. " With him," he wrote, "three or four Irish Captaines associate with a great fellowship of English rebells. . . They have burnt down a great towne of thine inheritance, Ramore, and other villages thereabouts, and murdered and brent both men, women, and children without mercy. The which enemies be yet assembled in woods and forts wayting to doe the hurt or grievance to the King's subjects that they can thinke or imagine."

This is a fair picture of the difficulties with which a Lord Lieutenant of those days had to cope ; and when badly paid and worse supported by the King and his Council we cannot be surprised if few reached the high standard of our best English Viceroy— Richard Duke of York.

CHAPTER VII.

ACTS OF SIGNIFICANCE.

WE have followed the O'Connor clan from comparative obscurity to considerable importance. We shall see how they gradually fell from the pinnacle of their pride. Their fall is to be ascribed to their connexions, hostile and friendly, with the Geraldines, and to their own unhappy dissensions. Some time after the capture of the King's Deputy the Fitzgeralds of Kildare and Desmond began to cast longing glances upon the rich pastures of Offaly, and to make themselves strong, with a view not only to repel their "rash intruding" neighbour, but also to seize his lands. The Earl of Desmond followed hard on the heels of the O'Connor as he was returning from one of the forays in Leix (1440). Twelve years afterwards (1452) James, Earl of Ormond, Lord Justice of Ireland, was compelled to put down the Midland septs with a firm hand. He overran Leix, burnt Airem, the property of O'Dempsey, and marched into Offaly, where the O'Connor submitted to him. Seven years pass and Con O'Connor was defeated by Thomas, Earl of Kildare, and taken prisoner. The next year (1460) the restless Con defeated the English, when Hussey or Hose Baron of Galtrim was killed. These Husseys claimed Birr under the grant of the town and the neighbouring lands of Ely O'Carroll made by King John to Theobald Fitzwalter, and by him transferred in part, i.e., Villam de Birre, to Hugh de Hose or Hussey, for military tenure. The Husseys of Galtrim were great warriors. Their war cry, Cor-deragh-aboe, or the cause of the great cast, was won by the courage of the Hussey, who slew O'Kelly and his squire at the battle of Athenry, already described.

And two years afterwards the O'Connor made his memorable incursion at the head of a thousand horsemen into Meath, when he laid the whole country waste and departed laden with spoils and gifts.

The English, accordingly, began in self-defence to plan a complete removal of this thorn in their side. John Fitzgerald, who was said to be "the best and most renowned general of the English," marshalled his forces in Kildare and the Deputy, Thomas, Earl of Desmond, arranged to meet him at a certain place with the Dublin contingent. But Con was on the alert and completely frustrated his enemy's plans by attacking the men of Kildare before they were joined by the Deputy, and defeating them with much loss. The next day he followed up his advantage by giving battle to the army that was on the march from Dublin and fighting on his own terms succeeded in putting it to a complete rout and taking prisoner the Deputy, Thomas, Earl of Desmond. The latter was taken to Carbury Castle, but was soon afterwards rescued by his own party. However, in 1468, the brave Con ventured too far into the mouth of the Norman lion and was taken prisoner himself, and Teige O'Connor, "the conqueror of both English and Irish," died of the plague.

Furthermore, as we frequently find in Irish history, tribal feuds and family troubles were effectual where foreign combination was unavailing. In the first place, a quarrel between the MacGeoghegans of Moycashel,

Westmeath, and the O'Connors of Offaly led to a series of disasters for the latter, and then MacGeoghegan, who had hitherto assisted the O'Connors against the English, and had themselves in 1329 defeated an English force under Lord Thomas le Botiller, now allied themselves to the English of the Pale ; and although the O'Connors were able to hold their own against the lords of Moycastle and Kilbeggan, they suffered a severe defeat in 1493, when Cahir O'Connor Faly and many of his kinsmen were taken prisoners by the MacGeoghegans.

About this same time it appears that the O'Connor had two of his own relations, Torlogh O'Connor and Cathal O'Connor hanged. It is from this point that we may date the downfall of the clan, which was so powerful when united, but when divided by internal disputes lay completely at the mercy of its foes. For Cahir himself was murdered in 1511 by his own kinsmen, doubtless in revenge for friends Cahir had caused to be murdered. From that murder, the feud which eventually split up the O'Connors in Queen Elizabeth's reign into the Queen's O'Connors and the Irish O'Connors, began in real earnest. This Cahir O'Connor, who is described as " a general entertainer of learned men and a distinguished military leader among the English and Irish," was attacked near the Monastery of Monasteroris, called after the Irish name MacFeoris, adopted, as we have already seen, by Sir John Bermingham, just as the names McWilliam Iochtar and McWilliam Uachtar were taken by the Connaught Burkes, who became more Irish than the Irish themselves, and affected Irish dress, customs and language. Within sight of the consecrated walls and hallowed ground of the abbey, which the hereditary foe of the O'Connors had built nearly two centuries before, the head of the clan was slain by his own relations, the sons of Teige. This was in the year 1511.

The seed of dissension thus sown bore a bitter fruit in the family of the reigning Prince of Offaly. Brian and Cahir were brothers. Of these Brian seems to have been the elder, but not necessarily the heir. They do not appear to have been very loyal or affectionate to one another. However, Brian, undisturbed by this family disagreement, which was nothing out of the beaten track of an O'Connor's life, arranged with the O'Moores and O'Carrolls to invade the English Pale (1521).

The Lord Lieutenant, at the time, was Surrey, a most capable and enterprising officer, who had already written a very strong letter to Henry VIII. in which he insisted that Ireland should be conquered by arms, and that to attempt to kill rebellion by pacific measures was impracticable. The King had advised his officer to win the Irish chieftains " by circumspect and politic ways," to obey the English laws, and "following justice, to forbear to detain rebelliously such lands and dominions as to us in right appertaineth." And his deputy is urged to appeal to the reason of these chieftains and their sense of fair play, and "to show unto them that of necessity it is requisite that every reasonable creature be governed by a law." By this means the King thought an entry could be made into the inaccessible parts of the country, and that " our lands detained by usurpation might be reduced to our possession." But he directs his Deputy to proceed "*politically, patiently,* and *secretly,* that the Irish lords conceive no jealousy or suspicion that they shall be constrained precisely to live under our laws or put from all the lands by them now detained."

But Surrey wrote on the 16th December, 1520, beseeching the King that "if the King's pleasure be not to go through with the conquest of this land, which would be a marvellous charge, no longer to suffer me to waste his Grace's treasure here." In this clause Surrey had struck home. For Henry VIII., though prodigal in his pleasures, was a miser in matters of State. He grudged the spending of the £17,000 a year that was required for the upkeep of a respectable army in Ireland for the defence of the four shores of the Pale. We shall see how his avarice led him afterwards (1532) to appoint the Earl of Kildare as Lord Deputy. And in an answer to another letter from Henry, in which the expenses of the standing army in Ireland were impressed upon the Deputy's mind, Surrey wrote back on the 30th June, 1521, saying—"After my poor opinion, the land shall never be brought to good order and subjection but only by conquest, which is, at your Grace's pleasure, to be brought to pass in two ways. One way is, if your Grace will one year set on hand to win one country, and another year another country, and so continue, till at length all be won." In Surrey's opinion, a force of 6,000 men were required: whereas the king was only willing to give 800, and the country could not be subdued in less than ten years, for, as he said, "the countries here be as strong or stronger as Wales, and the inhabitants of the same can, and do live, more hardly than any other people, after mine opinion, in Christendom or Turkey, and " may have three or four thousand Irish Skottes whensoever and as often as they will call for them." It is not, therefore, to be imagined that such a commander, alert and alive to all the difficulties of his task, could be found napping even by the astute O'Connor. Indeed, he managed to surprise O'Connor, and with the assistance of the Mayors of Drogheda and Dublin and the loyal nobles defeated the confederates, who retreated in different directions. O'Connor retired to his castle at Monasterois, a place of great natural strength, and leaving a strong garrison to defend it, made a dash for Westmeath, in order to draw off his enemy's forces from his own lands and towns. But while he was engaged in devastating the farmsteads of the English settlers, the Deputy had followed up his advantage by besieging the Irish garrison in Monasteroris with such vigour and skill that though it was " the strongest hold within the Irishry," they were fain to escape under cover of the night, and to leave the castle in the possession of the royal forces.

Surrey then employed his forces in ravaging the lands of the absent chieftain. He " destroyed much goodly corn and burnt many towns and houses." This had the desired effect of drawing the O'Connor away from the English settlements, and making him return to defend his own, but finding that Monasteroris was in the hands of the English, he withdrew to the recesses of his own bogs and woods, whence he made sudden and unexpected sallies upon the English, in one of which Edward Plunket, Lord Dunsany, fell.

After this initial exchange of courtesies, Surrey

withdrew his forces to the capital to collect a larger army, while O'Connor and his allies were left at peace for a time to prepare for another campaign, one of the saddest, but yet one of the most interesting, in the annals of Irish history.

In the meantime we may take a glance at the affairs of the English Pale, where life was now more intolerable than ever. We have seen how the English colonists had been deprived of their moustachios by a statute of Henry VI., lest they should be mistaken for Celts. A similar order was made in Edward IV's. reign, 1467, with regard to the upper lips of the Irishmen who had made their home in the counties of Dublin, Meath, Uriel (Louth) and Kildare, and had not been allocated to the various Irish towns in the country. The fact that there were a "multitude" of such people to be sworn as the King's liegemen within the borders of the Pale shows that the statute of Kilkenny was more honoured in the breach than in the observance. A feeble attempt was now made to assimilate these Irish people to their English neighbours in appearance and in name. They were ordered to remove "the beard above their mouth," to go "like an Englishman in apparel," and to "take to him an English surname of a town—as Sutton, Chester, Trym, Skryne, Cork, Kinsale, or colour, as white, black, brown ; or art or science, as smith or carpenter ; or office, as cook, butler ; and he and his issue shall use this name under pain of forfeiting of his goods yearly." From this assortment of worthy if not musical English names the Kinsellaghs, MacNamaras, O'Molloys, O'Shaughnessys and O'Morchoes had to take their choice under pain of losing their goods.

That was the humour of the statute. Upon this compulsory exchange of the Irishman's surname, and the threatened forfeiture of his property, a Celt of a later age might have moralised somewhat in the words of Iago in Shakspeare's Othello—

> Who steals my purse steals trash ! 'tis something, nothing,
> But he that filches from me my good name
> Robs me of that which not enriches him,
> And makes me poor, indeed.

At a recent meeting in Dublin a certain worthy citizen with an English name objected to having it "turned upside down in Irish." But what must have been the feelings of a Diarmaid O'Halloran when addressed as Jeremiah Black, or a Timothy McCarthy when styled Tim Brown, or a Cathal O'Carroll when called Charles White, or a Torlogh O'Donoghoe to have to assume the brief appellation of Terence Gray !

It was bad enough to lose one's moustache, the growth of which had been so anxiously watched and tended ; it was worse to be compelled to lay aside the picturesque and highly coloured garment in which the Irish, who rejoiced in colours, arrayed their muscular forms, and don the sober livery of an Englishman ; but it "was the most unkindest cut of all" to be shorn of their musical and high sounding names which they had carried with more or less distinction since the Milesian conquest, and which reminded them, not merely of their own family, but also of the sept with whose varying fortunes their deepest sympathies and highest sentiments were associated.

In the meantime, the Irish Parliament, which might have become a constitutional and representative assembly, had by reason of the lawlessness of the country, which made it dangerous for the country members of the Houses to attend at Dublin, Kilkenny, Drogheda or Trim (1416), at which places the parliaments were then summoned, and owing to the control exercised by the officials of the Crown, had been reduced to a condition of utter helplessness and uselessness. Before the ruin of the English Pale it had met regularly and transacted its business in an independent spirit. But it was now but a pliable instrument in the hands of the king and his advisers, and seems to have been only summoned when subsidies were required by the English Government for its foreign wars. The lords of the Upper House, peers, prelates and priors, were conspicuous for their absence. Nobles, like Desmond and Ormonde claimed exemption; while the bishops and abbots sent proctors to represent them. Hence the custom arose of summoning two proctors from each diocese, who sat with the knights, citizens and burgesses in the lower house, and claimed to be representatives of the clergy and entitled to vote. The knights of the shires, who had been summoned in Ireland since 1264 were not a strong body, as there were only four shires in the Pale, while the burgesses, who had been summoned since 1295, could only attend from a few towns. Many of these had not even gone through the formality of an election, having received the writ directly from the king. It would, indeed, be hard to find an assembly less deserving of the name of Parliament. It was simply a Dublin Council in the hands of the king's officer. But its history proves the truth of the saying, that " even a worm will turn." For this generally supine and invertebrate assembly

H

dared on one occasion at least to act with a spirit worthy of Stephen Langton, Simon de Montfort and other makers of England and founders of its freedom. It was when the Duke of York crossed the Irish Sea in 1459, having been deserted by his own forces, who were seized with a panic when Henry VI. marched against him at Ludlow, and threw himself upon the loyalty and devotion of the English Pale. He had been sent by Henry VI., who wanted to be rid of him, to Ireland as Lord Lieutenant in 1449, and had won golden opinions from Norman, Saxon and Celt by his noble character and high ideals. He had left Ireland in 1454 to assume the protectorate in England, but now returned to the land where "he had exceedingly tyed unto him the hearts of the noblemen and gentlemen," and was received in a different manner from that in which any other English protector was greeted. Although under the attainder of the English Government, in which the Lancastrian party had for the time gained the upper hand, the Irish house acknowledged Richard of York as its Viceroy, and supported by him asserted its independence and its right to be bound only by its own laws, and to coin money, and declared that no Irish subject was bound to answer any writs save those issued under the great seal of Ireland.

These were no mere words, as was proved by the terrible earnestness with which the Irish nobles, especially of the houses of Kildare and Desmond, some twenty years afterwards threw themselves into the cause of Lambert Simnel, who personated the Earl of Warwick, and was crowned in Christ Church Cathedral, Dublin, with great pomp by the Bishop of

Meath in May, 1486, a coronation which was attended by the Earl of Kildare, the Lord Deputy with "the lords of the Council and other great men of quality." The crown won by the future scullion and falconer of Henry VII. consisted of a diadem taken from an image of the Virgin in the nunnery of St. Mary. And the sham monarch was carried, according to an old Irish usage, upon the shoulders of an Irish giant "called Great Darcy of Platten" to Dublin Castle, and escorted by 2,000 German troops under Martin Schwartz, sent by the Duchess of Burgundy, who supported the claims of the pretender who was introduced to the Earl of Kildare by a priest, Sir Richard Symonds, as the son of the Duke of Clarence. In Smith's " History of Waterford," we read how John Butler, Mayor of Waterford, refused to receive the pretender, and how the Butlers collected their forces and prepared to resist the claims of Kildare's protégé. But numbers of the Earl of Kildare's faction, including Thomas Fitzgerald, his own brother, followed Simnel to Lancashire, and shared in his defeat at Stoke and the leniency with which the king treated him. And when the fraud was discovered the Irish still believed in him. He was followed by Perkin Warbeck, who landed in Cork in 1490, and personated Richard Plantagenet and found many adherents in Ireland, who suffered for their hotheadedness in Cornwall and on the block.

Even though the utterances of this parliament of 1459 were dignified and noble, they brought sorrow to Ireland, for they alienated the feelings of the Lancastrian party from Ireland and its parliament. And in 1492 Henry VII., who could not forget that the house of York was the popular party with the English of the Pale, or forgive the Geraldines' adherence to the Duke of York's family, superseded the Earl of Kildare and appointed Walter Fitz-Simon, Archbishop of Dublin, as Deputy in his room, and Sir James Butler as High Treasurer in the stead of Fitz-Eustace, the earl's father-in-law. And shortly afterwards (1494) sent over Sir Edward Poynings, who drove back the native Irish and summoned the historic parliament of Drogheda which, after passing a number of useful laws for the benefit of the natives and the protection of the dwellers in the Pale from the extortions of the great lords, took away all initiative from the Irish Parliament and reduced it to the dependent condition it occupied for centuries, when it was alternately the mouthpiece of the Geraldines and the Butlers, but in which men had once acted with spirit. Among the new regulations was one declaring it to be unlawful to incite the natives to war, to engage in private hostilities, and to practise coyne and livery. Owners of march lands were required to reside on their lands and under heavy penalties were ordered to see that no Irish rebel or enemy crossed the border. Citizens were not to become the retainers of the lords, and judges were only to hold office during the king's pleasure. The Statutes of Kilkenny (1367) were also renewed, with the exception of those relating to the use of the Irish language and the non-use of saddles —a custom which had become too general to be put down by edict.

The Statutes of Kilkenny may sound very terrible in our ears ; but it was a voice in the wilderness during the century and more, that elapsed between the date of its enactment and this Act of Sir Edward Poynings (1494). Its object had been like the Mosaic legislation, to raise a barrier between the English of the Pale and the Irish inhabitants, and to check every kind of communication between the two races. Hardiman described it as " no more than a peevish and revengeful expression Duke Lionel felt from the opposition he had met with and the loss of the lands he had come over to claim." The purpose of the Act which condemned marriage alliances, gossiped and fosterage with the Irish, the use of the Irish language, and the Brehon law, styled by the Drogheda Parliament as " the wicked and damnable law called Brehon Law," and the adoption of Irish customs and dress was to prevent the English becoming more Irish than the Irish themselves, and like the lotus eaters forgetting their own country. But the statute was in many respects a dead letter; for it was not founded on public opinion, was not granted in response to the demands of any portion of the English community, was resented by the English as well as by the Irish, and could not be enforced without a police or military force. Such a statute was a sign of weakness and savoured rather of hysterics than politics.

Poynings' Act of 1494, which is rather extravagantly styled by Ritchie as " the most disgraceful Act ever passed by an independent legislature," meant nothing more than the removal of the rag of power and the simulacrum of rule, which had been absurdly paraded by the Irish Parliament for some centuries, and the exorcism of the ghost of the spirit of freedom which had haunted for many years their Council Chamber, a strange visitant which on the occasion that it appeared, bewildered the members themselves and alarmed their opponents. Henry VII. was determined to remove whatever sting the Irish Parliament might still possess. And he may have had the idea of still further crippling the broken power of the English soldiers in the presence of the Celtic population, and of provoking the latter to repeat their incursions, so as to prevent the colonists from ever becoming a menace to the Welsh house of Tudor.

The clause of the Act which evoked so much criticism was to the effect that—" no parliament be holden hereafter in the said land (of Ireland) but at such season as the King's Lieutenant and Council there first do certify the king, under the great seals of that land, the causes and considerations, and acts affirmed by the king and his council, to be good and expedient for that land, and his licence thereupon, as well in affirmation of the said causes and acts, as to summon the said parliament under his great seal of England had and obtained ; that done, a parliament to be had and holden after this form and effect before rehearsed : and if any parliament be holden in that land hereafter, contrary to the form and provision aforesaid, it be deemed void and of none effect in law."

Consequently no parliament could be summoned in Ireland without the permission of the king and his council, and no bills could be introduced into any parliament so summoned without the king's consent. The Irish Houses of Parliament were in this manner reduced to an office for the registration of English law in Ireland. The result was not altogether so bad as represented ; for by this means the Anglo-Norman factions, the Butlers and Geraldines, whose councils and opinions were voiced from time to time in Dublin, as now one and now the other gained the predominance, were held in check. A sketch of these rival factions is required to explain the political situation which ended with so much disaster to the O'Connors, and will be given in the following chapter. It will be sufficient to add here that this was not the first or the last attempt to muzzle the Irish Houses of Parliament. In 1376 Edward III., desiring to obtain a grant of subsidies for his wars, had summoned the bishops, peers, and representatives of Ireland to a parliament in London. They attended, but under protest. The protest of the Archbishop of Armagh may be read in Leland's History of Ireland (1. 363-397) : "We do not grant," it ran, "to the representatives we have elected any power of assenting to burthens or taxes to be imposed on us or our clergy." In 1460 another declaration of independence was made ; Cromwell held the next union parliament at Westminster ; and in 1801 the parliaments were united.

CHAPTER VIII.

THE GERALDINES AND BUTLERS.

WE have said that one good result of Poynings' Act was the restraint upon the perpetual feuds of these rival houses of Kildare and Ormonde. This was a boon to the law-abiding gentry and citizens of Dublin, Kilkenny, Waterford, and other towns, whose peace was disturbed by the tumults caused by these nobles and the brawls of their retainers and followers in the streets, and who, utterly indifferent for the most part to the *casus belli*, might well exclaim with Mercutio —" A plague o' both your houses !" For just as Verona was kept in perpetual ferment by the Montagues and Capulets, the towns and villages of the Pale were disturbed by these rival factions, whose battle cries *Cromabo* and *Butlerabo* resounded at every hour of the night, but were made penal offences by the new Act.

A brief review of these distinguished families may not be out of place. The Butlers of Ormonde, which eventually became all powerful in Ireland, and still retains much of its former prestige, are descended from Theobald Walter, a nephew of Thomas, Archbishop of Canterbury, who was made hereditary Chief Butler to King Henry II. Theobald obtained grants of land in Kilkenny and Tipperary. One of his descendants, Edmund le Botiller, was created Earl of Carrick in 1315, and his son, James Butler, who married a kins-woman of Edward III., was created Earl of Ormonde

(Oir ¦Mumhan or East Munster) in 1328, and was made Lord Lieutenant the following year. In 1391 the Earl of Ormonde purchased Kilkenny Castle from the descendants of Strongbow's granddaughter Isabel, and the influence of the family was gradually extended by successful marriages in England. In Ireland, this house by degrees became omnipotent in Kilkenny and North Tipperary, where the English colonists had established many castles, towns and monasteries. But in the city of Dublin the house of Kildare, living in greater proximity to the metropolis, was naturally the stronger.

The greatest representative of this family was the gallant marquis who held Ireland for King Charles II. against Cromwell, but whose army was defeated by Colonel Jones in the battle of Rathmines, then some distance outside the city walls. The peaceful citizens of that prosperous and populous township little dream of that fateful night in March 1649 when a gallant little force of 1,500 of Ormonde's troops under Captain Purcell set out in darkness to assault the city, which was in the hands of Jones, the Parliamentary general, but their plans miscarried, and, like the Highland Brigade that marched upon death at Magersfontein, were cut to pieces, and then the main body in the camp being suddenly attacked by the Dublin garrison, who had followed up their success with lightning speed, were completely routed.

The Butlers were always at variance with the Geraldines ; and doubtless from a spirit of rivalry which dictated the smallest details as well as the main lines of their policy, selected opposite sides in every civil war. Around the Lancastrian standard were to be found the Butlers, while the Geraldines were Yorkist to the backbone. And afterwards the Butlers became the staunchest supporters of the English Crown ; while the Geraldines frequently followed an opposite course, and produced some worthy rebels.

The Geraldines, the rival house of Kildare, are said to have been of Florentine origin, and this connection is mentioned in the Earl of Surrey's sonnet on one of the earl's sisters, afterwards Lady Clinton, whom he greatly admired during his term of office—1520-1522.

> From Tuscane came my Ladye's worthy race,
> Fair Florence was sometime her ancient seate,
> The Western Isle whose pleasant shore doth face,
> Wild Cambre's cliffes did give her lively heate.

One record that Campion saw mentioned a Geraldine, the first Earl of Kildare, in the year 1289, and another "saith there dyed a Geraldine, the fourth Earle of Kildare, in anno 1316." The eldest son of the earl was called Baron of Ophalye. The same authority states that he read of a Geraldine " Lord of Ophalye " in the year 1270.

An interesting story is told of the manner in which the Leinster Fitzgeralds took for their crest an ape with a broken chain. Woodstock Castle, near Athy, went on fire, and all the inmates were saved but the infant heir, who was left behind in the flames. Suddenly to the delight of the terrified people a scream was heard on the battlements and a great ape was seen making its way along the parapet and down the sides of the wall into safety with the babe tenderly held in its mouth.

This family became in the following century all powerful, reached the zenith of its glory in

Henry VIII's. reign, and delighted to measure its strength with the Ormondes. Neither family could like or trust the other. A remarkable case in point was the conference between Sir James Ormonde and the great Earl of Kildare in S. Patrick's Cathedral.

This Earl of Kildare had been appointed Lord Deputy by Henry VII. in 1496. He had been attainted by Poynings' Parliament and sent a prisoner to the Tower, which he left to take up the position of Governor of Ireland. It is said that he owed his promotion from his precarious position, which might have led to the block, to his own presence of mind and adroitness in the royal presence. For when accused before the king by the Archhishop of Cashel and the Bishop of Meath of having burnt down the Cathedral of Cashel, the earl admitted it. " Spare your proofs," quoth he, " I own I did burn the church, but I thought the Archbishop was in it." When advised by the king to provide himself with good counsel, he answered : " If I may choose I shall have the best counsel in England." And when the king enquired who that might be, he replied, " Marry, the king himself." The bishop then made many charges concluding with the words—" All Ireland, sire, cannot govern this earl." " Then," said the king : " the earl shall rule all Ireland."

This story may be apocryphal, but the fact remains that the king, a wise monarch with a shrewd knowledge of human nature, had seen the failure of the policy of governing Ireland through exclusively English officials, and had decided to entrust the Government to the most turbulent and powerful nobleman, who might possibly be converted by the complimen

into a trusty supporter. So it fell out. For the Earl
of Kildare never wavered in his allegiance to Henry VII.
Another consideration which weighed with the king
was that of expense. Of a saving disposition, he saw
in the generous and open-handed Irishman one who
would be likely to undertake the duties of Government
without the emoluments of office.

Returning to Ireland as governor for the king, the
earl strove to carry out his compact loyally. He
attacked the Irish insurgents, and defeated them in
several places. He made himself strong in the land
and his name feared. He became reconciled with the
Archbishop of Armagh, but his conference with Sir
James Ormonde was not equally successful. Invited
to a personal interview to explain his conduct, Sir
James marched with a large bodyguard to Dublin,
where the citizens and followers of Kildare armed
themselves in self-defence. S. Patrick's Cathedral, the
place appointed for the interview, became rapidly
filled with armed men. These soon grew impatient
at the length of the conference, and the retainers of
both noblemen discharged their arrows in every direction, damaging the church and its ornaments, for
which profanation the Mayor of Dublin was condemned, it is said, to walk barefoot every year on
Corpus Christi Day. Of this unpleasant duty the
Reformation has relieved the Lord Mayors of that
city. In alarm Sir James Ormonde took refuge in
the Chapter House, bolting the heavy door after him.
Having pacified his followers, and quelled the tumult
with a few stern words, Kildare hastened after
Ormonde, and entreated him to come forth. But he
refused. Whereupon a piece was cut out of the door

by order of Kildare, so that they might clasp hands through the door. But Ormonde hesitated, and then Kildare passed his hand through, and the other clasped it. The door was then opened, and the two noblemen embraced in view of their followers. This door, which witnessed this dramatically-conceived, but hollow, compact is among the well-preserved treasures of the cathedral.

Although the interview ended with a show of friendship there was little love lost between the rivals. This was demonstrated by the fact that shortly afterwards Kildare gave his daughter, Margaret, in marriage to Pierce Butler, Earl of Ormond, a rival of Sir James, who is described by Stanihurst as "a plain, simple gentleman, saving in feats of arms." But Margaret, his countess, who espoused the quarrel of the Butlers against the Geraldines, then under Earl Gerald, who had succeeded his father in 1513 as Lord Deputy of Ireland, seems to have inherited the masterful and resourceful character of her father. Here is Stanihurst's vignette of her : " a lady of such port that all estates of the realm crouched unto her, and such a politician that nothing was thought substantially debated without her advice. She was tall of stature, and masculine ; very bountiful, a fast friend, a bitter enemy, seldom disliking whom once she liked, not easily liking whom once she disliked." It may have been through her influence that Pierce, Earl of Ormonde, was made Lord Deputy on the recommendation of the noble and gallant Earl of Surrey, who departed from these shores, amid universal regret, in 1521. This Pierce was called Pierce the Red, and it was with regard to his oppression that the very unceremonious message was

sent to Henry VIII. from Gillpatrick of Ossory :
" Stand my lord king, my lord Gillpatrick has sent me
unto thee to say that if thou dost not chastise Peter
the Red he will make war upon thee."

The Earl of Kildare, the father of Margaret Butler
—Henry VII's nominee—proved an excellent ally of
England. During his term of office, 1496-1513, the
Crown regained the authority it had lost, and the
Pale was secured against the encroachments of the
tribes. But Kildare was not content with merely re-
building the fenced cities and border castles of the
colony, he carried his arms into Connaught in order
to check the turbulence of Ulick Bourke, Lord
Clanrickarde, who also rejoiced in the name of
McWilliam. Supported by his northern allies, O'Neill
and O'Donnell, and the trained bands of Dublin and the
Pale, Kildare met the forces of Connaught and the
clans of Munster, including the O'Carrolls of Ely, at
Knocktuadh (Knocktow), near Galway city, and dispersed them with great slaughter, entering the city on
the following day. In the battle of Knocktuadh,
fought in the same picturesque district of Connemara,
to which the descendants of Conmac, son of the famous
Queen Maev, have given their name, and which had
witnessed the half mythical battle of Moytura, between
the Firbolgs and the Tuatha De Danann, Nugent,
lord of Delvin, behaved with gallantry. Kildare's
forces were inferior in numbers, and many of his
officers advised a retreat. Upon this Nugent spurred
his horse forward against the Irish, and hurled a spear
with such dexterity that it struck one of the Burkes,
and then rode back to his own troop, which immediately charged the enemy. It is urged by Sir John

Davis against Kildare that "his journey was not made by warrant of the king, or upon his charge, but only on a private quarrel of the Earl of Kildare." Private animosity lay at the bottom of the whole matter. The Lord Deputy's sister, Lady Eleanora Fitzgerald, had married Henry O'Neill, and their son, Turlough, had a quarrel with another O'Neill. The Lord Deputy invaded Ulster to support his nephew, while Ulick Burke, Lord Clanrickarde, who had a private grudge against the Deputy, took the opportunity of gathering the western clans against him.

The result, however, was good for the English power, for it showed the Irish "rebels" and "enemies" that the days of English decadence were ended, and that the King's Deputy was not only prepared to take the offensive, but likely to prove dangerous ; and it crushed for a time the power of the O'Briens of Thomond, who had been a veritable thorn in the side of the English, from the days (1369) when Murragh-en-Ranagh, or Morris of the Fern, collected his lawless bands in the wilds of Clare, so called from the *clar* or wooden bridge across the Fergus river, and sweeping over the hills, destroyed Killaloe, Buttevant, Inchiquin and other towns, and demonstrated the truth of the Welsh historian's words—"When the Irish are bad, you can no where meet with worse; but if they be good, you can scarcely find better." By Poynings' Act of 1494 an attempt was made to silence for ever the voice of Anglo-Irish independence ; by the battle of Knocktow in 1497 the Irish septs received a salutary lesson.

CHAPTER IX.

SILKEN THOMAS AND THE O'CONNORS.

WE are now drawing near to one of the most interesting, but, from the Irish standpoint, one of the most disastrous campaigns in the history of the Dukes of Leinster and of the O'Connor clan, which culminated in the foolish and fatal rebellion of Silken Thomas.

In 1513 Henry II's Deputy, the Earl of Kildare, during a campaign against the O'Carrolls of Ely, which will be noticed in the chapter on that clan, and was succeeded by his son, Gerald, one of the most brilliant and most unfortunate of the Geraldines. At the very beginning of his office he was attacked by Wolsey, who had been made Chancellor in 1515, and hated the Geraldines. In consequence of Wolsey's representations, the earl was summoned to London in 1519 to answer the charge of assuming sovereign power in the land. But his wit, presence, and courage carried him out of his difficulties. He replied to Wolsey's accusations before Henry VIII. in the same manner as his father had defended himself in the presence of Henry VII. "Would, my lord," he said, " that you and I had changed kingdoms but for one month. I could gather more crumbs in that little space than twice the revenues of my poor earldom. Upbraid me not with such an odious storm. I slumber in a hard cabin; you sleep softly on a bed of down. I serve under the cope of heaven, you are served under a gorgeous canopy. I drink water out of a skull; you drink wine out of a golden cup. My courser is trained to the field, your jennet is taught to amble. You are begraced, belorded, crouched and knelt to, but I find small grace with our Irish borderers except I cut them by the knee."

The case looked black against the earl. He had, indeed, made common cause with the " Irish enemies " in many a conflict, and was more popular with the Irish chieftains than his rival, the Earl of Ormonde. But his personal popularity had won him many friends at the English Court, where he married the Lady Elizabeth Grey, a daughter of the house of Dorset and he was finally acquitted, and attended Henry at "the Field of the Cloth of Gold," (1520), where his splendour and extravagance were conspicuous. The Earl of Surrey, who had been Lord Deputy, resigned in 1522, and in 1523 Kildare returned to Ireland to find a strong party against him, and many of his castles destroyed by the Earl of Ormonde, who was now ordered to resign office in favour of his rival. But Kildare did not enjoy his ascendency long. He was ordered to arrest one of his friends, Desmond, who was carrying on an intrigue with Francis I. of France, the enemy of Henry VIII. ever since that unfortunate wrestling bout at the Field of the Cloth of Gold; but he did not do so.

Summoned to London to explain, he was cast into the Tower from which the good offices of his friends at last set him free. He returned to Ireland with Sir William Skeffington (1530) and succeeded him as Lord Deputy in 1532. But his fortunes were materially affected by two alliances which he had previously made. He gave his daughters in marriage to two

I

Irish chieftains, Fearganainm (the man without a name) O'Connor of Offaly and Bryan O'Carroll of Ely, in order to strengthen his position against the powerful house of Ormonde and to win popularity among the Irish "enemies." But the consequences of these alliances proved fatal to the earl. For owing to his enforced absence in England the O'Connor had risen in revolt and treacherously seized the person of Richard Nugent, Lord Devlin, who was Lord Deputy at the time (1526-1528), and thrown him into prison. Concerning this outrage Sir Piers Butler, who had by order of Henry VIII. resigned his title, Earl of Ormonde, in favour of Sir Thomas Boleyn, and taken that of Earl of Ossory, wrote a virtuous letter saying—" After the taking of the Baron of Delvin treacherously by the Earl of Kildare's son-in-law O'Connor, all the Irish determined to have joined in aid with the said O'Connor for the destruction of your English Pale through the practice of the said Earl of Kildare." He also adds—" Kildare's object at this time is to compel the Irish to combine and confederate with him, having no regard to the King's Deputy. He would make all the land believe that the Deputy is sent only to be his instrument "—words which were calculated to rouse the ire of a monarch whose policy might be summed up in the words of another potentate, *L'état c'est moi.*

In 1525, Kildare had written an equally self-righteous letter concerning the misdemeanours of the Earl of Ormonde, which is preserved in the Carew manuscripts. In it he stated that " all the churches for the most part, within the counties of Kilkenny and Tipperary, are in such extreme decay by provision, that no divine service is kept there, and it shall be well proved that few or none laboureth to the apostle of any benefice there without the consent of the said earl or my lady his wife, by *whom he is only ruled*, which are the maintainers of all such provisions, in so much as they lately maintained certain provisos against the said earl's son, being the Archbishop of Cashel, contrary to the king's letters directed in the favour of the said archbishop. If the king do not provide a remedy there will be no more Christianitie than in the middle of Turkey."

Sir Piers had thus his revenge upon his brother-in-law for the criticism passed upon himself and his countess, whom Campion described as "a rare woman, and able for wisdome to govern a whole realme had not her stomacke (pride) overruled herself." He also made capital for himself out of his rival's connexions with the O'Connors and O'Carrolls—connexions which show the importance and prestige of those septs. His wife, to whom Kildare referred, was a singularly able person, and assisted her husband during his term of office as Lord Justice, to which he had been elected by the King's Council in S. Mary's Abbey in Diuelin (Dublin), who were overawed by his army of Irishmen, "having captaine over them O'Connor, O'More, and O'Carroll" (1528). Stanihurst, whose vignette of her has been elsewhere cited, states that she was "the only meane at those dayes whereby her husband's country was reclaimed from the sluttish and unclean Irish custom to the English habite, bedding and house-keeping."

Another event which hastened the ruin of Kildare was, strange to say, the fall of Wolsey, his enemy, whose proceedings as Lord Chancellor against Kildare for conniving at the evil deeds of his cousin of Desmond are recorded in Campion's History (pp. 164-171). The fall of his great foe in 1529 not only freed the chief of the Geraldines from uneasy apprehensions but also from a wholesome restraint. Kildare seems to have let himself "go," as the phrase is, after Wolsey's disgrace; for, when sent over to quell the rising of the O'Connors, who had, in the meantime, seized the Deputy, the Baron of Delvin, he seized the opportunity of revenging himself on the Earl of Ossory and the Butlers for all the evil they had wrought him. Of a turbulent and ungovernable temper, which was the common characteristic of the men of his age, Kildare had many qualities which endeared him to the Irish. For he was, like his father, "not forgetful of benefits, and not unmindful of injuries." A story, which is given by Ware in his *Annals*, reveals the quality of his temper. The earl had been wounded by a shot from the castle of Birr, which he was besieging, and as he lay groaning in his pain, a common soldier standing near him said : " My lord, why do you sigh so ? I myself was thrice shot with bullets, and yet am whole," to which the earl replied : " I wish you had received the fourth in my stead." It was, probably, the same Earl of Kildare who drew a skean, or Irish dagger, upon the Bishop of Kildare, in the presence of more than 300 persons, in the hall of the house of Connall. (Carew MS. 1. 151.)

Having the reins of government in his hands, he simply exercised his power to advance his own family and friends, and to overthrow his enemies. He raided and harried the lands of Ormonde in a merciless manner. Followed by an armed rabble—which circumstance gave some foundation for the Earl of Sussex's statement to Queen Elizabeth in 1560—" On the faction of the Geraldines depend all the evildisposed men in the realm "—he wreaked his vengeance here and there, and conducted himself in a manner which would seem outrageous to anyone possessed of statecraft. But Kildare was no statesman. And his recklessness spelt ruin for himself and his house. For he gave his foes the very handle they wanted against him. The result was that charges of treason and misgovernment were made against the earl by the council which gave a sad picture of the Pale and its sufferings in a document it presented to the Master of the Rolls in 1533—a very damning document against the Earl of Kildare, the Lord Deputy. Among the things complained of by the council were —(1) that neither English " order, tongue, or habit " was used, nor the king's laws obeyed above twenty miles in compass ; (2) the taking of coyne and livery and other extortions; (3) that owing to default of English inhabitants Irish tenants were being admitted ; (4) that the English lords and gentlemen, instead of keeping English yeomen, employ horsemen and knaves who live upon the king's subjects, and that they keep no hospitality, but live upon the poor ; (5) the liberties of the temporal lords ; (6) the black rents and tributes levied by the Irish upon the king's subjects ; (7) that "when the Deputies go upon the Irishmen by the aid of the king's subjects for redress of their nightly and daily robberies, they keep all they get to their own use, and restore nothing to the poor people "; (8) the frequent change of

Deputies; (9) the negligent keeping of king's records, and appointment of unlearned and incompetent clerks to the offices of the Four Courts; and (10) the loss of the king's revenues, customs, and manors. This State Paper, signed by two archbishops, the Bishop of Meath, the Prior of Kilmainham, the Abbots of St. Thomas's, St. Mary's, and Louth, and three judges, reveals an unfortunate state of affairs in the Pale, for which Kildare was at once taken to task. He was summoned for the fourth time to England to answer these charges, but was reluctant to go. But before he went he committed two more grievous faults, which hastened his own downfall. He removed out of Dublin Castle all the king's arms, artillery, and munitions of war for the fortification and furnishing of his own castles, in case his enemies should attack them in his absence; and he appointed his son, Lord Thomas, a vain youth, called Silken Thomas, to act as his vice-deputy. On his arrival in London the earl was cast into prison, and, with the express design of forcing the hands of the Geraldines, the cruel report was spread by a letter, which reached the hands of Silken Thomas, that Kildare had been executed, and that a similar fate was in store for his uncles.

Driven to desperation by this cunningly-devised document, Silken Thomas resolved to cast off his allegiance, and to join the O'Connors and O'Neills, who were in revolt. But instead of seizing the castle and the city, when his foes were unprepared, he devised a theatrical exodus from his office, which gave them the necessary time. Galloping into the city, at the head of a large troop, he rode to S. Mary's Abbey, where the Council was sitting, and, bursting into the chamber with his followers, he advanced to the foot of the dais, and proceeded to renounce his allegiance to the king. Archbishop Cromer, his father's friend made a strong but futile remonstrance and appeal in the English language, which the Geraldine's followers did not understand. But while Lord Thomas stood irresolute, his Irish bard broke into a song of praise of the silken lord in the Irish language, which completely turned his foolish head, and, in his excitement, the boy seized the sword of state and hurled it to the ground, and strode out of the Council Chamber amid the martial strains of his bard's song and shouts of "Cromaboo." The rubicon was crossed in accordance with the Latin saying, "Quem Deus vult perdere dementat" (1534).

Among the staunchest of the Geraldine's allies at this time were the O'Connors of Offaly with whom he was related. They also suffered in his subsequent disasters. As this is not a history of the House of Leinster, we may hurrry over these ill-advised and wanton deeds of the young lord, described by the *Four Masters* in glowing language, and his plunder of Fingal, on which the city of Dublin, then ravaged by a pestilence, depended for corn ; his seizure of the children who had been removed to the country for safety by their anxious parents ; his futile assaults on the city which were repulsed with loss by the trained bands and valiant citizens, who took courage when they perceived that the arrows of the enemy were headless, and seized his cannon and dispersed his Irish gallowglasses ; and his barbarous arrest and murder of Allen, the Archbishop of Dublin, who was escaping to England in a vessel which unfortunately was stranded near Howth, and the unhappy prelate kneeling before the young lord and pleading for mercy was " brained like an ox." For the execrable deed he and his accomplices, John Telynge and Nicholas Wafer, who took the archbishop prisoner and brought him to Artayne, and John Fitzgerald, Oliver Fitzgerald, James Delahide, Edward Rorke and " divers others evil-disposed persons who most shamefully, tyrannously and cruelly murdered and put to death the said arch-bishop, were duly excommunicated, accursed and anathematized." " The place," writes Campion, " is ever since hedged in, overgrown and unfrequented in detestation of the deed."

Forces at last arrived from England under the com-mand of Sir William Skeffington, whom the Irish called "the Gunner," and Sir William Brereton. And Lord Thomas having in vain sought the assistance of Piers Butler, the Earl of Ossory, with whom he offered to divide the dominion of Ireland, but who stiffly replied—" If my country were laid waste, my castles won and prostrated, and myself an exile, yet still would I persevere in my duty to my king "—placed a strong garrison in his castle at Maynooth, which he deemed impregnable, and betook himself with the majority of his followers to the bogs and woods of Offaly. Then he moved from place to place, gather-ing followers and placing garrisons in his castles at Rathangan, Leix, Carlow and Athy, while Skeffington. the Deputy, lay ill in Dublin. But in March the following year, 1535, Sir William Brereton assumed the command, and marched with a well-equipped army and a siege train of artillery to attack the castle of Maynooth. After a siege of some twelve days a breach was made in the walls, and the governor, Christopher Paris, who is said to have earned the reward of Judas, ended the matter by betraying the castle into the hands of the English, who carried it by assault with but slight resistance. The news of the fall of the fortress and the noise of the English cannon caused Kildare's half-armed kerne and gallowglasses to disperse in all directions in a general *sauve qui peut*. Silken Thomas, who found a refuge with the O'Connors of Offaly, the O'Moores and O'Briens, having failed in his attempt to procure aid from France, Spain, or the Pope, was finally induced by Sir Leonard Grey to surrender himself under promise of the king's pardon, and was sent to the Tower, where his father had died a few years before of grief and shame for the madness of his son.

Here he was soon afterwards joined by his five uncles who had been invited to a banquet by the Lord Deputy, and were arrested by his orders and conveyed to the Tower. For the king's wish was to destroy the obnoxious race root and branch, and his promise of forgiveness was but a pretence. For within twelve months the uncles and their ill-advised nephew paid the penalty for belonging to a house which had grown so dangerous in the eyes of the English monarchs, being executed at Tyburn.

The king's hope of annihilation was, however, disappointed. For two sons of Gerald, Earl of Kildare, by his second wife, the Lady Elizabeth Grey, escaped his vengeance. The elder of these, Gerald, was brought by Thomas Leverous, afterwards Bishop of Kildare, to Lady Mary O'Connor, who protected him for a time in the wilds of Offaly from the dangers that

threatened him.   He was then sent to the French
Court by his aunt, who discovered that her husband,
O'Donnell of Tyrconnell, was about to betray him to
the English Govermnment, and finally found a refuge
with his relation, Cardinal Pole, at Rome.   In his
period of exile his life was on one occasion provi-
dentially preserved for the restoration of his family.
Hunting in Italy, his horse fell into a chasm and was
killed.   The boy's fall was broken by some branches
on the side of the precipice, to which he had clung for
some hours, until he was rescued from his perilous
position by some travellers, who had been attracted to
the place by the barking of the young earl's dog.

After Henry VIII.'s death he returned to England,
and was kindly received by Edward VI., who gave
him some of his family honours.   Eventually he returned to Ireland in Mary's reign, and was put into
possession of his father's estates, but he was regarded by Elizabeth as the most dangerous person
in Ireland.

During the period of his exile the Butlers had
taken an ample revenge.   The lands of Kildare were
plundered and harried.   The peasantry suffered
greatly, and their loyalty to their ancient lords, the
Geraldines, was intensified by the cruelty of the
Butlers.   Cowley, writing to Cromwell in 1538, said :
" I assure your lordship that this English Pale, except
the towns and some few of the possessioners, be so
affectionate to the Geraldines, that for kindred,
marriage, fostering, and adhering as followers, they
covet more to see a Geraldine to reign and triumph
than to see God come among them ; and if they might
see this young Girol's banner displayed—if they

should lose half their substance, they would rejoice more at the same, than otherwise to gain great good.

The siege of the great castle of Maynooth, which ended in so much disaster to the Geraldines, is fully described in the Deputy's report of the 26th March, 1535. to be found in the Carew MSS., vol. I., p. 65. As Maynooth was the first feudal castle in Ireland which was besieged in regular form, and battered by cannon, the report of the siege and capture may prove interesting :—

"On 14th March I, your Deputy, with your army, besieged the castle of Maynooth, which Thomas Fitzgerald so strongly fortified with men and ordnance, 'as the like hath not been seen in Ireland since any of your most noble progenitors had first dominion in the land.' Within the same were about 100 able men, of whom more than sixty were gunners. On the 16th 'your ordnance was sent to the north-west side of the dungeon[1] of the same castle, which did batter the top thereof on that wise, as their ordnance within that part was dampned.' Then your ordnance was bent upon the north side of the base court of the castle, 'at the north-east end whereof there was now made a very strong and fast bulwark, well garnished with men and ordnance ; which the 18th, 19th, 20th, 21st, and 22nd days of the said month did beat the same by night and day on that wise, that a great battery and a large entrance was made there.' On the 23rd being Tuesday next before Easter Day, a galiard assault was given, and the base court entered. About sixty of the ward of the castle were slain, and of your

---

[1] Donjon or keep.

army only John Griffin, yeoman of your guard, and six others. We next assaulted the great castle, which yielded, wherein was the Dean of Kildare, Christopher Paris, captain of the garrison; Donagh O'Dogan, master of the ordnance; Sir Simon Walshe, priest; and Nicholas Wafer which took the Archbishop of Dublin, with divers other gunners and archers to the number of 37."

Christopher Paris was the governor who betrayed the castle; and it is remarkable that he with the other thirty-six prisoners whose lives were preserved by appointment until they should be presented to the Deputy and then to be dealt with according as the Deputy and council thought fit were, as the Deputy grimly writes, "put to execution as an example to others." The Deputy showed the spirit of English "fair play all round," by not excepting the traitor from the doom he had planned for the betrayed. Henceforth the English guns were masters of the situation. The Gallowglasses (Galloglach), or foreign mercenaries, principally Scotch, steel-capped, mail-coated, and armed with heavy axe and two-handed sword, and the fighting clansmen or kerne, half-naked and equipped with javelins, light axes and skians, who often proved more than a match for the trained troops of the Pale, could now be mowed down with the same ease, if not rapidity, as the Arab hordes and Zulu impis of modern times by British fire. Under the old system of warfare the great feudal piles might bid defiance to any assaulting party; but now the ammunition—almost an English monopoly—had changed the aspect of affairs, and supplied the English settlers with a substitute for the bow, with which they had, in spite of many statutes, ceased to practise.

Although the Irish were not able to obtain artillery, they altered their mode of fighting in order to cope with the English on more equal terms. An interesting picture-plan of the battle of Bel-an-Atha-buidhe, preserved in the library of Trinity College, represents the infantry of O'Neill, the Earl of Tyrone, as harquebusiers supported by masses of pikemen. The gallowglasses have disappeared, and the cavalry are armed precisely as the English. The latter, however, were supported by artillery of which the Irish had none.

Occasionally the Irish were able to take the ordnance of the English. There is a ford in the King's County, called Bel-atha-nabh-Fabcun, the ford mouth of the Fabcun, from a battle fought there between the sons of Moalroona O'Carroll, and the sons of John O'Carroll, who were supported by the Earl of Ormond (1532), in which the sons of Maolroona were victorious and took from their opponents a piece of ordnance called Fabcun.

CHAPTER X.

THE capture of Maynooth caused consternation among
the O'Connors and other Irish adherents of the
Geraldines. But with their ready wit they speedily
found a way out of their difficulty. It was time that
they needed; time for them to recover themselves;
time for the English Deputy, Lord Leonard Grey, to
lose the advantage gained by Skeffington. Accordingly, they made temporary submissions. On January
20, 1536, O'Connor, the most important of the midland
chiefs, tendered his submission, engaging on his part
to allow the Deputy and his army to pass through his
dominion without hindrance from him or his clansmen,
and even to make proper roads for their passage.[1]
O'Byrne of Wicklow followed suit. And thus the
Deputy was enabled to move at once against the
Desmonds of Munster. But while he was engaged
in taking the castle of Loughgyr, "a stronghold in no
less reputation in those parts than Maynooth in the
North parts," and taming the pride of the O'Briens
by capturing the castle of Carrick-OGunnel and destroying the splendid bridge[2] across the Shannon
called O'Brien's bridge, with a castle of hewn marble
at each end, the O'Connors were busily engaged in
repairing their losses and collecting their forces. They
were encouraged by the mutiny which arose among
the Deputy's troops on account of bad pay.

[1] Carew MSS. Vol. I., p. 86.
[2] An interesting account of the capture of this bridge is given in the
Carew MSS., I., 88.

But Lord Leonard Grey, one of the most vigorous of the English Deputies, was undaunted by troubles without and fears within. And as Chancellor Alen wrote to Cromwell in his letter of the 12th July, 1537 —" My lord deputy proceeded on his journey into O'Chonour's country the Tuesday after Trinity Sunday, entering into the same on the west side, betwixt O'Mulmoy, McGoghegan's and O'Molaglyn's countries, neighbours and aiders of the said O'Connors, on which side of his country any host hath not passed with carts heretofore, by reason of the dangerous way, being all woods and marshes."

His objective was the castles of the O'Connor, who was not only abandoned by his neighbours, the O'Mulloys, McGeoghegans, O'Melaghlins and O'Moores, but was also betrayed by his own brother, Cathal Roe. The *Four Masters* sum up the disastrous results of the campaign in the words—" O'Conor Faily, that is Bryan the son of Cahir, was expelled from his territory, and after many of his people had been slain, all his castles were taken and demolished by the Saxon Lord Justice, that is Lord Leonard, and it *was through the conspiracy and at the instigation of O'Connor's own brother, Cathal Roe, these acts were perpetrated.*"

This Irish chieftain, like another Judas, led the English forces against the castle of Bragnot, " wherein there was left a good ward, well victualled, well ordnanced, and well manned, environed strongly with wood and moor." But the ill-fated garrison could make but feeble resistance, as Cathal had a confederate behind the walls whose treachery placed the defenders at the mercy of the assailants. The fortress was seized and the garrison secured, all but Cathal's man being led out for immediate execution. Alen, who seems to know nothing of their betrayal, states—" his lordship achieved the same, heading all the ward, all save three, which were preserved to show his lordship the ways of another castle of the said O'Connors, that in the Irish tongue he named the castle of Dengin, that is, in English, the castle of most assurance." The writer proceeds to give an account of the natural defences of this " castle of most assurance," which had become a " doubting castle " for its gallant defenders. The approach to it was by a broken-down causeway, laid down over an impassible moor.

To this fortress of " Daingean "—a name cognate with the English donjon—the traitor led the forces of the Deputy. The erection of this old castle is recorded by the *Four Masters* as having taken place in 1546. But they were evidently alluding to a later fortress, built by Sir William Brabazon some years after the events to which we are referring, when the head-quarters of the O'Connors consisted of a huge circular mound in the midst of a marsh and almost surrounded by the bog of Allen ; and to make approach more difficult, artificial obstructions had been carefully placed in the only accessible places. But Cahir's knowledge again proved of untold advantage to the English, and the military were led over the quaking bog and sinking morass up to the very vallum of Dangan.

Alen informed Cromwell that the Deputy had fag-gots made for the repair of the causeway, which had been broken down, and for the filling up of the great double ditches, " so strong and so large as have not been seen in this land heretofore." The English troops engaged in this work were protected by two companies, one under Martin Pellis and the other under Mr. Seintlowe's captain. But the garrison made a successful assault and killed several of their foes, wounding Seintlowe's captain ; but the other captains succeeded in entering their fortress on their very heels. Brian fled, but his brother was rewarded for his noble services by being made Lord of Offaly by the English Governor.

The present town of Philipstown was built on the site of Dangan, which changed its name in the reign of Mary, and the trembling of the houses, when a heavy vehicle rumbles through the streets, reminds one that the town is built on a bog, which recalls the doings of Cathal Roe and Martin Pellis.

In connection with the taking of Dangan, it is interesting to read that the English lost their only one piece of ordnance, and at once sent a message to the Governor beseeching him "to be a mean to the King's highness that there may be another sent thither with speed, or his Grace's Deputy can't prevail against Irishmen which have garrisons." This speaks rather well for the valour of the Irish.

The brave Brian was not, however, discomfited by the loss of his title and possessions, and he had the apparent audacity to venture into the Pale and demand the restoration of his rights. But his cool request was not granted, while his brother Cahir was created Baron of Offaly and made tenant of the Crown. Exasperated by his bad luck, Brian once more had recourse to arms, and getting assistance from his friends in Connaught he marched into his own lands and defeated his brother, who was taken unprepared and

K

drove him out of the country. The English court were greatly vexed at this upset to their plans. A very strongly-worded letter was written by Lord Chancellor Cromwell, Wolsey's friend, to Lord Grey urging him " eftsoons to handle the matter of O'Connor's with such dexterity as he may be hanged as a terrible example to all Irish traitors." The writer went on to say— " The expulsion of him was taken very well, but the permission of him to have such a scope to work mischief at his pleasure, no doubt he must needs be remaining in despair of restitution, was neither wisdom nor good precedent. Redub it, my lord, in the just punishment of his traitorous carcass. And let his treason be a warning to you and to all who have to do for the King's Majesty there never to trust a traitor after, but to use them without treaty after their demerits."

This was sound advice, and it would have been well for the English governor had he acted upon it. But the O'Connors were as cunning as they were warlike. After successfully harassing the invaders' flanks, they returned without the guidance of Cahir through the wild tracks and dense forests of country which was utterly unknown to them, but every inch of which was known to him. The wily Bryan took advantage of the heavy rains, when the Deputy was practically powerless, to put in a plea for immunity, and was granted a safe conduct to Dublin. Of this permission Bryan took advantage in order to obtain an interview with his brother Cahir, and became duly reconciled to him, and together with him laid deep plots for the recovery of their dominions. But their funds were well-nigh exhausted, and they had little means of carrying on the war with any hope of success, and were at last reduced to make overtures to the much-exasperated but too confiding Deputy Lord Grey. The meeting took place at the ford of Kinnegad, the English forces drawn up on the north side of the stream, and the clansmen, full of fight and courage, lining the southern bank, the boundary of the dominion of Offaly, for which they were ready to die at a moment's notice.

The result of the interview was eminently satisfactory, according to Lord Grey's version, the said Bryan greeting him " with humble reverence, submitting to the King's highness, confessing his offences, and did utterly refuse (resign) all his title in Offaly, and in all black rents and fees that can be had of the King's subjects." In a word, Bryan promised to be a good and quiet boy again, and with all due reverence to farm the land as a tenant of the Crown, promising to give pay out of every ploughed land " three shillings and four pence, Irish, by the year," and was pardoned and reinstated. Cahir, who had received the land from the king as his tenant, naturally, even though a traitor himself, resented this worse than " punic faith," and withdrawing his forces retired to a strongly-fortified house. But Bryan now proved the traitor. With evident satisfaction, he led the English on the trail of his brother, and at last ran him to earth in one of his strongholds. It is said that the place was so closely besieged that the refractory Cahir with difficulty escaped, and only in his shirt. But the fugitive, seeing the folly of further fighting, gave in with a good grace, and was received with favour again by Lord Grey, who thus missed the opportunity of making the O'Connors "terrible examples to all Irish traitors," as the king's highness desired.

The Deputy, however, had his hands full. The power of the O'Neill was threatening in the north, but was crushed by him at Belahoe (1539), and Ireland was quiet for a year. But no sooner had Lord Grey left the country than the O'Connors broke out afresh (1540), and captured and destroyed Castle Jordan, in Meath, on the borders of the Pale. A hosting is made against them, and there is a nominal peace for some years, during which the conciliatory St. Leger, the Deputy, sought to come to terms with the native Irish. A remarkable sight was witnessed when all the Anglo-Irish nobles and the Irish chiefs, including the O'Dempseys, O'Dunnes, O'Moores, O'Molloys, with the O'Byrnes, O'Carroll's and O'Connors made their submission to the Deputy (1540). This was the fourth general submission of the Irish. The others had been made to Henry II., John, and Richard II., respectively. In their indentures of submission, the Irish lords, O'Neill, O'Donnell, Rory O'Moore and others, agreed to recognise the king as the supreme head of the Church of England and Ireland, and as their liege lord and king, at the same time renouncing the authority of the Roman pontiff. And in St. Leger's parliament at Dublin the English lords and Irish chiefs sat side by side, accepted and confirmed the Act of Supremacy, and passed a bill conferring on Henry the title of King of Ireland (1541). It was a gala day for Dublin. The city was *en fête*, bonfires were lit, and salutes fired. Wine flowed freely, and prisoners were set at liberty. In their temporary exhilaration, the Irish chieftains threw down their caps, skeins and girdles in acknowledgment of King Henry. O'Neill, O'Brien and McWilliam went to England to the king who advanced them to the degree of earls and granted them several counties by Letters Patent. But the Brehon Laws prevailed over nearly all the land. Connaught, Ulster and Munster had not been yet reduced to shireland, and though Munster was divided into counties, no justice of assize dare execute his commission in them.

The Irish chieftains seem, however, to show a surprising docility and loyalty. In 1546 the Earls of Tyrone, Desmond and Thomond, with the O'Carroll, O'Connor, O'Mulloy and Fitzpatrick, sent a Latin letter to the king congratulating him on the peaceful state of the country ; stating that no man in Ireland, were he as old as Nestor, has seen the country in a more peaceable condition, and promising to strive to " answer to right and law as exactly as the others who from their cradles and earliest infancy have been well educated in the same." [1]

But we find the O'Connors disturbing that peace, which seems to have been like that which precedes the storm, by raiding Kildare, Clane and Carbury with the O'Kellys, whose lands, then called Caellen, are now included in the county of Kildare. In retaliation the English invaded Offaly. Thereupon Bryan, with the O'Moore's of Leix, burnt down the town and monastery of Athy (Ath-brodain—the bloody ford), which was then one of the keys of the marches of Kildare. The Lord Justice then proclaimed the O'Connors traitors, and sent letters to their allies to leave them and be pardoned. This they did, and

[1] State Papers, Ireland. Vol II., 3, 562.

O'Connor, left alone, fled to Connaught, where he was attacked and deprived of a great quantity of his supplies by some of the Irish who were friendly to the English. In the meantime, Sir William Brabazon had overrun all Offaly, and erected a castle at Dangan, the name of which was afterwards changed to Philipstown, in honour of Queen Mary's consort. While the English Lord Justice was securing his country, Bryan O'Connor was trying to levy forces to attack him. And feeling himself sufficiently strong to do this, the next year he crossed the Shannon with his clans, but on his march to Leinster they melted away, evidently alarmed by the fact that none of their ancient allies had rallied to the banner of the O'Connors. Bryan was, therefore forced to submit. And this time he had no mild Lord Grey to deal with, but a resolute and determined man who brought him to England " at the mercy of the king." It was Sir Edward Bellingham who accomplished this feat, with 600 horse and 400 foot, and who, according to Sir John Davis, was " the first Deputy who, from the time of Edward III. to Edward VI. extended the borders of the English Pale by beating and breaking the O'Moores and O'Connors and by building the forts of Offaly and Leix." The Book of Howth gives him the following good character :—
" After him Sir Edward Bellinghame, a good man, a very good payer of all men, and never took anything but that he paid for ; and in his time Afale (Offaly) and Lexe was won and a strong fort was built in every of them ; and after being sent for into England there died. This man had cesses worse than Selingere ; but for his own horses wholly was kept in his own stables, and paid for all he took and was a true-dealing

man. He could not have bide the cry of the poor. He never in his time took anything of any man, but that he truly paid for ; he wore ever his harness, and so did all those who he liked for." Of his military capacity, his enemy, Alen, writes—" My Lord Deputy is the best man of war that ever I saw n Ireland, having since his coming hither, done more service to the king than was done—after the repressing of the Geraldines—in all the king's father's lifetime, notwithstanding all his charges." It was no disgrace to the O'Connor to be subdued by this honest and brusque officer, who is reported to have said to the man he committed to prison—" Content thyself, for I will do no worse to thee than I will do to the best of the Council, if he displease me."

It would have been well for Ireland if his officers and the Irish Council had carried out the plan of winning the Irish " by sober ways, politic drifts, and amiable persuasions of law and reason," but feeling their impotence, while without a police force, to grasp with the situation, they were compelled to have recourse to sterner measures of plantation. Accordingly English settlers were planted in Leix and Offaly, from which the tribes were driven, and two forts, one called " The Governor" in Faly, ond the other "the Protector " in Leix, were built to defend the settlers, among whom were the Barringtons, Cosbies, Breretons, Pigotts, Browns, Hovendens. In the instructions given to Sir A. St. Leger, Lord Deputy 1550, and to Sir James Croft, Lord Justice 1557, the following passage occurs which throws light upon the situation : " As the Counties of Offalye and Leix, lately called O'Connor's Country and O'Moore's Country, are now in good towardness to be wholly in our hands and possession, and yet not in perfection, the Deputy and Council are to take order for the full and ample possession of the same countries and also for the surveying thereof, and to let this to farm or otherwise for terms of 21 years, allowing the farmers one or two years rent free." To this there is an allusion in the words of the historian regarding the Bellinghams, to wit, that they built " two large courts " at Maryboro' and Philipstown, and " began to let these lands for rent as if they were their rightful inheritance." But during the whole of Edward's reign the fighting continued, the Irish shooting down the settlers, and the settlers shooting down the Irish. But in Mary's reign the O'Connor and his ally the O'Moore, who had in the meantime failed to secure favourable terms from the English Court, were set free. The former firebrand was released at the entreaty of his daughter, Margaret. This young lady, whose natural charms were enhanced by all the accomplishments of the age in which she lived, courageously faced the perils of a voyage across the Channel and a journey through England to the Court of Queen Mary, who, in consideration of her connection with the great English family of Kildare and her religion, admitted her to an interview. The heroic daughter pleaded her father's cause with such eloquence that Mary, very unwisely —from the English point of view—allowed Bryan to return to his native land (1553).

The inevitable consequence of O'Connor's return was that the country was in a blaze again, and on this occasion the O'Maddens, the O'Moores, the O'Molloys, and the O'Carrolls assisted the O'Connors in carrying fire and sword through Offaly and the neighbouring districts. All the hostile septs rose like one man, and directed their operations principally against the Irish who were loyal to England, and the English settlers in Offaly, which was now to be made shireland.

Instead of granting the O'Connors better terms than her predecessors, Queen Mary pursued their policy. In fact while Lord L. Grey and St. Leger had felt that the O'Connors had been treated with great harshness, doubtless owing to their connection with the Geraldines, and had sought to give them better terms, the Government of Mary was responsible for the complete extermination and plantation of the King's and Queen's Counties, and the districts of Offaly, Fercall, Ely and Leix, which were created shireland by the Act of the third and fourth Philip and Mary. In the first Act—the cruellest Act of Confiscation ever placed on the Statute Book—the Lord Deputy was authorized to grant to all their Majesties' subjects, English or Irish, estates in fee-simple " in the countries of Leix, Slewmarge, Offallie, Irrie and Glenmalire, which belong of right to the King and Queen's most excellent Majesties, of late wholly possessed by the Moores, the Connors, the Dempseys and other rebels, and now by the industrious travaile of the Earl of Sussex, brought again into the possession of their Majesties." By the second Act these countries were created shires being entitled Queen's County and King's County, with Philipstown and Maryborough as their chief towns. Sheriffs and other officers were appointed to complete the work. And in 1556 a system of colonization was introduced into the district of Leix, which was divided between the new English settlers, 160 in number, and the Irish natives. All the country beyond the bog was allocated to the Moores. The head of each sept was made responsible for the conduct of his followers, who were to obey the laws of the realm, while the English settlers were ordered to keep open the fords and destroy their fastnesses, and to cause their children to learn English, to abandon Irish customs and fosterage, and to build a church in every town within three years.

In the days of King John there had been an attempt to make twelve shires in Ireland. Henry VIII. had divided Meath into Meath and Westmeath, but this was practically the first creation of shireland outside the Pale. In the making thereof Thomas, Earl of Sussex earned his laurels for " having broken completely the two most rebellious and powerful Irish septs in Leinster, the Moores and O'Connors," but the planting thereof with the new settlers sowed the seed of an internecine struggle between the settlers and the tribes, while the Government looked impassively on at the cruel deeds wrought and endured on either side.

One of the most terrible of the atrocities that were perpetrated in connection with the settlement of the midland counties took place at Mullaghmast. This remarkable eminence, which rises to the south of Athy, had been long associated with the fortunes and traditions of South Leinster. Here Conn of the Hundred Battles, marching to enforce the Leinster tribute, was defeated by Eochy of Leinster. Here Lewy Leeshagh of Ulster defeated the Munstermen in two successive battles at the fords in the vicinity and drove them out of Leinster. Upon its brow is found an ancient rath, circular, and made of earth and of considerable extent and height. This rath was an ancient fortress and residence of the kings. Here was held in olden times the Naasteighan or the assembly of the states, the beginning of this word *Nás* is still preserved in the name Naas. Upon the summit of the rath were sixteen conical mounds, in which the elders sat, while all around them lay the pillar-stones and other emblems of Sun-worship. One of these called Gobhlan is about seven feet high. With regard to this ancient Hill of Carmen, the tradition was that it should be one day the scene of a terrible conflict between the English and the Irish, and that the mill-race hard by would run red with the blood of the slain for twenty-four hours. To a conference on this historic hill the Irish chiefs and principal men of the inhabitants of the new counties were summoned. Suspecting nothing, the O'Connors, O'Carrolls, O'Moores, O'Molloys, O'Dempseys and O'Dunnes came in large numbers on New Year's Day, 1577. It is said that but one returned.

Foreseeing the troubles that might arise in connection with the plantation of Leix and Offaly an Act was passed by the Government of Philip and Mary authorising the Land Commissioners of those days to declare the land of any turbulent chief shireland, which meant that it would be governed according to English law, and that the chief had no longer any authority, but was himself intimidated by the erection of a gaol in his ancient " town " or district, and that his Irish dress and customs might lead him to a closer acquaintance with the inside thereof.

The O'Connors found it hard to raise their heads after this cruel and cold-blooded massacre. But again the hostile chieftains owed the restoration of their lives and lands to the good offices of a woman, the ladies of the fighting clans showing as much superiority in the arts of peace and piety as their husbands did in the art of war. For Lady Mary O'Connor protected the young earl, last scion of the Kildare family, in the forest wilds of Offaly, and Elizabeth was ultimately induced to restore the titles and lands of this ancient family to him.

Some years afterwards (1583) occurred a strange event in the annals of the O'Connor sept, which is related by Cox in his *Hibernia Anglicana*, and which recalls the scenes of single combat which was so frequent in the highland clans of Scotland. It was a dispute between two of the O'Connors. Conor MacCormack O'Connor stated that Teige MacGillpatrick O'Connor had treacherously and foully murdered some of his followers. Teige, it would appear, belonged to the O'Connors who were ranged on the side of England in the stormy times of the sixteenth century, and had been only too glad to wreak vengeance on the Irish O'Connors for their extermination of his relations. And when accused by Conor before the English Court he challenged his opponent to decide the dispute by mortal combat. The challenge was accepted, and the next day was appointed for the contest. When the hour for the fray was come, the two combatants were accommodated with seats at the opposite ends of the inner court of Dublin Castle. Sir Henry Wallop and Adam Loftus, Archbishop of Dublin (Lords Justices) were the judges, and there was a large sprinkling of the military element present, attracted by the remarkable character of the proceedings. The pleadings were then made and the oath administered to the litigants, each of whom maintained the justice of his quarrel. Fenton, the Secretary, and some attendants then approached the combatants and searched them to see if they carried the skian or dagger. They were then armed with sword and target—the weapons chosen by Teige. At the sound of the trumpet the combatants dashed into the lists and began the fray which was to prove fatal to one or both. Teige soon showed his superiority. He was a greater master of his weapon and was stronger and quicker, while his opponent recklessly exposed himself. Three times Teige's sword penetrated his body, and at last, exasperated by his wounds, Connor threw aside his weapons and rushed like a tiger at Teige, and closing with him sought to strangle him. But he was weakened by loss of blood and could not retain his grip, and then Teige struck him to the ground, and having cut off his head, laid the ghastly offering before Sir Henry Wallop and Archbishop Adam Loftus, the Lords Justices, who must have witnessed with horror this terrible combat, to which the Irish often resorted in settlement of disputed claims.

In 1597 we find the O'Connors again in the field. There is a pass in Westmeath, a dangerous defile through a wood, now called Tyrrellspass, from a victory Tyrrell and the O'Connor won over the English there. This Tyrrell was a dashing captain of cavalry in O'Neill's army, then fighting Elizabeth in the North. He had been sent by his general with a small body of men to create a diversion and to prevent the Anglo-Irish of the midlands from joining the army that was marching north against him. In this Tyrrell was successful, for a strong force mustered in Mullingar under Baron Trimleston with a view to join Lord Burgh, the Deputy, turned their attention to Tyrrell's little force. The latter was now joined by O'Connor Faily, a warrior of great bravery and skill, and a plan of campaign was formed which was eventually crowned with complete success. Tyrrell posted half his forces under O'Connor in the hollow of the road to the rear, and with the rest prepared to receive the attack, which was not long delayed. He then retreated slowly, and the English forces following impetuously rushed into the ambuscade. The O'Connor and his men leaping out of their hiding places attacked the enemy, who were then surrounded and almost annihilated. One man, it is said, escaped to Mullingar. The O'Connor himself displayed prodigies of valour, and his hand, it is said, was so swollen from the use of his sword that the weapon had to be filed through before it could be released.

Tyrrell then entered the English part of Offaly and made " great preys, slaughter, taking of towns and of people, of plunder and of booty." He then marched south to meet Mountjoy at Kinsale, and to be defeated with his master.

In 1599 the ill-fated Essex entered Ireland with a great army. He marched through Leinster into Munster, the O'Connors hanging on his flanks. And on his return he was again assailed by this indomitable

sept and others; and completely out of patience
despatched force after force against him. And with
that unthinking obstinacy which persists in adopting
the same hard and fast methods of warfare that have
ever proved unavailing in a struggle of this nature he
sent detachment after detachment of heavy cavalry
into bogs and glens and mountain passes, where they
were at the mercy of the foe. And thus the flower
of the English host found a grave in the bogs and
woods of Offaly. Sir Henry Harrington with 3,000
men, were defeated so frequently by the O'Connors,
O'Moores and O'Tooles that the earl decimated his
brave but badly led soldiers for their cowardice, but
really for his own folly, *pour encourager les autres.*
Such an action, unsoldierlike and brutal, was in keeping
with much of his strange conduct.

The last we see of this famous sept is in a hot
encounter with the English of Meath and the Connaught men under Owen O'Connor. The latter were
suddenly attacked, as they were plundering a small
town, Giolla Bindhe, in Cluain-ni-Murrois, near Geashill, and not expecting opposition were taken unawares.
It was, indeed, a case of a hundred flying at the rebuke
of one, for it would appear that the Calvach, the heir
of Offaly, had only a few men at his heels when he
came upon the spoilers. An incident is said to have
occurred at this juncture which shows that the Irish
grasp of a humourous situation was then, as now racy
of the soil. As the Calvach rode into the town where
the kerne of Connaught were busy with their plunder,
an hotel proprietor, who had borrowed a cauldron
from him, ran up and pointing to one of the spoilers
who was carrying off a bronze cauldron on his back,

said, " There is your cauldron, you can have it now,
kerne and all." " I accept it," said the Calvach, and
taking aim with a large stone he hurled it at the man,
and the stone struck the bronze with such a crash
that the Connaughtmen thought they were surrounded
and fled in confusion. But the Calvach was at their
heels and smote them hip and thigh with a great
slaughter between Giolla Bindhe and Cluain-Aine in
Crioch-na-gedoch in Westmeath. The night came to
the rescue of the vanquished, and the victors returned
with the chief religious emblem of Connaught, the
Buacach Phatraig or mitre of Patrick, which had
always been kept at Elphin until that ill-fated expedition of Owen O'Connor. The last warlike action
recorded of the clan is the invasion of the English
Offaly and the burning down of many of the castles
of the English, in revenge for which the Lord Justice
went down to Offaly in August of 1600, as the Four
Masters say, " with many harrows, great iron rakes
and a great deal of scythes and sickles, and cut down
and destroyed the crops of the country, ripe and
unripe." After this cruel action the fighting clan
disappears as a clan from history, although many
distinguished men, including the late Judge O'Connor
Morris of Gortnamona, in recent times, represent them
worthily. And individuals now and then emerge
from the obscurity that has lowered upon their house,
evincing the military genius and ability of the warrior
clan, which have not been diminished by untoward
circumstances or unkind fortune. Not the least among
them was Arthur O'Connor, the friend of Grattan
and Lord Edward Fitzgerald.

It has been observed that the Irish annalists devoted

themselves almost completely to "feats of broil and battle," and bestowed but little attention upon the social and literary progress of their nation. This was due to the unhappy divisions of Ireland. The annalist confined himself to the glories and triumphs of his own tribe, reserving his spleen and wrath for their enemies, Irish and English. The Book of Leinster, for instance, depreciates the men of Connaught and Munster, while it magnifies the deeds of the Leinstermen. One grows wearied of these blood-stained annals which give as distorted a view of Irish humanity as the Records of Newgate would give of English morality.

It is, therefore, a pleasant change to read of the gentler pursuit of learning and law, which were encouraged by those very chieftains who are paraded as very monsters by the admiring historians of their tribe. In the Annals of Duald MacFirbis, cited by Dr. O'Donovan, there is an account of two entertainments given by Margaret, the wife of O'Conor Faily in 1451 to the learned men of Ireland. At Killeigh "there gathered the number of 2,700 persons, as it was recorded in a roll for that purpose, and that account was made thus :—The chief kindred of each family of the learned Irish was written in the roll by O'Connor's chief judge, and his adherents and kinsmen, so that the aforesaid number of 2,700 was listed in that Roll with the arts of poetry, music and antiquity. Every one as he was paid was written in that Roll for fear of mistake, and was set down to eat afterwards. The hostess, Margaret, was in the gallery of the great church of Da Sinchall (the two Sinchalls, Sean-Sinchell and Sinchell-og), clad in cloth of gold,

L

her dearest friends about her, her clergy and judges too. Her husband, Calvach O'Connor, himself on horseback, by the church's outward side, to the end that all things might be done orderly and each one served successively. And first of all she gave two chalices of gold as offerings that day on the altar to God Almighty, and she also caused to nurse or foster two young orphans. A second feast given on the festival of the Assumption is described as being " nothing inferior to the first day."

Nor is the fighting clan without its religious associations. Killeigh Abbey, the church of the field, founded in the sixth century by S. Sincheall, was and is the favourite resting-place of all who boast the O'Connor name. The ruins of the original building are still to be seen. The roof is of rough hewn stones. Here the most warlike of the O'Connors, O'Connor Faily, established a monastery for Franciscan Friars. Here Murrough O'Connor, the bravest of the race, who had taken the Sheriff of Meath prisoner, was interred after gaining " the victory over the world and the devil." Here Margaret, " the best woman of her time in Ireland, for it was she who gave two general entertainments of hospitality in the one year to the poor " (*Four Masters*) was buried. Here Fionngula, daughter of Calvach O'Connor, the most beautiful of the O'Connors, took the veil and lived for forty-nine years " in a chaste, honourable, pious and devout manner." Here in the cemetery of the church of the field that nestles under the long ridge, repose all that is mortal of the princes and princesses of the fighting clan of the O'Connors of Offaly.

CHAPTER XI.

THE RISE OF THE O'CARROLLS AND O'MULLOYS.

THE O'Carrolls of Ely are another of the fighting clans who made the subjugation of Ireland an extremely difficult task to the English Lord Deputies and settlers. Though they never succeeded in bagging a Viceroy and keeping him prisoner until a ransom and hostage were given for him, they displayed a certain amount of natural taste for warfare that was extremely disagreeable to their more peaceably disposed neighbours. It is true that we do not find them carrying on long and organised campaigns like their friends in Offaly, but sallying from their strong castles—their "small piles of little importance, the chiefest whereof is Limwaddon," as Dimmock describes them in his Treatise on Ireland (1600), they were able to inflict many a crushing blow on their adversaries.

Ely O'Carroll, to call the clan by its proper name, derived its descent and domain from Eile or Ely, seventh in line from Cian or Kian, a son of the famous Oliol Ollum, King of Mumha, now known as Munster, for Moonster (Mumhan-stadr), the place of Mumha. According to O'h-Uidhrin Ely O'Carroll was divided into eight tuatha or districts, over which O'Cearbhaill or O'Carroll was the ruling chief. The territory of Ely is almost coterminous with that part of the King's County which belongs to the diocese of Killaloe, and includes the baronies of Clonlisk and Ballybritt. Ikerrin and Elyogarty, in Tipperary, were detatched from it at an early date and given to "Ormond." Birr, the ancient Biorra, or plain of water, the Umbilicus Hiberniae, or centre of Ireland, according to Giraldus Cambrensis, seems to have been the head-quarters of the tribe when they first emerge into history. According to the poets, they were a hospitable, fierce, and yellow-haired race, to whom the neighbouring tribes were compelled to pay tribute.

Speaking of Ossory, the poet O'Dugan writes :—

> There are three tribes who possess it,
> The Clan Carroll who are free from opposition,
> They are as fierce as leopards under their leaders.

The war-cry of the clan was Showeth-aboe, which must have been at one time heard far and wide. For we find in the Book of Rights that the king of Caiseal (Cashel) paid tribute to the king of Eile :—

> Eight steeds to the King of Eile of the gold,
> Eight shields, eight swords are due,
> Eight drinking horns, to be used at the feast,
> Eight coats of mail in the day of bravery.

And again :—

> The stipend of the King of Eile, of the gold,
> From the King of Caiseal, of the banquets,
> Six shields and six bright swords,
> Six bondsmen, six bondswomen.

Up to the slopes of Sliabh Bladhma (Slieve Bloom) the O'Carrolls of Ely held sway, and were found to furnish fewer forces than the other kings to the Ard-ri. There was gold in the country in these days, the gold from which crosses and chalices, torques and chains, bracelets and bodkins, were fashioned, and with which the warrior's sword was inlaid and the lady's mantle inwoven.   And in gold Ely was rich, for the

O'Carroll was " King of Eile of the Gold." The chief was also rich in cattle and herds, that found pasture on the green slopes of the hills and in the well-watered plains of Ely.

A bard, O'Heerin, who died in 1420, thus alludes to this princely race :—

> Lords to whom great men submit
> Are the O'Carrolls, of the plains of Birr,
> Princes of Eile, as far as tall Slieve Bloom,
> The most hospitable land in Erin.
> Eight districts and eight chiefs are ruled
> By the Prince of Ely, of the land of herds ;
> Valiant in enforcing the tributes
> Are the troops of the yellow-ringletted hair.

It appears that Ely came into notice at a very early period. The story is given in Keating's and Comerford's histories of Ireland. In 212, Fergus of the black teeth reigned in Ireland, when the king of Ulster gave a great feast at Magh Breagh—the Plain of the Wolf —to which Cormac MacArt was invited. But the guest falling under the displeasure of the king, the cruel but curious order was given that Cormac's fair beard—of which the possessor was proud—should be burnt. Cormac immediately applied to Thady, who was then Chief of Ely, for assistance, and overthrew the king of Ulster in a great battle, and wiped out the disgrace of his burnt beard in the blood of his foes. To Birr, the seat of the pagan worship of Fen, which is preserved in the name Seffin, and the chief stronghold of Ely O'Carroll, came the good S. Brendan, S. Columkill's friend (See Adamnan's *Life of Columkill*), whose prophetic gift, long life, and profound piety formed the theme of many a legend, to spread the light of Christianity and to found a monastery, about 550 A.D. S. Brendan, according to the

Four Masters, died in 571 (Nov. 29), in the same
year that a battle was fought at Tola, a plain between
Saigher and Clonfert Molua, where the men of Ossory
and Ely were defeated by Fiachna. To his foundation Colgan refers in the words—" Birra monasterium
in Elia in Mumonia." Some of these abbots of Birr
were men of renown. S. Killian, a successor of S.
Brendan, died in 690, Seanchan, Abbot of Birr
and Killoughy, died in 791, and MacRiagail, who
died in 820, wrote a copy of the Gospels known as the
Codex Rusworthianus, and was kept at Stowe. The
work concludes with the words—" Quicunque legerit et
intelligerit istam narrationem, oret pro MacReguil
scriptore." The *Rerum Hibernicarum Scriptores
Veteres* gives an account of this document. Ely
O'Carroll had also its native saint, Albaeus, the second
patron of Munster after Patrick, who was born here
and said to have been exposed in his youth, as the
legend reporteth, in a place afterwards called Rath.
The same authority states that in 1284 "Geoffrey St.
Leger, the second founder of the cathedral church of
St. Canice, recovered by combat—the combatants I do
not find recorded—the manor of Seirkeiran in Ely,
now in O'Carroll's country," while Kiaran, or Pyran,
born in Ossory, was the first bishop of Ossory and
lived at Seir Kieran. Hanmer writes of Albanus,
another of these primitive saints—" He founded Cluain
Findglaise and Cluan Conbruno, and went into Ely
where he baptised and converted unto the faith,
thousands." Birr was not only the meeting place of
the waters, as some explain the name, from the meeting of the Brosna and the Camcor, " the river called
the Abhan Chara," which flows from the Slieve Bloom

and forms the boundary of Meath—it was also the meeting place of the kings of Ireland and Munster and Cashel. The *Four Masters* mention that a meeting took place here in 825 between Conchobhar, son of Donchadh, king of Ireland, and Feidhlimidh, son of Crimhthann, king of Munster, and the *Annals of Ulster* give 826 as date for "a kingly parlee at Byre between Felim and Connor."

Hither the " foreigners of the Boyne," as the *Four Masters* describe the Danes, penetrated in 841, plundering both Birr and Saighar. Of this inroad of destruction, Ely O'Carroll has a perpetual record in the name Oxmantown, or the town of the Ostmen. Through here, in 852, Felim of Cashel, the archbishop king of the south, passed in his terrible expedition to Tara, plundering and slaying all the Irish that came in his way, instead of forming a coalition against the invaders. Here the tribe of the O'Connors, the Ui Failge, were defeated and many of them slain, with Cinaeth Cruach, in 949. From here a strong detachment of the O'Carrolls marched to join the standard of Bryan Boroihme, and helped to hurl the ruthless invaders—the Vikings of the North—into the sea on the strands of Clontarf. In 1121 the town lay under the fear and distress of a terrible siege. For Torlogh, the son of Roderick O'Connor, king of Ireland, had collected a great army and "encamped near Birr for some months," and then, to the infinite relief of the O'Carrolls, he was forced by the heavy snows and bitter cold of winter to withdraw to Connaught again. The history of the O'Carrolls begins with a sacrilege —the murder of a king, O'Hendersgeol of Cathluighe in South Munster, who was stabbed as he was leaving the church, and fell dead on the threshold (1154). And twenty years afterwards, Rughry O'Carroll, king of Ely, was slain by his own brother on an island (Inis Clothrann) in the Shannon, and in 1170, the *Annals of Boyle* says the Synod of Birr was held here. It is the story of a red-haired and red-handed race that we are now reading. But when we remember the fierce times in which they lived, and the wild and ungovernable passions of a people who had never experienced the blessing of peace, who had but half learnt the lessons of Christianity, and who had imbibed from their parents that inborn love of fighting which has now been happily turned by English influence into more useful but not less vigorous channels, we may not judge them harshly, though we may congratulate ourselves on the fact that their day is over, and their dread is past.

The English invasion should have had at any rate one good effect in making the isolated tribes and principalities of Ireland forget their private feuds for a moment and combine to some extent against their common foe. But the clansmen of the different tribes would not amalgamate; they had been so long accustomed to hate and fear, to distrust and dislike their neighbours. And so they presented an easier task to the Anglo-Normans than they had doubtless anticipated. It was in consequence of their dissension that the English king was able to portion out their dominions to his favourite and trusted knights, and the latter were not afraid to occupy that part of the land that fell to their share.

It seems that Henry II., without consulting the wishes of the O'Carrolls, had made over the estates of

Ely O'Carroll to Theobald Fitzwalter, the ancestor of the powerful Butlers of Ormond, and that the treacherous John, with an equal disregard for his father's promises, sold the same lots to Walter de Braosa for a large sum of money, so that Fitzwalter had to purchase Braosa's claim before he could take possession. This he at once proceeded to do, having granted part of Birr to Hugh de Hose or Hussy. The O'Carroll opposed his entrance into his dominions, but suffered defeat, losing his own life in the battle. The English invaders were now greatly aided in their conquest of Ely by the unpatriotic action of Moriertagh MacBryen of the Mountain (an Slieve, *i.e.* Tuatharra), a Tipperary neighbour, who seized the opportunity while the O'Carrolls had their hands full, to overrun their country (1207). According to the *Annals of Clonmacnoise*, this highland chief besieged the castle of Byrre, and at last burnt the whole town. He then attacked the Castle of Kinnetty and the castle of Lothra, and broke them down and destroyed them, thus leaving the country of his neighbours completely exposed to the incursions of Fitzwalter and his men.

Kinnetty, as we have already seen, was one of the frontier fortresses of the O'Carroll sept. The tower, built on a spur of the mountain range of Slieve Bloom, served to protect the O'Carroll's country from the invasions of the foreign Danes and the native Irish. That castle, with others belonging to the sept, now fell into the hands of the English, who profited by O'Bryen's campaign by occupying and restoring the castles of Durrow, Birr and Kinnetty (1213). The English having already erected a castle at Athlone, the central plain of Ireland was now dominated by their spearsmen, archers and cavalry.

But the O'Carrolls were not conquered. Far from it, for when defeated in the field they had strongholds to flee into, even those at Clonlisk, Dunkerrin, Emil, and Lemivanane, or Leap. Behind the stout walls and deep trenches of these fortresses they were safe until gunpowder was brought to bear upon them. Then only did they yield.

At Clonlisk, the meadow of the fort, two miles from Shinrone, the O'Carrolls "of the redddened spears" were able to inflict a defeat upon a force of English who were marching to surprise them from the south, but who found in Shinrone (the seat of the Seal) a veritable ambush of fierce and nimble warriors. Intestine feuds from this time forth helped to decimate the ranks of the O'Carrolls. The men of Ossory, on the one side, and the fierce kerne from Arran on the other, proved relentless and persistent foes. The Lord of Ely was slain in battle on his own lands as he was leading his men against the Ossorians, and James, Earl of Arran, took Teige O'Carroll, his own brother-in-law, prisoner, and kept him confined for eight years. But Teige escaped from his dungeon, to be afterwards slain by Lord Deputy Scrope (1407).

But amongst the fiery chieftains of this race some few were found who had more pious aspirations than to live the life of Ishmael, with their hand against every man and every man's hand against them. For, as we found an O'Connor withdrawn from the scenes of blood to the studies of the cloister, so we find Thady O'Carroll desirous of retiring into a more obscure but pious existence. But his clansmen and the lords of

Eastern Munster prevailed upon him to remain as he was, so he compromised matters by paying a visit to the Pope (1396), and afterwards was received at the Court of King Richard II., who was preparing an expedition to Ireland. But he seems to have been the solitary member of the reigning family that evinced such a desire, for those who went before him and those who came after him were conspicuous for the Berserker rage which has ever distinguished the Celtic race.

THE O'MULLOYS OF FEARCALL.

The O'Carroll had warlike neighbours who never refused to give him the pleasure of a fray. Right up to the town of Birr in Ely ran the ancient territory of the O'Maolmuaidh or O'Mulloy, called Fearcall, which may mean either the man of the wood or the man of the churches. The district is very bare and bleak and contains the ancient battlefield of Moylena, according to O'Flaherty's Ogygia, but there are traces of plantations known as the " Great Wood of Fearcall," near Broughall Castle at Frankford, one of the principal seats of the O'Mulloys, and at Dowris, near Whigsborough, or Cloneen, as it used to be called. Eglish, the name of the barony, which corresponds with *ecclesia* or church, supports the other derivation, which also receives some colour from the number of ancient churches in the district. Among these are Drumcullin, Kilcormack, Killyon, Ralyon, and Eglish. The O'Mulloy, who was variously styled king, prince, and chief, ruled this district, which comprised the baronies of Eglish and Ballyboy, lay in the ancient Kingdom of Meath, and between the O'Connors on one side and the O'Carrolls on the other. He was of the race of the Southern Hy Niall. O'Dugan thus describes him :—

> The Prince of Fearcall of the ancient swords
> Is O'Molloy of the free-born name ;
> Full power was granted to him,
> And he held his own country uncontrolled.

The O'Mulloys appear early and frequently in the Annals of the Four Masters. In 1175, O'Maolmuaidh (O'Mulloy), lord of " Ferkale," was treacherously slain by Roderick, son of Conor MacCoghlan. In 1382 Fergal Roe, son of MacGeoghegan, chief of Kinel Fiacha was treacherously slain by the people of Fearcall, when Fergal O'Mulloy, and the son of Theobald "were the persons who attacked him, and Myler Maintin was he who struck him." This may have been in revenge for the murder of Cian O'Carroll, the " illustrious heir," by Hugh O'Mulloy, who struck him with a javelin in 1380. In 1410 Torlogh and Teige, the sons of O'Mulloy, were slain by the people of Glenmalire, showing that they had quarrels with their neighbours on every side. In 1454 there was a dispute for the chieftaincy, which caused a schism in the sept for some time, for Theobald O'Mulloy and the grandson of Cosnavach O'Mulloy were appointed chiefs "in opposition to each other." And seven years afterwards Theobald, "lord of the half of Fearcall, was killed by O'Mulloy of the wood." In 1533 the lord of Fearcall was treacherously slain by his brother Peregrine and his nephew Art in the plain of Lynally, and his brother Cahir " was nominated the O'Mulloy." In 1582 Donald, the son of Theobald O'Mulloy, was slain, and "his death was the less lamented on account of his having endeavoured to supplant and expel his father, in order that he might assume his place." In 1585 Conall O'Mulloy, the lord of Fearcall, attended Queen Elizabeth's Parliament in Dublin, and in this reign the princes of this house were appointed royal standard bearers of Leinster. Cox, in his account of Lord Deputy Russell's progress in Ulster in 1595, states that O'Mulloy carried the English standard on one day and O'Hanlon of Armagh on the next. In virtue of the office they carried as arms a mounted knight with the British standard in his hand and the family arms on his shield. And on his death in 1599 his son Calvach took his place " by the power of the Queen," although there were gentlemen of his lineage who objected to and opposed him "according to the law of the Irish concerning that title." It would seem that certain of his family were wise in their generation, but their politics seemed rather uncertain. However, their lands and people suffered during the Elizabeth wars, although they seem to have but once fought with the O'Connors and other septs against the queen's forces. For the district was invaded by Lord Leonard Grey in 1537, who, according to Mageoghan, took the castles of Eglish, Birr and Modereny and, according to the *Annals of Boyle*, the castles of Modrymore and Broghill also. In 1580 Lord Grey, with 150 cavalry and six companies of infantry, reinforcements from England, overran the territories of Offaly, Fearcall, Kinelyagh and Ely. Camden and Mageoghan inform us that he pacified the O'Carroll of Ely but caused O'Mulloy, lord of Fearcall, to be put to death "as a seditious person." In 1600 the *Four Masters* relate that Hugh O'Neill, lord of Tyrone, marched into

Fearcall, where he remained nine days and the people submitted to him ; and that he then "proceeded over the Sliebh Bloom mountains." On this occasion O'Neill sent three bands to plunder and harry the territory of Ely O'Carroll, and he then marched south to Roscrea. The next year, 1601, he returned, and with several other chiefs who "were expeditiously conveyed across the Shannon at Shannon Harbour ; from thence they proceeded to Delvin MacCoghlan, to Fearcall, to the borders of Slieve Bloom, and into Ikerrin." By these raids Fearcall was greatly cut up, but the O'Mulloys continued to hold their own and to retain their property for a considerable time, one estate, Clonbella, being still in the hands of an O'Mulloy.

The chief burial place of the sept was Kilcormack Monastery, which was found for White Friars by Odo O'Mulloy. Mr. Archdall informs us that as well as being the place for the interment of the chief, this monastery was the scene of an inhuman murder, for in 1525 Charles O'Mulloy and his followers drew Hugh and Constantine O'Mulloy out of the church and put them to death "before the gate of the convent." In 1548 it and Saighir Chiarain, Seir Keiran, were burned down by the English and O'Carroll. The principal fortresses of this sept were Broghill Castle near Frankford, Caislean-na-Hegailse or Eglish Castle, Kiltubrid Castle, Rathmackilduffe, the Castle of Dowris, Le Porte Castle and Ballindown. Broghill Castle, still a splendidly preserved keep, with high walls in places, ten feet thick, was the chief residence of the O'Mulloy. In 1537 it was, however, surprised by the Lord Deputy. In the great hall lavish hospitality was given to all, the O'Mulloys being said to have entertained 900 men at the close of the sixteenth century. The property passed into the hands of the Marquis of Lansdowne through Sir William Petty. It is now owned by Mr. Christopher Banon, D.L., whose ancestor, Frank MacAuley, of the tribe mentioned by O'Dugan—

> The Fair MacAuley rules over
> The entire of the ports of Calrie.

gave its name to Frankford. Kiltubrid Castle stood once on an island and was known as Island Castle, but the land has now been completely drained. It is not far from Kinnetty, and Drumcullen. Shane O'Mnlloy lived at the Castle of Dowris in 1607, and Le Porte Castle stood on Lough Coura, since drained, near the present Whigsborough. These castles were on the frontiers of Fearcall facing Delvin (Dealbna Eathra), the county of the MacCoghlans, while Ballindown, "the town of the Dun or Earthen Fort," is nearer to Birr.

This glimpse of the O'Carrolls neighbours may prove of interest. To return to this class, we find that the good and pious Thady O'Carroll, who wished to retire to the seclusion of a monastery from the world and lawless life of his time, was succeeded by a warlike O'Carroll, who was speedily involved in a war with the Butlers of Ormonde, who eventually entered Ely and burnt down two of his fortresses (1432). Fifteen years, enlivened by the usual border feuds between the Irish and their English neighbours passed, and another enemy of an even more pernicious nature appeared, sparing neither high nor low, priest nor peasant, Norman nor Celt. Hussey, Baron of Galtrim, and 700 priests are said to have died of the plague (1447). The O'Carrolls, however, seem to have come well out of it, for in 1460 we find them in power, and, according to Macgeoghegan, compelling the counties of Kilkenny and Tipperary to pay forty livres yearly. Great pressure, however, was brought to bear upon the Lord Deputy, the Earl of Kildare, by the English of the Pale to release them from the tyranny of the O'Carrolls, and he besieged them in the castle of Lemivanane, or Banan's leap, which he failed to take, and on his return for reinforcements fell sick at Athy and died 1514. So the *Four Masters* say. But his son, Gerald, assumed the reigns of government and marched against this castle, now known as Leap Castle, and took it, although "it was doubtful," say the *Four Masters*, "if there was in that time a castle better fortified and defended than that, until it was demolished on its guards." This happened in 1516. This fortress is as formidable as it is forbidding, being of great strength and of equal antiquity. It is still in splendid preservation and full of interesting points for the antiquarian, oubliettes, crenelles, machicolations, etc. A capital view of the surrounding country may be had from its grim parapets. Right opposite is a splendid specimen of a rath, with a raised platform of earth for the chieftain's residence, with which the castle, which is said to have been built by the Danes, was connected by a subterranean passage. Mr. and Mrs. Darby—the latter of whom is widely known under her *nom de plume* of Andrew Merry— take much pride in their fine old baronial residence, which has been for the last three centuries in the possession of the Darby family, which was connected by marriage with the O'Carrolls.

CHAPTER XII.

The Fall of the O'Carrolls.

WE now come to an unpleasant episode in the history of the sept, a family dispute, which did more to weaken its power than any foreign oppression could have done. To cut a long story short, when John, son of Maolroona O'Carroll, died in 1485, the chieftainship of the sept was claimed by another O'Carroll, who was elected on account of his splendid qualities. This was the famous Maolroona O'Carroll, who, according to the *Four Masters*, was "the most distinguished man of his tribe for valour, prosperity, and excellence, to whom poets, travellers, ecclesiastics, and literary men were most thankful, and who gave, and entertained, and bestowed more presents than any other who lived of his lineage." But though devoted to literature, the patronage of all that was excellent, and the dispenser of princely hospitality, this, the best of the O'Carrolls, was, like the British Prince Alfred, equally proficient in the arts of war. For, while he was "the anvil of knowledge, and the golden pillar of the Elyans," he was also "the supporting mainstay of all persons, the rightful victorious rudder of his race; the powerful young warrior in the march of tribes; the active triumphant champion of Munster." This Maolroona O'Carroll was as popular among the English as he was among his own people. For he wooed and won no less a bride than the Lady Fitzgerald, daughter of the Earl of Kildare. Her sister had been

M

previously wedded to Bryan O'Connor of Offaly. But Maolroona died, unlike most of the O'Connors, however, in his own castle on S. Matthew's Day (1532), after he had heard of the defeat of the Earl of Ormond by his sons, who took many horses, and some ordnance at a ford which was called Bel-atha-na-bh Fabcun, in memory of the achievement. His eldest son, Ferganainm, or the "man without a name," was chosen to succeed him. But the sons of John O'Carroll, the former chief, who had distressed the closing years of Maolroona by conspiring with his foes against him, at once took the field against Ferganainm, and, seizing the Castle of Birr, continued to harass the supporters of Ferganainm, who entreated the Lord Deputy, the Earl of Kildare, his uncle, to come to his aid. This the latter did without delay. And taking on his way the Castle of Killurin, in Geashill, the Castle of Eglish, and the Castle of Ballindooney, or Ballindown, where the sons of John had fortified themselves, he proceeded to storm the Castle of Birr. During the attempt on this fortress, which he assailed from the Monastery of Birr, the Earl was wounded in his side by a bullet, but still persisted in the attack until the place was stormed. The earl was recalled shortly afterwards to England to give an account of his stewardship, and to answer among other things why he, a person of English descent, had, in spite of the statute of Kilkenny, allowed his daughters to marry the Milesian Irish, and was committed to the Tower by Henry VIII. There he died shortly afterwards (1535).

In the meantime he was succeeded by Lord Grey, whose presence was almost immediately required in the country of the O'Connors and O'Carrolls. For

" Silken Thomas" had commenced his absurd rebellion, and induced the only too willing clans to rally round the standard of revolt. Down to Offaly and Ely came the new Deputy, and took the castles of Eglish, Birr, Modereny, Modrymore, and Broghill, but not before much destruction had been wrought by Ferganainm. However, this proved an instance of the soft answer turning away wrath, for while O'Connor was driven from his land, and was followed by the unrelenting hatred and unremitting severity of Lord Grey, the O'Carroll succeeded in conciliating him and throwing dust in his eyes when he tendered his submission to him in Dublin Castle. It was one of the charges made against this unfortunate nobleman that he had over-looked the outrages that Ferganainm had committed, and was too partial to the Geraldines (1541). It would have been better for these Viceroys had they and their daughters seen less of the fascinating O'Carrolls.

However, the King himself, Henry VIII., in 1539 concluded a treaty [1] with Ferganainm on the conditions that the latter was to pay tribute for Ely O'Carroll, to furnish forces to the king, and to give the deputy passage through his dominions whenever it was neces-sary. Poor Ferganainm, however, did not long survive this new settlement of the question, for the unhappy man, now infirm and blind, was treacherously killed in his own castle of Clonlisk (Clonlis) by Teige, his kinsman, the son of Donagh, and the grandson of John O'Carroll, and by one of the O'Mulloys. The *Four Masters* give a full record of it. It was a

---

[1] A copy of this treaty—concordia facta inter Regem et O'Karroll Capitaneum Patriæ Ely O'Karroll—is preserved in Sir W. Betham's *Irish Antiquarian Researches.*

terrible scene, the assassins seemed to have got a secret entrance into the castle and attacked the blind prince unawares, but he defended himself with such vigour while some of his attendants, most of them unarmed, hurried to his assistance, and presented their defenceless bodies between the miscreants and their king, and thus obtained the glory of dying with their master (1541).

Now ensued a decade of fighting with varying fortune, but out of which the O'Carrolls seem to have emerged the best. Trusting more to their natural wit than to the force of their arms, they secured favourable terms from their invaders, who saw that it would be wiser to treat the sept at all events with more apparent consideration than they had done. But it is questionable if there was any sincerity on either side. In 1548 it is said that Thady O'Carroll (Thady being the same as Teige or Tadg), made an arrangement with Brabazon by which he engaged himself to supply the king with forces, and that shortly afterwards he surrendered his dominion of Ely O'Carroll to King Edward VI., who restored it to him with the title of Lord Baron of Ely. But this statement is not well authenticated. It is queried by Ware. It is certain, however, that this Thadeus was able to secure possession of Birr and to inflict a defeat on the English settlers. But Thadeus did not live long to reap the fruits of the victory, which were not, however, fated to be lasting. For he was slain by Cahir O'Carroll, who became Baron of Ely, and who perished as he deserved by the sword of another rival, William O'Carroll. The seed of dissension, sown by John O'Carroll and fostered by the English, did indeed produce a harvest of blood in 1554.

This William wisely tendered his submission to the English, and was acknowledged by them as the successor to the title of Lord of Ely, and having promised to fight for the King and Queen of England, and to send Queen Mary a number of horse and foot, was made Governor of Ely by Royal Patent (1557). This was all the wily William desired. The moment the Deputy's back was turned he began the old game of plundering the English settlements, in spite of the fact that the Deputy, before he had withdrawn, had taken hostages from William and his confederates for their good behaviour, which did not last long. For we find that after his return, the Earl of Essex was obliged to send an expedition through Fearcall to punish the O'Mulloys, and advancing with great rapidity to Lemyvanane Castle, now called Leap, he took William by surprise, and the latter only escaped by the swiftness of his horse. Teige O'Carroll was then put in the Governorship in his place by the English Deputy, who saw the advantage of promoting division in the ranks of the O'Carrolls, which was not hard to do among so quarrelsome a sept. But William was not done with, for he returned in an unexpected manner to his favourite stronghold, Caislean-an-Leime, the Castle of the Leap, and after slaying the English garrison, was once more master of Lemyvanane. His triumph, however, was but short-lived, for he was afterwards severely defeated by the soldiers of Essex, and had to draw in his horns. It was at this time that the districts of Leix and Offaly were made into the shires of King's County and Queen's County;

Ely, which was omitted at the time, being included in King's County afterwards. Dangan then became known as Philipstown, Maryborough being created the capital of Queen's County.

Under the 8th of March, 1576, we have an interesting document drawn up by "Betwyxte Sir Henry Sidney, Knight, Lord Deputy of Ireland, for and on behalf of the Queenes's Most Excellent Majestie, of those parts, and Sir William O'Kerroll, of Lemyvanan, in the countrie called Elye O'Kerroll, and now to be parcell of the King's County." This was a deed of surrender, a full copy of which is given in O'Donovan's translation of the *Four Masters*. Its chief interest nowadays arises from the list of thirty-six landed proprietors who held the land of Ballybritt and Clonlisk, under the O'Carrolls. The evident object of O'Carroll in delivering his possessions to the "Queene's most honourable Court of Chauncerie of Ireland" was to secure them by letters patent, one of the conditions of the surrender, for his illegitimate sons, of whom he had four—John O'Kerroll, Teige O'Kerroll, Calloghe O'Kerroll, and Donoghe O'Kerroll. And this he managed to do, and so excluded the legitimate heir, his own brother, Donoghe Keoghe O'Kerroll, from the succession.

But the Irish septs of Ely, Leix, Offaly, and Fearcall still continued in a restless and unpacified condition. While giving fair words to the English Deputy they ceased not to prey upon each other, and to plunder the property of the settlers, like the moss-trooping Scots of border fame. One of these expeditions (1579) against Birr terminated fatally. For we read that Conal Buighe, the son of Gillpatrick,

the son of Pierce O'Moore, was slain at Birr in the
territory of Ely, and the historian's comment is that
" it was better that he was killed, for it was to plunder
the town that he had come." But while the Irish
wolves were quarrelling in their dens, the English
bloodhounds were on their trail, tracking them to their
lairs. Lord Grey, reinforced by cavalry and infantry
from England, was upon them, and " pacified " the
O'Carrolls and the O'Mulloys. On his return the
Deputy released a hostage, William, the son of
Ferganainm, whose tragical death has been described.
But the unfortunate man was not fated to enjoy the
liberty of his native air, for as he was returning he
was attacked by some of his enemies of the O'Connor
clan who were displeased at his release, and who
" slew him at once and left his body exposed to the
claws of wolves and ravens." But the murdered man's,
son, John, was chosen to be the Lord of Ely. He,
too, did not enjoy his honours long. For Teige's
perfidious example was doomed to be perpetuated.
John O'Carroll was stabbed the very next year, 1582,
" with abominable and unprofitable treachery " by
Mulroona, the son of Teige Caoch, the son of Ferganainm. The assassin then became a victim of
assassination, falling three months afterwards by the
hand of a brother of the man he murdered—Calvagh
O'Carroll.

This Calvagh O'Carroll was then nominated chief of
the clan, which position he managed to hold for fifteen
years. He is described by the *Four Masters* as " a
warlike, defending man, and a strong arm against his
English and Irish neighbours ; he was a knight by
title and honour, by authority of his sovereign." In

the Parliament convened by Sir John Perrott at Dublin (1585), this Calvagh O'Carroll, with his neighbours, the O'Mulloy, O'Madden, and MacCoghlan of Delvin, was a distinguished figure. But there is an indelible blot of shame on his escutcheon. For it appears that Calvagh had hired some of the MacMahons from Monaghan to help him in the plundering expeditions, but when their time for payment came he had no funds to settle with them. With unspeakable truculence he conceived the idea of "removing" them. Accordingly in his castle of Lemyvanane, where O'Banan made his immortal leap, he made a great feast in honour of his mercenaries. But at the end of the banquet, when the revellers were overcome with the pleasures of the table, the orders were given to close the doors, and the perfidious host, violating all the traditions of hospitality, which we.e often of more weight in the eyes of the Celt than the laws of God, caused his armed retainers to fall upon the defenceless men who had fought his battles, and slew them to a man.

For this act of unparalleled atrocity, Calvagh paid the penalty. The O'Neills from the north invaded his land, harrying and carrying all before them, and in June of the following year his life was taken "by some inferior gentlemen of the O'Carrolls and O'Meaghers." Such was the melancholy end of a great warrior, whose crimes prevent us from regarding him as a hero. When we compare the callousness and perfidy of such men— the prevalent type of the Celt at the close of the sixteenth century—with the gallantry and chivalry of their English contemporaries, of whom Sir Philip Sydney is an example, we cannot but lament the fact that his life of constant rapine and murder tended to foster all that was low and cunning, and banished all that was generous and noble from the heart of the Celtic chief. There was nothing to encourage but much to impede the spirit of chivalry in the associations of the Irish chieftain, who knew himself to be safe in his stronghold from the representatives of the law he had so basely broken. It was well for Ireland that a new race was coming to infuse higher ideas and better customs into the wild but warm blood of the Irish clans, who when trained and disciplined have proved on many a field and in many a clime that they are inferior to no race in the game of war and the arts of peace.

In the last year of the century that had witnessed so many distressing scenes and doughty deeds, we find that the O'Carrolls, who were then posing as dutiful and loyal, though, we need hardly add, little trusted servants of the Crown, were ordered to invade the O'Mulloys of Fearcall, who were at this time living in the heated atmosphere of family feuds and open sedition. This order the O'Carrolls must have been only too willing to obey. Sir Charles O'Carroll appears in command of 100 men in the muster roll of the Lord Deputy Mountjoy, dated 26th March, 1600, and Captain Mulrooney O'Carroll as commanding 100 foot in O'Carroll's Country in the same and the two following years.

The seventeenth century saw many changes in this powerful sept. When the so-called " undertakers " were planted in Ely, O'Carroll, to the disgust of the dispossessed, but to the advantage of our poor distressful country, those of the O'Carrolls who fell in with the existing order of things fared well, while those who did not for a time defied the English from behind their stout fortresses of Emill, Dunkerrin, or Frankfort, Lemvanane, and Clonlisk.

On an inquisition held in the year 1612 Teige O'Carroll was found to possess some ninety acres, but Lord Thurles, on behalf of his father, the Earl of Ormond, declared that the said Teige had surrendered his claim to the earl, and held the property as the latter's tenant. The O'Carroll afterwards disputed this statement when he found that Sir Laurence Parsons had been given possession of Birr, but after petitioning the king three times the decision was given against him. Thus ends the connection of the O'Carrolls with their old town, which now, thanks to the genius, enterprise, and wealth of Sir Laurence and his worthy successors, was transformed from being the headquarters of a lawless predatory chieftain, and the scene of murders and rapine, into the centre of culture, civilization, and religion—as it once was—in the midland counties of Ireland. Birr rapidly improved. Its streets were lighted, its poor were employed and protected, glass was manufactured in the Bigo factory, chimneys were erected on the houses, and single women were forbidden, under pain of being exposed for three days in the stocks, to sell liquor. The " Black Castle " of Birr—a forbidding ruin that stood prominently above the river's bank, presents a significant contrast with the handsome baronial residence which has taken its place, and which has stood as many sieges and seen as much fighting under its valiant defenders—whose history in places reads like a romance—as any other castle in the land. In 1639 we read of a search made by Sir William Parsons, of Birr, and Captain William Paisley, Provost-Marshal of Munster, in the castle of Clonlisk, where O'Carroll was suspected of plotting a conspiracy. The bird was flown, but the searchers found a quantity of muskets and pikes and a secret chamber, which had been used in former times for coining money. Another stronghold of the once powerful sept was Dunkerrin, the fortress of the ash tree, which afterwards passed into the hands of Thomas Francks, who obtained by grant the lands of Coologe and Castleroan, and became known as Frankfort Castle.

But the last memoirs of the O'Carrolls are associated with Emmell, a castle that had long been in their possession, and one that, like the others, except Leap castle, which, strange to say, is now held partly in the O'Carroll name and right, was taken from them. The Irish Rebellion of 1641 hastened the climax. Then the O'Carrolls, Mulloys, Kennedys, and the neighbouring septs rose and burnt down the castles of the settlers, and in many cases murdered the inmates. This cruelty was not, however, universal. Many instances of gallantry and courtesy extended by the rebels to the English, notably the polite treatment which Lady Anne Parsons received from Colonel Moore, who besieged Parsonstown, relieve that story of some of its repellent and melancholy features. The tide of fortune turned, and Emmell was granted by Cromwell to Captain Rose, and its owner had to take up his abode in Cullenwaine, where he died in 1681.

He was succeeded by his son, Long Anthony Carroll, who made a supreme but ineffectual effort to retrieve the fortunes of his ancient house. However, he was

able to recover Emmell.   For Captain Rose, not feeling at all safe among such determined and dangerous
neighbours, who had been the loyal supporters of the
House of Stuart, to which he and his late general
officer, the Lord Protector, had proved traitors, was
glad to dispose of it by deed of sale to Long Anthony
in 1676.   Anthony now became regarded as the lord
of Ely, and endeavoured, with some success, to unite
the scattered fragments of his sept.   However, the
revolution of 1688 burst upon the land, fanning into
flame the now dormant elements of party strife and
hatred, and Anthony, like all the Irish chieftains, remained loyal to the king.   Their loyalty cost them
dear.   Anthony armed his men, and took part in a
great many encounters under the brilliant leadership
of Sarsfield.   In one of his expeditions he seized
Nenagh, which was then in the hands of a party who
had ever been opposed to the Stuarts.   And although
the castle was dismantled and its walls had not been
rebuilt since Ireton demolished them in 1651, he
thought of making it his headquarters for his operations
in Ormond.   However, he was forced to abandon it
on the approach of General Leveson against him, so
he evacuated the town after burning it down to prevent it being of use to the Orange party.   There is no
doubt that his movement was accelerated by the report that a strong body of William's men were marching against Emmell.   Those men never reached their
destination.   The gallant Anthony was before them.
And as the Dutchmen were endeavouring to pick their
way through an Irish bog at Barna, the Place of the
Gap, the Celts flew upon them like wolves upon their
prey, and the scene of the slaughter that ensued bears

the name of " the Bloody Togher," or pass through the bog.

But when King James fled, Anthony showed his wisdom by returning to his estates and submitting to the new condition of things, which he could not alter, with a good grace. Finally, the lavish hospitality of Anthony's great grandson, Richard O'Carroll, who was compelled to mortgage his castle and estates, extinguished the flickering glories of this illustrious house.

CHAPTER XIII.

THE DEFENCE OF THE PALE.

SIR JOHN DAVIS alleges as reasons why the country was not subdued until his time (1603). (1) "The faint prosecution of the war" and (2) "the looseness of the civil government." When discussing the superficial nature of Henry II's. conquest he points out that Henry very unwisely gave the Irish lords the style of "kings." The word "Rex" is preserved in Hoveden's record of his agreement with Roderick O'Connor. And from the twelfth year of King John to the thirty-sixth year of Edward III. no royal army came from England to make an end of the war, but during that period "the chief governors of the realm, at first called Custodes Hiberniae and afterwards Lords Justices," maintained an ill-paid and ill-governed army in the country. The English subjects in Ireland were continually cessed and taxed to maintain this army because little treasure came out of England to pay the soldiers' wages. Consequently in all the Pipe-Rolls of Henry III., Edward I., Edward II., and Edward III., there is the entry "In Thesauro nihil" (nothing in the treasury) because the officers of the state and army had exhausted the little there was."

We do not imply that the officers or their men were well paid according to modern standards, in those days. Sir John Davis informs us that 6s. 8d. a day was the pay drawn by Lord Lionel as general, but

this was doubled when he was created Duke of
Clarence. Then he was allowed for eight knights 2s.
each, per diem; for sixty-four esquires 1s. each; for
368 mounted archers from Lancashire, 6d. each; and
for twenty-three archers from Wales, 2d. each, per
diem. When Lord Lientenant 1361-1369, James, Earl
of Ormonde, Lord Justice in 1364 was allowed for
twenty armed " hobblers," as Irish horsemen who
served on " hobbies " were called, 6d. each, and for
twenty unarmed "hobblers" 4d. each, per diem.   In
the time of Sir William Windsor (Lord Lieutenant
1369) the charge of the kingdom amounted only to
£11,200, while the revenue, according to Sir John
Davis, did not rise to £10,000 any year during the
reign of Edward III. In the year 1442 the revenue
only amounted to £4,877 2s. 4d.   And in the same
year—one of perfect peace—the Executive and
military establishment in Ireland cost only
£7,982 6s. 8d. The force itself consisted of 9 officers
and 532 men, who were maintained at an annual cost
of £7,175 13s. 4d.—a small force and outlay compared with the Dublin police and the cost of their
maintenance, and utterly inadequate for the purpose
of protecting life and property in the Pale, had they
not been supported by the levies of the Pale and the
Earl of Ossory. The force was divided in this way : Sir
Anthony St. Leger's retinue, 2 officers and 100 horsemen (£1,360 16s. per an.) ; Mr. R. St. Leger's retinue,
2 officers and 100 horsemen at the same cost; Mr.
Brereton's retinue, 2 officers and 150 archers; the
Master of Ordnance, 3 officers and 100 hackbutteers.
The Treasurer of this empty treasury had an escort
of 40 horsemen ; the Knight Marshal had 1 officer

and 32 horsemen ; and the Clerk of the Check, 10 horsemen. Lord Leonard Grey had introduced in 1535 the plan at first effectual, of sending flying columns supported by artillery, through the country, which checked the lawless here and there for a moment, but, of course, led to no permanent settlement of the country. But when we consider the slenderness of the means at his disposal, the paucity of his troops and the smallness of his treasury we wonder at the success of his enterprises and the extent of his operations. In 1536 when he invaded Munster, which was in revolt, he had an army of 1,023 men, 323 of whom were Irish levies ! In 1560 the Irish revenues of Elizabeth were £8,351, £500 of this came from the lands of Leix and Offaly, while the outlay was £9,400, a deficit of £1,049. The expenditure was as follows : —£1,500 for the Lord Lieutenant; an escort of 50 horsemen, £700; 100 horsemen to attend him, £1,400 ; 200 footmen to do the same, £2,600 ; 100 kerne, £600; 100 footmen for the fort of Offaly, £1,300 ; 100 footmen for the fort of Leix, £1,300, a horseman being paid £14 per an. ; and footmen £13. Ireland was, financially in those times a dead loss to England. During the first 16 years of Elizabeth's reign the loss in hard cash in those days was £370,779—a sum which would have established a magnificent exhibition in London or Dublin, or founded a noble university.

The principal source of the King's income in Ireland was the customs, which were chiefly raised on hides, rents of land and various subsidies. Queen Elizabeth, for instance, had certain " bonaught for gallowglass upon Irishmen living on the border of the

Pale " to the value of £4,000 (Carew MS. I., p. 300). These sums were rather uncertain, and the difficulty of collecting them was so great that in Henry VI's. reign the Duke of York on his appointment as Lord Lieutenant was to have all the King's revenues there and 4,000 marks yearly for England. When the Brotherhood of St. George was instituted by 14. Edward IV. a subsidy of poundage on all exports and imports—the hides and goods of freemen of Dublin and Drogheda excepted—was granted to pay the standing army of 200 men, of whom 120 were mounted archers, at 6d. per diem ; 40 were horsemen at 5d., and the rest at a lower rate. Sir Edward Bellingham, Lord Justice in Edward VI's. reign, the first Deputy to extend the borders of the Pale by breaking the power of the Moores and O'Connors and building the forts of Leix and Offaly, had but 600 horse and 400 foot, whose pay amounted to £1,216 per month. In those years, at any rate, the Irish taxes and revenues were spent on Irish concerns —if the upkeep of the army may be considered so— and were miserably deficient for the purpose. The slenderness of the means placed at their disposal is an excuse for the almost proverbial rapacity of the lieu-tenant and their deputies at which the English Government winked. We are strongly reminded of the publicani under the Roman Empire, whose extor-tions were connived at, provided they did not commit the Empire in any way, by the story of the doings of the English officials almost from their first appearance in the land.

Of this rapacity, a few instances will now be given Henry Marleburrough informs us in his *Chronicle*

N

that Lord Thomas of Lancaster, the Lord Lieutenant, landed at Carlingford in 1406, and was received in Dublin by the Earl of Kildare, one of the Lord Justices, whom he had arrested and detained in the Castle of Dublin till "he had paid three hundred markes fine." The unhappy Earl, whose colleague, strange to say, was James, Earl of Ormonde, in the meantime "lost all his goods, being spoiled and rifled by the Lord Lieutenant and his servants." Shortly after this action, which reminds one of the exploits of the modern bushranger, this royal governor was wounded in a skirmish at Kilmainham, and returned to England, leaving as deputy in his place the warlike William de Botiller, Prior of Kilmainham. The same chronicler also states that in 1419, on the festival of Mary Magdalene, the Lord Lieutenant, John Talbot, went over to England, leaving as his deputy Richard Talbot, the Archbishop of Dublin, and carrying with him the curses of many "because hee being runne much in debt for victuall and divers other things would pay for little or nothing." In the Parliament that met in November, 1420, "were reckoned up the debts of the Lord John Talbot, which amounted to a great summe." Spenser comments on the rapacity of the governor and his official. He requests "that no offices should be sold by the Lord Deputy for money, nor no protections brought for reward, nor no beeves taken for captaincies of counties, nor no shares of bishoprics, nor no selling of licences for exportation of prohibited goods and specially corn and flesh." A contemporary of Spenser, Richard Boyle, a young gentleman who first landed at Dublin in 1588 with but twenty-seven pounds and three shillings in his pocket and two changes of raiment, a rapier, dagger and taffety doublet was made Earl of Cork in 1620, and left vast estates behind him. However, he may have been a fortunate speculator, as many of the English immigrants were more lucky and more provident than the old inhabitants of the county. It was to him that Sir Walter Raleigh sold his house and estates in Youghal in order to provide himself with ships to attack the Spaniards, and it was he who quarrelled with Laud and Strafford over the removal of a family monument from the east wall of the choir, where the altar used to be, of S. Patrick's Cathedral.

To go back some centuries, we find Sir Ralph Ufford, Lord Deputy in 1344, acting in the most unknightly manner towards the Earl of Desmond, of whose castles at Castleisland and Iniskisty in Kerry he got possession by treachery, and hanged the Knights, Sir Eustace De La Poer, Sir William Grant, and Sir John Cottrel. Camden gives a vivid picture of this ruffian, " at whose death the common sort truly and heartily praised the only Son of God." " Being dead, he was folded fast in a sheet in a coffin of lead to be interred in England and with his treasure not worthy to be bestowed with such holy relics "—the historian sarcastically remarks—" his countess (the widow of the Earl of Ulster) in horrible grief of heart went over to England; and she, who at her coming had entered the city of Dublin so gloriously with the King's arms and ensigns, attended by a numerous guard of soldiers, and a long train in her procession through the streets; for a short period living in royal state as Queen of Ireland, was now, at her going forth from the same city obliged to pass stealthily through a postern gate of the castle to avoid the clamour of the common people calling upon her to discharge her debts." How that noble but rather dishonest dame must have sadly meditated upon the unstability of human greatness as she departed in disguise from Dublin on the 2nd of May, 1346, *taking her money for greater security in her husband's coffin !*

Another Lord Deputy, Sir Stephen Scrope, who held office in 1401 and again in 1406, was converted by his wife who was not "a miserable sott" like Lady Ufford, from being a character like Ufford into a gentleman and a popular governor to boot. Campion tells us that his wife, hearing of his misconduct and extortion in Ireland, declared she would in no wise assent to live in his company there unless he swore a solemn oath on the Bible that willingly he should wrong no Christian creature in the land, but that duly and truly he should see payment made for all expenses. This oath was faithfully kept by the Deputy who "recovered a good opinion, schooled his caters, enriched the country, continued a plentifull house, remissions of great fines, pardons of lands and lives he granted so charitably and discreetly that his name was never uttered among them, without many blessings and prayers." Lady Scrope's example illustrates both the influence of a good wife and also the misconduct of which a Lord Deputy could be guilty with impunity in those days of misrule in the English Pale.

When speaking of these distinguished Governors of Ireland we may not omit the name of Prince John,

Lord of Ireland (1185). Campion gives an interesting account of the loyal and handsome manner in which the boy-governor, who was accompanied on this occasion by the celebrated Giraldus Cambrensis, was received by the Kings of Thomond, Desmond and Connaught who "put themselves in the bravest manner they could to meete him," while they sent on before them to Waterford Irish gentlemen with rich presents. "And these men as they are very kind hearted where they list to show obedience made unto the Childe their Lord the most joy and gladnesse that might be, and though rudely yet lovingly and after the custom of their country, offered to kisse him, with such familiarity, as they used towards their Princes at home." But the result was contrary to their expectations. For, instead of receiving a gracious acknowledgment of their homage, they were thrust rudely back by two of the Norman Guard," " pick thankes," who " shooke and tore the clownes by the glibs and beards unmannerly and churlishly thrust them out of the presence." This was a grievous insult which is even more graphically described in Hanmer's account, which is taken from Giraldus Cambrensis, who was present. He says, " one made courtesie, another kneeled, some tooke him by the hand, other some offer to kisse him. The new gallants and Normans set them at nought, laughed at their mantles and trooses (trousers), derided their glibbes and long beards, one takes a sticke and pats the Irishman on the pate, another halls the mantle and pricks him behinde with a pinne, some have their glibbes and long beards pulled and departing have flappes on the lippes, thumps on their neckes, and the doores clapt

on their heeles with divers other abuses and undis-
ereet entertainment."

Camden's description of the dress affected by the
better class of Irishmen at the time may help to
explain the indignation of the Irish chieftains at such
treatment : " The hair of their head they wear long,
and nothing set they greater store by than the glibbes
or tresse of their haires ; and to have the same plucked
or twitched they take it for a contumelious indignitee.
They use linen shirts, and these, verilie, exceeding
large, with wide sleeves, and hanging side down to the
very knees, which (shirts) they wont to stain with
saffron, Little jackets they have of woollen, and those
very short ; breeches most plain and tight ; over these
they cast their mantles, with a drape fringed purple,
and the same daintly set out with sundrie colours,
within which they lappe themselves in the night and
sweetly sleep on the very ground. Such also do the
women cast over the side garment that they wear
down to the foot."

Greatly incensed by the indignities they had
suffered at the hands of this Norman Rehoboam and
his satellites whom Giraldus describes as "great
talkers, boasters and swearers, very proud, and
despisers of others, very forward to claim position,
profit and honour, but very backward to undertake
any dangerous service," the Irish envoys went back
to the kings "turned them home with great oathes
and leagues" from "a Boy peevish and insolent,
governed by a sort of flatterers, younglings and
prowlers." " The entertainment," however, was not
altogether one-sided. For John and the "beardlesse
boys " were promptly ordered back into England and

censured by Henry II., who appointed John de Courcy
"the strong man" of the kingdom to quell the storm
their silly behaviour had raised.   John did not forget
the lesson.   For when he returned in 1210—the year
after the notable massacre of the Dublin holiday party
in Cullenswood by the O'Birnes and O'Tooles of
Wicklow on Black Monday—he treated the Irish
chiefs with greater respect, reformed the coinage and
appointed twelve English shires with sheriffs to rule
over them, and when he went to war with France in
1213 was supported by an Irish regiment of 300 men.
In the 12th year of his reign both the Benches and
the Exchequer Court were erected (Sir John Davis),
and there are great keeps at Nenagh, Limerick, and
Roscrea, said to have been erected in his reign.

As a general rule the lieutenants and their deputies
did nothing, according to the English Chronicler, but
extort money from the English and Irish aristocracy,
"make great preyes upon the neighbouring Irish,"
receive grants from Parliament, run heavily into debt,
and carry home with them the curses of the plundered
merchants of Dublin.   In consequence of these extortions the colonists had begun to leave the country in
great numbers, but in 1353 they were checked for a
time by a royal proclamation forbidding the departure
of any ecclesiastic, noble or able-bodied man from the
shores of Ireland.   In 1356 a royal order was issued
that no one born in Ireland should thenceforth hold a
command in any of the King's castles or towns.   A
brilliant scheme was this for the encouragement of the
English colonists !   They were compelled by law to
remain in Ireland in order to defend the territory of
the English King from the inroads of the Irish and

to provide the English-born deputy with a suitable
field for his embezzlements; and at the same time
because of their having been born in Ireland they
were treated as " Irish rebels," unfit to hold the
smallest office or post in connexion with the Saxon
Government. It is not, therefore, to be wondered at
that many Anglo-Norman houses withdrew from their
allegiance to England, adopted Irish ideas, and promoted the policy of " Ireland for the Irish." Among
those who had been converted to the new policy by
the injustice and tyranny of the English officials were
the Le Poers, one of whom had been infamously
hanged by Sir Ralph Ufford, the Lord Justice (1344),
the St. Aubyns, De Roches, and the De Cantillons.

In 1361 Lionel Duke of Clarence came over as Lord
Lieutenant to save the situation, but only made
matters worse than before. Opening his campaign
with a well-equipped English army he made no efforts
to conciliate those who were still wavering between
their allegiance to the King of England and their love
for their native land, but estranged them still more by
his proclamation forbidding any English colonist to
join his army or approach his camp. But his campaign was not crowned with many laurels. And he
withdrew to England when he found the subjugation
of Ireland a hopeless task. On his return in 1367 he
held the parliament in Kilkenny which passed the
celebrated statute by which an undisguised effort was
made to drive a permanent wedge between the still
loyal English of the Pale, the "degenerate" English
throughout the country who had been obliged by
circumstances to adopt the native customs and the
native Irish themselves. By the provisions of the

historic enactment every connexion between the English of the Pale and the Celts, such as gossipred, fosterage, and intermarriage, was made illegal, and sale and barter between the two races in time of war was denounced as felony. The wearing of Irish garments, the use of the Irish language, the submission to Brehon laws, by which every penalty was commuted to a fine, the giving of coyne and livery, or food and fodder to soldiers billeted upon them, the riding without a saddle, the keeping of "kerns, hoblers or idle men" by the English subjects, were strictly prohibited. Irishmen were also debarred from entering English monasteries and Irish bards from English lands.

The framers of this statute not only desired to separate the English subjects from the "rebel" and native Irish by a barrier that no man might cross ; they also wished to remove all occasions of hostility between the two nations. To this end they enacted that on the one hand the cattle of Irish people pastured on English lands without consent of the owner should be impounded until compensation should be made, but on the other hand, that cattle so impounded should be kept safely for their owners under heavy penalties; and that the Irish should receive due notice of the new regulation. They also declared that in the case of a debt the creditor, whether English or Irish could not make the family or tribe of the debtor responsible for the debt. For it was a feature of the Brehon law that the whole sept could be made liable for the eric or debt incurred by a single member. They also ordered that " no difference of allegiance shall henceforth be made between the English born in Ireland and the English born in England, by calling them English hobbe or Irish dog, but that all be called by one name, the English lieges of our lord the King." Those who persisted in calling these names were to be imprisoned for a year and afterwards fined.

Those regulations were strict but not harsh. Fair play was intended for all. But the English and Irish in Ireland were henceforth to be treated not as one nation but as two distinct peoples. And while the English subjects of the Pale were prohibited from all friendly intercourse with the Irish, they were also debarred from every hostile encroachment, by section 26, which ordained that if any peace or truce made by the justices or sheriff " between English and Irish shall be broken by any English and thereof be attainted, he shall be taken and put in prison until satisfaction be made by him to those who shall be disturbed or injured by that occasion, and he shall moreover make fine at the King's will."

The English Government had apparently abandoned the hope of anglicising the Irish and recovering the degenerate English, and now directed its efforts to check the steadily advancing de-anglicisation of the English settlers, and to shepherd, after the hireling fashion, the few loyal sheep in the wilderness. This measure, a wise one for the time, had there been a sufficient executive to support it, was followed by an order (1368) for the return of absentee landlords under pain of forfeiture of their lands. Had the Government nursed its own subjects more kindly, or maintained them more loyally, there would have been no need for any such edict. But owing to the indifference

of the people in England, and the injustice of the
English governors in Ireland, life in the English Pale
had become intolerable. Reduced to pauperism by
legal taxation and illegal embezzlement, depleted by
constant conscriptions, worn out by perpetual campaigns, insulted and harassed by the officials who employed their temporary banishment from the English
court like the *publicani* of evil fame, so that "an
officer of the king who enters very poor could in one
year heap up more wealth than men of great estates
in many," the English of the Pale were sorely tempted
either to return to England, or to join the ranks of their
countrymen who were stigmatised as " Irish rebels."
Richard II., who is not conspicuous for aught save
magnificent conceptions, struck the nail on the head
when he wrote regarding the English who had become
de-anglicised by English misrule—" To us and to our
council it appears that the Irish rebels have rebelled
in consequence of the injustice and grievances practised towards them, for which they have been afforded
no redress ; and that if not wisely treated and given
hope of grace, they will most likely ally themselves
with our enemies."

In the meantime the Irish tribes were regaining
lost ground and assuming the aggressive. Acting independently of each other, the tribes made the work
of their subjugation a matter beyond the range of
practical politics. The various English colonists had
to cope with the tribes in their vicinity, but the English Government had to settle with the tribes in rota-
tion. In the course of time they were compelled to
buy off their hostility ; but before they were reduced
to such straits they made some attempt to keep them

in their place. This was by no means easy when there was no military executive or police to patrol the country; and when the forts and castles of the previous settlers had been destroyed and the settlers themselves dispersed. Out of their hiding places in the bogs and hills the O'Connors and O'Carrolls and the O'Byrnes and O'Tooles came with great numbers and courage. And in 1368, the very year after the Statute of Kilkenny had been passed, the Irish Parliament made a strong but ineffectual appeal to King Edward III. to help them, stating that the Irish with his other enemies and rebels, continued to ride over the country in hostile array, slaying those who opposed them, despoiling the monasteries, churches, castles, towns, and fortresses of the English without reverence for God or Holy Church "to the great shame and disherison of His Majesty." At this juncture (1371), De Cotton, the warlike Dean of S. Patrick's, raised a strong body of men and marched against the O'Byrnes, who had made a descent upon Carrick-imayne, and when Newcastle-MacKinegan, on the Wicklow frontier, was threatened, and none of the English officers would undertake its defence, marched to its assistance, and held the castle for five days with thirty-six men, for whose keep he had pawned his own goods.

But the Government would do nothing. They not only left the defence of the king's dominions to individuals like Dean de Cotton, and other warlike ecclesiastics like Thomas Canley, Archbishop of Dublin and Lord Justice (1414), who defeated the O'Moores and O'Dempseys near Kilka. "Praying in procession with clergy and his men . . . he slew one hundred of the Irish enemies," and Richard Talbot, Archbishop

of Dublin, who, in 1419, " being Lord Deputy made
an assault upon Scotties, and slue thirty of the Irish
neere unto Rodiston "—(Marleburrough's *Chonicle*),
but they attempted to violate the constitutional
liberties of the colony. In the Parliament assembled
at Kilkenny, 1374, the Lord Lieutenant, Sir William
de Windsor, announced that the king, in consequence
of the expenditure required for foreign affairs, was no
longer able to defray the expenses of maintaining
soldiers for the defence of his territory in Ireland ; and
Sir Nicholas Dagworth, on behalf of the Crown, demanded a contribution from the prelates, lords and
commons, there assembled, for that purpose. As they
declined, the viceroy issued writs requiring them to
elect representatives to be sent at their own expense
to England to confer upon the matter with the king.
A strong protest against the violation of their rights
and privileges was made by the clergy, nobles and
commons of the Pale, the ecclesiastics stating bluntly
—" we do not grant by any means to the representatives we have elected any power of assenting to
burthens or taxes to be imposed on us or our clergy,
to which we cannot yield by reason of our poverty and
daily expense in defending the land against the Irish."

But while they were engaged in wordy warfare in
Kilkenny, the Irish " enemies " and " rebels " poured
like the " Harpies " of Virgilian fame upon their lands.
The Wicklow tribes, the O'Byrnes and O'Tooles,
attacked Newcastle and dismantled it, and cut off Wicklow from the English lines. Limerick was assailed by
the O'Briens ; Youghal by the De Roches ; Art
MacMurrough Kavanagh after raiding and slaying
all over the counties of Kilkenny, Carlow, and Kildare

was bought off by the sum of eighty marks, while Murrough O'Brien received a hundred to withdraw from Leinster. At this time there was the magnificent sum of nine marks in the Irish treasury. The balance was made up by the following subscriptions and levies —" From the Prior of the Hospitallers, sixteen marks; from William FitzWilliam, a horse price twenty marks; from Robert Lughteburgh, a horse price twenty marks; from John More, a bed, price thirty shillings; from Sir Patrick and Robert de la Freyne, seven marks and ten shillings." This list will give a fair idea of the state to which the English colony in Ireland had been reduced. This was the price they had to pay for the honour of being portion of the British dominions; while her wealth and strength, and the wealth and strength of England, had been squandered by the English monarch, Edward III., in a foreign campaign, which after thirty-five years of wonderful success and brilliant victories ended in shame and grief to his country and the breaking of the noblest heart of the age—a sad frustration of the hopes which men had of the king, of whom the quaint *Chronicle* of Henry of Marleburrough says—" In the beginning of whose reign there was great likelihood of good successe to follow. For then also the Earth received fruitfulnesse, the Ayr temperature and Sea calmnesse."

But the picture of the Pale is not altogether one of unredeemed misery. It had its moments of relief and also of brilliance. On many occasions the intestine feuds of the Irish spelt safety for the English colonists. Under the year 1260, Hanmer states that " the Carties placed the Divells in Desmond," where they became so strong that for twelve years the Desmonds durst not put plough in their own country. " But at length," he says, "through the operation of Satan, a bane of discord was throwen between the Carties and O'Driscolls, O'Donovaies, MacDonoch, MacMahonna, MacSwines and the inhabitants of Muscrie (Muskerry), in so much that by their cruell dissention, they weakened themselves on all sides, that the Desmond in the end overcame and overtopped them all." An historic instance of the policy of allowing the Irish to destroy one another occurred during the civil wars of 1278 between MacDermot de Moylargs and O'Connor of Connaught, when the latter king was slain. The Lord Justice (Sir Robert de Ufford) when called to account for permitting " such shamefull enormities under his government," replied that "in policie he thought it expedient to winke at one knave cutting off another, and that he would save the king's coffers and purchase peace to the land; whereat the king smiled." (Hanmer, p. 107.)

It is also but bare justice to Ireland to point out that on many an occasion forces from Ireland, Norman and native, released English troops from a difficult position. When Henry III. took the reins of authority into his own hand, and began to give the world a specimen of misgovernment, he made an expedition in 1245 against David ap Llewelin, Prince of Wales; but was completely foiled by him, and his army was surrounded and reduced to great straits, as Powell, a writer cited by Hanmer, informs us. In the meantime some ships from Ireland and Chester brought victuals to the camp. But it was to Ireland that Henry looked for aid. As the authority quoted wrote —"the king all this while expected the arrival of

Maurice Fitz Gerald (the Lord Justice) with his Irish forces, mused with himselfe, fretted with himselfe, the wind serving and yet said nothing ; at length the Irish sayles are descryd, a shore they come, and Maurice Fitz Gerald together with Phelim O'Conor in battle array present themselves before the king." The result was that the Welshmen were overthrown, and the English troops, with the assistance of the Irish, were victorious. Another time also in his Welsh wars, being hard pressed, Henry III. sent to Ireland for succour and did not ask in vain. Hanmer's *Chronicle* (p. 378) relates this incident also.

But such moments of brightness were few and far between. The horizon was black with gathering clouds ; and storms continued to break forth upon the unhappy Pale, bound hand and foot on the altar of self-renunciation by the two lines of policy, government by corrupt officials and "no Irish need apply." [1]

---

[1] In the Compositio realis (1514) between the Archbishop of Dublin and the Dean and Chapter of S. Patrick's we find the same principle laid down—"the ancient custom of this Church is confirmed and ratified that all Irishmen by blood and nation, and all who conform to them in mode of life, are shut out from being members of this cathedral." The same policy continued in the Church of Ireland until Archbishop Whateley's time, all the best appointments being reserved for Englishmen.

CHAPTER XIV.

MISRULE AND OPPRESSION.

BEFORE the Reformation both Church and people were in an evil case. The reports of the visitations, preserved in Theiner's monumental work, of the various Sees in Ireland, as they became vacant from time to time, are not pleasant reading. The famous church of Clonmacnoise, where S. Columkille was received with great honour by the pupils of S. Kiaran more than 900 years before, is described in 1515 as "almost ruined, unroofed, with one altar and only covered with straw. . . . Here Mass is seldom celebrated." The town itself is described as consisting of "scarcely twelve cabins built of wicker work and mud, close to which flows a river styled in the language of the inhabitants, Sinin." In the church itself was "the body of an Irish saint, of whose name the writer is ignorant.' So perished the glory of the Divinity School of the Church of Ireland in the west, and the name of its illustrious founder, S. Kiaran Macantsoir, or MacEntire, the son of the carpenter, generally known as S. Kiaran the younger. The see is said to be worth "thirty ducats, at which sum it is assessed in the Books of the Camera. The proceeds are derived from barley and oats." This would be about £15, if the ducats were gold. In the Inquisitio, 38, Henry VIII. (1547), the prebend of Wicklow is described as worth "communibus annis xlvil, xiiis, ivd." This was quite a large income, as the archdeaconry of Glendalough had been valued at 10 marks (£7) in the Pope's valuation of 1306, but at 100 marks (£70) in the king's visitation of 1615. But the ordinary income was "*nil*," the usual entries being "nil propt. guerr.," "nil quia vasta." The report of the town (civitas) of Ardagh, to which see Henry VIII., appointed Roger O'Moleyn in 1517 presents a similar picture of decay. The *civitas* is described as "in spiritualities subject to the Archbishop of Armagh, Primate of all Ireland, in temporalities subject to the king of England." It is in the island of Hibernia, "called by the barbarians Irlandia. The part of it nearer to England is more civilised, but the rest is wild. A large number of the inhabitants even live with the cattle in the fields and in caves. Few wear shoes and almost all subsist on plunder. The land itself produces nothing but oats and horses, both excellent and victorious, being more swift than the English ones, the lighter in colour, having the easier motion."

The report of this visitation of Ardagh, which is found in Theiner's *Vetera Monumenta*, p. 521, states that the cathedral church had but one altar and that exposed to the air, and that it was served by only one priest who seldom officiated at Mass; that it was without sacristy, bell-tower and bell, and sustained scarcely the necessary equipment for one Mass. The town contained but four cabins and very few inhabitants on account of their constant feuds with their neighbours, who would not allow a certain Bishop William to exercise any temporal authority over them and destroyed the town. Even St. Patrick's cathedral was no exception. We read that in 1474 that "the divine service of God is daily withdrawn," and that no espers were said on St. Patrick's eve.

Indeed, all the documents, public and private, that have come down to us from those days, reveal a condition of society deplorable in the extreme. Lawlessness, rapine, murder and perpetual warfare made our unhappy island a den of furies. The Scotch mercenaries who passed over into the north, to settle and to offer their services to the various chiefs who happened to be at war, added fresh fuel to the flames that were extinguishing whatever hopes of peace and prosperity were fostered in Irish hearts. Of these a detachment was cut to pieces by Shane O'Neill to please Queen Elizabeth—the rashest act he ever perpetrated. For at Clandeboy the Scots under Alexander Oge (or Young) and MacGilly Asspuke took a terrible revenge (1567). Few of the English justices cared for these things. One of them, Lord Justice Arnold, grimly informed Lord Cecil, who was much shocked, that he acted "with the Irish as with bears and bandogs, so that he saw them fight earnestly, and hug each other well, he cared not who had the worst." At times even the Government seemed to encourage these feuds, not that any great encouragement was required. For we find the Archbishop of Dublin instructed in 1520 to establish concord between the Earl of Desmond and Sir Piers Butler, also to enfeeble and weaken the strength of the native Irish "as well by getting their captains from them as by putting division among them, so they join not together."

But the unhappiest of all the inhabitants of Erin, if we except the English subjects of the Pale whose condition beggars description, were the tenants on the estates of the great Norman barons, who had become more or less Irish in the course of time. These noblemen, for all their Irish pretensions, treated their tenants with the hauteur of the Norman and the cruelty of the Celt. Subject to all the impositions the feudal lords exacted from their tenants, and to the support the Celtic chieftain demanded of his tribesmen, these unhappy people, who were principally Celts, were ground down to the earth, and their wrongs had no redress in a court presided over by their tyrant, who cared neither for British nor Brehon law. And in the King's Courts which sat in Dublin there was even less chance of fair play for these unfortunates. For these courts, presided over by English officials, were notoriously corrupt and practised extortion on all who placed themselves in their power, surpassing in corruption even the infamous Chancery Court of last century, and compelling the tenants to sell their land and freeholds rather than " be under the said extortion." [1] And before they could enter these "cities of refuge," the tenants had to run the gauntlet of their own masters, who had, as Archbishop Allen wrote to Cromwell, made laws among themselves, "that whosoever under any of their rules pursue any action at the king's law shall forfeit five marks." The Royal Commission held in 1537, like other Commissions, did nothing save bringing to light many of these unjust impositions. But the condition of the Pale was the worst of all. The forms of exaction and extortion to which its inhabitants were subjected were legion. These are detailed at length in the document sent from the council in 1533 to the Master of the Rolls, which led to the arrest of the Earl of Kildare in the following year. The document mentions, in addition

---

[1] State Papers, Henry VIII. Vol. II., pt. 3, p. 9.

to coyne and livery, "cuddies, gartie, taking of caanes for felonies, murders and all other offences, alterages, biengis, saulties and slaughteaghes."

Another document, twenty years earlier, mentions "carting, carriages, journies, and other impositions for hosting and journies and woful war." Moreover black rents and tributes were wrung from the unhappy people for the payment of the Irish enemies. And yet when their property, taken by these enemies, was recovered by the king's forces, maintained on cesses levied on the Pale, the Deputies kept it for their own use, in vulgar parlance, purloined it. Campion tells us that it was James, Earl of Desmond, and his son, Thomas, Deputy in 1463, who put upon the "king's subjects within the counties of Waterford, Corke, Kerry, and Limericke the Irish impositions of coyne and liverie, carting, carriages, loadings, cosherings, bonnaght and such like." He describes these customs as "the very nurse and teat of all Irish enormities," and denounces the everlasting cess wrung from the poor tenants by the Deputy and his gallowglasses, who "eat out the farmers, beggar the country, and foster a sort of idle vagabonds ready to rebell if their lord command them, ever nusseled in stealth and robberyes."

This was a precedent, evil but rapidly learnt, and in consequence the king's subjects in the south and in the Pale lived in extreme poverty and debt. Patrick Finglas, Baron of the Exchequer, 1515, says—"There is not eight of the lords, knights, esquires, and gentlemen of the four shires but be in debt and their land be made waste, and without brief remedy be had, they must sell their lands and go to some other land," while a letter from a Mr. Deythyke, of Dublin, dated 3rd

Sept. 1533, reveals an equally hopeless state of affairs in the city. In it he speaks of the prolonged fasting from flesh in the city, where he hopes many saints may be found. But this fasting, he slyly remarks, is not a work of supererogation but a case of the fox, "say of hens when he could not reach them," for "all the butchers of Dublin hath no so much meat to sell as would make one mess of brawes ; so as they use white meat in Dublin, except it be in my Lord of Dublin's house, or such as have of their own provision." The next famine in Dublin was owing not to the scarcity of stock in the county, but to the constant robberies of cattle at night, and the restless state of the country which made it dangerous to go even a mile out of the city to buy meat. But the Deputy would not listen to any complaints for "the wind hath blown him so in the eyes that he cannot hear them !" This is an instance, we presume, of "the Irish bull." The robberies this poor gentleman describes must have been of an alarming nature. "There hath been," he states, "five or six preys taken out of St. Thomas within this ten days, so that one butcher for his part hath lost 220 kine." The result was that "the poor butchers lie remediless and have closed their shops, and have taken to making of prekes (prayers), thinking there is a new Lent." The great ordnance for the Government of Ireland in 1534 prohibits a great number of these impositions. We learn from this document that different lords and gentlemen within the four shires were wont to compel their tenants and adherents to give them night suppers, which went by the euphonious name of *cuddies*, and that these self-invited guests brought with them as many others as they could, to

the great oppression of their own tenants and the disturbance of the King's subjects for a great number of
miles round in whose stables they put up their horses
and grooms,

They were also in the habit of taking "a peck of oats
of every plough in seed time, called the great horse's
peck"; and when the King's Deputy or any other
lord came to visit them, they added the expenses of
entertainment to the rent of their tenants. These
great lords and captains also compelled the King's
subjects to send their own carts and men to draw stuff
to their own buildings, and labour there at their own
charges, and by personal threats wrung gifts of money,
cattle and horse, called *bienges*, from the King's subjects in the march or frontier.

The Lord Deputy's Book of 1537 declares that
" there is no march borderer, lord, knight, esquire or
gentleman but hath more thieves belonging to him
than true men." Such ruffians were allowed to rob
and spoil the King's subjects, and were protected from
punishment by their masters. The lords marchers,
who were paid for the defence of the King's subjects,
also permitted the neighbouring Irish septs to plunder the lands of the smaller gentry and farmers, on the
understanding that theirs should not be touched. And
if they desired to possess any man's freehold, they
suffered, which means encouraged, the Irish to raid
that freeholder's property and drive his cattle, until
the unhappy man was forced to sell his freehold to
them on their own terms. Moreover, these poor freeholders had not only to pay for the lord's protection,
which was generally of the nature described; they had
also to defray the expenses of any guests he chose to

entertain, and to keep his gallowglasses, servants and horses, for as his report says : "the greatest captain of the English borders will keep no horse or boy in his own house for the most part." They were also subject to the insolence of the lord's sons and the outrages of his servant without hope of redress. For, should any of these be accused of stealing, and arrested, they were at once released on payment of a fine, which went, not to the plaintiff, but to their master, so that the latter was interested in encouraging the misconduct of his own people.

The tenants of the Pale could not even call their own houses, much less their own souls their own. They could not sell a pig or a cow without paying a fine to the tyrant, who took from them everything he required at his own price, frequently a "song." A favourite practice was the regrating of provisions. The lord, with his followers, would come to the market and buy up everything, wood and coal and provision, and sell them again at his own price. They erected weirs on the rivers, committed riots, made penal laws, neglected their own children, wore the Irish dress, spoke the Irish language, and frequently took the holdings from an English occupier and gave them to native peasants. In consequence of their lawlessness the greater portion of the land was uncultivated and the pastures were not stocked. For the gentry were crushed as well as the tenantry by the lords, who acted as absolute monarchs of all they surveyed, worried the Deputies, and gave many an anxious hour to the king and his council who, in addition to perpetual unrest, had to endure heavy financial loss yearly in the upkeep of the little army in Ireland. The only policy that paid then, as now, was that of the Irishman who, when asked his politics in the United States, said : " I am always agin the Government." So we find Sir Gerard Shaneson, writing to Sir Thomas Fitzgerald : " What, thou fool! thou shalt be more esteemed in Ireland to take part against the king ; for what hadst thou been if thy father had not done so ? What was he set by until he crowned a king (Lambert Simnel) here ; took Garthe, the king's captain, prisoner ; hanged his son ; resisted Poyning and all Deputies ; killed them of Dublin upon Oxmantown Green ; would suffer no man to rule here for the king but himself ? Then the king regarded him, made him Deputy, and married thy mother to him. Or else thou never should have had a foot of land, where now thou mayst despend 400 marks by the year."

What offended the English most of all was the adoption of the Brehon law and its system of eric, or compensation for injury fatal and otherwise to property and person. It was with the greatest difficulty that the sheriffs put down the Brehon law in the shire land. The story is told that when Sir William Fitzwilliams informed the Maguire that he was sending a sheriff into Fermanagh, which had been made a county, Maguire replied, " Your sheriff shall be welcome to me ; but let me know his ericke or the *price of his head, aforehand*, that if my people cut it off, I may put the ericke upon the country."[1]

Under the Geraldines the condition of the king's subjects of the Pale naturally became worse than ever. Coin and livery were exacted for their ever increasing

State Papers. Henry VIII. Vol II., 3, 174.

band of hired assassins—gallowglasses and and kerne
—from the unfortunate English, who were eaten up
"as it were bread." The captain of the marches and
his kinsmen, called the Welshmen, in addition to "coin
and foys," or horse meat and man's meat, took certain quarterly payments called Byerahe, as Justice
Suttrell states, often amounted to 13s. 4d. from the
farmers.

We find the wives of these great lords as tyrannical
as themselves. We read in the letter of Patrick
Finglas that "the deputies' wives go to cuddies and
put coyne and livery in all places at their pleasure and
do stir up great war." These grand dames levied
all manner of impositions upon their unfortunate
tenants. Of these, Lady Poer of Waterford bore an
unenviable reputation. When the Deputy or any
visitor of importance stayed at her castle, she made
her tenants give mertyeght or a contribution towards
the expense of meat and drink and candles for her
guests. In cases of litigation she demanded two
shillings in the pound, as her fee from both plaintiff and
defendant, after the manner of the Irish Brehon, and
perhaps in emulation of the Milesian princess, who is
described by Caesar Otway as taking on herself the
office of Brehon, and from the Moate Granoge, or
Moat of Little Grace, now known simply as Moate in
Westmeath, "adjudicating causes and delivering her
oral laws to the people." If a tenant had his cow or
horse stolen, he was required to pay a fine of five
marks for his negligence. If he refused to obey her
sergeant, he was promptly fined, and if one declined
to give coin and livery he had to pay an additional
fine called *kyntroisk*. And she not only required

coin and livery for her own boys and horses, but also
for her guests, both English and Irish, chiefly at
Easter and Christmas, which became the most miserable instead of the most blessed periods of the year
for the tenant. When her daughters were married a
dowry of sheep and of cattle was "lifted" by her
ladyship from her farmers and villagers, and she made
her journeys to Dublin and England at the expense
of her tenants.

But it is hardly fair to the Irish gentry to regard
the degraded Earl of Desmond as a representative
either of Irish gentry or nobility. Hooker describes
him much in the same way as General Cronje might
have been described by a British officer. "This earl,"
he writes, "was very rude both in gesture and apparel,
having for want of nurture, as much good manners as
his kerne and followers could teach him." The Deputy,
Sir William Bellingham, brought this uncivilized
nobleman to his house and then undertook a task
worthy of Hercules to "instruct, advise and inform"
his unwilling guest. He is said to have made a new
man of him by literally bringing the earl to his knees,
for he ordered him "to kneel upon his knees sometimes
an hour together before he knew his duty." This
degenerate peer had, however, lost English civilization
without acquiring Irish. For there was an Irish culture
still extant which was not indifferent to art and literature, and often indulged in the sweet luxury of thought
and poesy and music. We can hardly believe that
the O'Connors, who built their stately castle at Daingean in 1537, or the O'Donnells, who lived also in their
Elizabethan mansion in Donegal, lived like savages
and drank like Bohemians, while the country gentlemen

of England were studying the lessons of chivalry in the writings of Malory and Spenser. With regard to the condition of the masses the opinion of the Irish Council of 1533 may be cited, which was to the effect that " if there were justice used among them, they would be found as civil, wise and polite, and as active as any other nation." While with regard to the other classes James Stanihurst, the Speaker, as Campion writes, said in the Irish House of Parliament in 1570, before Trinity College was founded, "In mine experience who have not yet seen much more than forty years, I am able to say that our realm is at this day an half deal more civil than it was since noble men and worshipful with others of ability have used to send their sons into England to the law, to universities, or to schools." The Speaker referred also in his speech to the project of a university which had been shelved for the time, and moved "the erecting of grammar schools within every diocese."

An interesting letter from Sir John Harrington, one of the attendants of the Earl of Essex in his unhappy expedition to Ireland (1599), describes the northern Earl O'Neill and his sons, and whom he met at Carlingford. The O'Neill behaved himself remarkably well, excusing his own hard manner of life and comparing himself to the wolves. The writer says it were needless to describe "The O'Neill's fern table and fern forms spread under the stately canopy of heaven," and remarks, "that his guards were chiefly beardless boys without shirts; who, in the frost, wade as familiarly through rivers as water-spaniels. With what charm such a master makes them love him I know not; but if he bid them come, they come; if

he bid them go, they go; if he says do this, they
do it."

The sons of this earl seem to have been nice
intelligent boys. Sir John Harrington found "the
two children of good towardly spirit, their age between
thirteen and fifteen, dressed in English clothes, like
the sons of a nobleman, with velvet jerkins and gold
lace, of a good, cheerful aspect and freckled faces ;
not tall of stature but strong and well-set, both of them
speaking English." He presented them with a copy
of an English translation of Ariosto, with which their
father was greatly pleased and "solemnly swore his
boys should read all the book over to him." Hugh
O'Neill himself is said to have been very accomplished,
and as Plowden writes : "spoke four modern languages
with the fluency of a native." The humour of the
earl was shown in his suggestion that when he went
in English dress to the Viceroy's Court he should
be attended by a chaplain in saffron robes, so that he
might divert the attention of the English crowd from
his master. He did not disguise his contempt for the
de-anglicised Englishman, as in the case of Barret,
whose convictions he regarded as a matter of con-
venience, saying of him : "No matter, I hate the
English churl as if he came yesterday.' But he
showed an open disregard for religious plundering and
destroying churches and monasteries on his way to
Kinsale, so that a Spanish officer exclaimed that
"Christ did not die for the Irish," and Lord Essex
said, "Hang thee! thou talk of a free exercise of
religion ! Thou carest as much for religion as my
horse." In Camden's *Elizabeth* we have a sad picture
of the fallen chief, who in 1598 defeated the English

at the Yellow Ford (Beal-an-atha buidhe, Ballyboy), where, as Fynes Moryson says : " The English, from their first arrival in the kingdom, never had received so great an overthrow as this," and who surrendered to Lord Mountjoy in Mellifont Abbey on the 30th March, 1603, six days after Elizabeth had passed away. The brave nobleman, who had never rallied his forces since their crushing defeat at Kinsale, now reduced to despair, entered the presence of the Deputy, who failed to show the generosity and courtesy that gallant gentlemen always extend to the vanquished. It was indeed " vae victis " here, and yet these were the days of the Sidneys ! The defeated earl, in mean and shabby attire, cast himself down at the threshold of the door and made an abject confession of his crimes against her gracious majesty and most solemn promise of atonement. Moryson (ii. 179) gives the terms of submission, which included absolute surrender of all his lands and titles and renunciation of the King of Spain, and a promise to abstain from " intermeddling with the urriaghs or fostering with them or other neighbour lords and gentlemen outside my country, or exacting black rents of any urriaghs or bordering lords." The unhappy man rode into Dublin two days afterwards a prisoner of state to learn that he had surrendered all too soon. But his mistake was a fortunate matter for Ulster, which had been reduced to a desert by his rebellion. An eyewitness, Moryson, says, " No spectacle was more frequent in the ditches of the towns, and especially in wasted countries, than to see multitudes of these poor people dead with their mouths all coloured green by eating nettles, docks, and all things they could rend up above ground."

The one redeeming feature of the country was the prosperity and growth of the seaport towns. The quaint old town of Galway, with its interesting Claddagh or fishing quarter, and the Moorish gateways, and the celebrated house of Lynch, the Irish Brutus, was at the zenith of its fame in the reign of Henry VII., during which time its enterprising burghers, as Hardiman relates in his " History of Galway," "planned the cutting of a passage from Lough Corrib to the sea, as well as repairing their city after a fire, paving their streets, building an hospital, extending their wall and erecting quays." It is hoped that the same strenuous spirits of improvement may again become embodied in the city of the tribes. This and other cities on the seaboard thrived and prospered while the rest of the island was sunk in torpor and decay, simply because they were allowed to work out their own salvation in their own fashion without let or hindrance from feudal lord, Irish chieftain, or those harpies of the Pale—the officials sent from England

Limerick is described by William Body in 1536 as a "wondrous proper city and a strong and standeth environed with the river Shenon,[1] and it may be called little London for the situation and the plenty." The writer goes on to say that its ancient castle, still a formidable structure, was in "need of reparation." It is indeed as much a sign of its own commercial enterprise and republican independence as a proof of the deputy's laxity and the Council's feebleness to find

[1] Sıonaınn (Shin-an) not Shannon, was the proper pronunciation Mr. Body's spelling was more accurate than ours.

this city of the barren land, Luimneach, carrying on war by sea and land and concluding treaties with the rival city of the great marsh of Munster, *Corcach-mor-Mumhan*, now abridged to Cork, in 1520. This reminds one of the long and internecine struggles between the rival republics of the sea, Venice and Genoa, in the thirteenth and fourteenth centuries.

The troubles of the inhabitants of the Pale were, however, mitigated in the course of time. But they had, like many a patient, to be worse before they could be better. It was in Elizabeth's reign that matters began to amend. To the skill and courage of the Dublin bands and soldiers references are made in the histories of the period. They assisted in punitive expeditions organised by Sussex and Sidney against Shane O'Neill; and it was only with their assistance that Sir Henry Sidney "to the inestimable benefit of the realm brought under obedience the disordered countries of Leix, Slewmargy Ofalie, Irrye and Glenmalire then late possessed by the O'Connors, O'Mores, O'Dempseys and other Irish rebels." And "with a fair company" under John Usher, Sheriff, and Patrick Buckley, they helped Sussex to attack and defeat a roving Scotch pirate, James MacConell, who was afterwards connected with the notorious Shane O'Neill, to the misfortune of both. Their young men were well taught in the foreign universities of Paris and Louvain and also at Oxford and Cambridge. Their houses were furnished "with plate, furniture, and apparel." Their towns were walled and populous, and their home produce and foreign trade was increasing when Sidney (11th Elizabeth) held a parliament in Dublin for the purpose of imposing a tax on wines, which called forth so angry a remonstrance from the gentlemen of the Pale that a parliament was not summoned for many years after. Sidney, in his parting oration (given in Campion) to the parliament after the defeat and death of Shane O'Neill (1570), defended his policy of maintaining an armed garrison in Ireland, and contrasted the condition of life in the Pale at the time with that which prevailed in a previous age. "Consider," he said, "the effect of an army wrought in these few years, for doubt whereof you are nothing so oft nor so lamentably pelled as your ancestors were, which of you durst be stored with coyne, knowing the rebels' mouth watered thereat? Which of them had leisure to build, to lie soft and warm, to take his ease in his own home? Which of them were plated or jewelled, or attired themselves, their wives and children sumptuously, after their calling, as ye do now? If your bags be full where they dwelled homely; if you sleep on feather beds, where they slept on couches, if you be sumptuous, where they were scant, you have the more cause to honour that sceptre, that so directeth you and to love her warrant that procureth you this quietness, the mother of all your wealth and prosperity."

CHAPTER XV.

Legal and Other Reforms.

THERE are many interesting notices of Ireland and its inhabitants in the writings of Spenser, Fynes Moryson, Sir John Davis, Campion, and others. Spenser well describes the pasturing capacity of the country: " For though the whole tract of the country be mountainous and woody, yet there are many goodly valleys amongst them, fit for fair habitations, to which those mountains adjoined will be a great increase of pasturage, for that country is a great soil for cattle, and very fit for breed ; as for corn it is nothing material, save only for barley and oats, and some places, for rye." Fynes Moryson, Secretary of Lord Mountjoy (1600-1603) also remarks upon " the plenty of grass which makes the Irish have infinite multitudes of cattle, and in the heat of the last rebellion the very vagabond rebels had great multitudes of cows, which they still, like the nomads, drove with them whithersoever themselves were driven, and fought for them as for their altars and families. He says they carried on " a frequent, though somewhat poor, traffic for their hedes—the cattle being in general very little, and only the men and the grey-hounds of great stature." For fear of thieves and wolves, which became so numerous and daring as to enter the villages and suburbs, the cattle were driven into the bawns of the castles, where they were allowed to stand all night without so much as a lock of hay.

Very little hay was made, doubtless owing to the
dampness of the climate as much as to "the sluggishness" of the people, and that little was kept for the
horses.   "Their horses," he writes, "called hobbies
are much commended for their ambling, grace, and
beauty; but Ireland yields few good horses for service
in war, and the said hobbies are much inferior to our
geldings in strength to endure long journies, and
being bred in the fenny, soft ground of Ireland, soon
lamed when they were brought into England." With
regard to sheep, Fynes Moryson remarks, "they
abound in flocks of sheep, which they shear twice in
the year, but their wool is coarse, and merchants may
not export it." The reason why they were forbidden
was that the poor might be employed in turning it
into cloth, "namely rugs, whereof the best are made
at Waterford, and mantles, generally worn by men
and women, and exported in great quantity." They
had such plenty of linen cloth that "the wild Irish
used to wear thirty or forty ells in a shirt, all gathered
and wrinkled, and washed in saffron because they
never put them off till they were worn out."

The same writer also notices the great recuperative
power of the country, which "in a short time after
the rebellion appeared like the new spring, to put on
the wonted beauty;" the "excellent marble near
Dublin, Kilkenny, and Cork;" the "excellent fishes,
as salmons, oysters (which are preferred before the
English), and shell-fish, with all other kinds of sea-
fish;" the "frequent lakes of great circuit yielding
plenty of fish; "such plenty of pheasants, as I
have known sixty served at one feast;" and "very
many eagles, and great plenty of hares, conies, hawks,

called goshawks, much esteemed with us, and bees."
He is of opinion that the mountains would yield
abundance of metals if the public good were not
hindered by the seditious and slothful character of the
inhabitants, that if the Irish were industrious in
fishing " they might export salted and dried fish with
great gain." He comments severely on the indolence
of the people. Although the country had " great
plenty of birds and fowls, by reason of their natural
sloth they had little delight or skill in birding or
fowling." Again, he says : " the best sorts of flowers and
fruits are much rarer in Ireland than in England,
which, notwithstanding, is more to be attributed to the
inhabitants than to the air," and remarks that the Irish
might have abundance of excellent fish, " if the fisher-
men were not so possessed with the natural fault of
slothfulness, as no hope of gain, scarcely the fear of
authority, can in many places make them come out of
their houses, and put to sea." And the consequence
was that Scots and Englishmen employed as fisher-
men " make profit of the inhabitants' sluggishness."
Lord Mountjoy, a devoted angler, must have felt indignant at this neglect of his favourite sport. There
were, however, other explanations for this remissness.
In the first place, there was no encouragement given
to the people to make an effort to improve themselves.
For instance, the Irish were not permitted to build
great ships for war, but had " little ships in some sort
armed to resist pirates, for transporting of com-
modities into France and Spain, yet no great number
of them." It is no wonder that the Irish had then
small skill in navigation, but Fynes Moryson is con-
fident that " the nation being bold and warlike,

would, no doubt, prove brave seamen if they shall practise navigation, and could possibly prove industrious therein." Again he points out that "in time of peace the Irish transport good quantity of corn, yet they may not transport it without licence, lest in any sudden rebellion the king's forces and his good subjects should want corn." These were acts of repressive legislation at the time.

Again, he comments upon the dampness of the soil and air, which caused lateness of harvest and indolence of spirit, besides feebleness of body. When describing Lord Mountjoy, he says, "he took tobacco abundantly, and of the best, which, I think, preserved him from sickness, especially in Ireland, where the foggy air of the bogs, and waterish fowl, plenty of fish, and generally all meats, with the common sort always unsalted and green roasted, do most prejudice the health." He also states that the country people had an excellent remedy for the rawness of their air and the looseness of the body, the country disease, in their *aqua vitae*, vulgarly called usquebaugh. And when treating the ague, the women gave the sick man no meat, but milk and some ordinary remedies. He also notes that Ulster and the western parts of Munster yield "vast woods, in which the rebels, cutting up trees and casting them in heaps, used to stop the passages therein, as also in fenny and boggy places to fight with the English," but he was deceived in his expectation of finding Ireland woody, "having found in my long journey from Armagh to Kinsale few or no woods by the way, except the great woods of Offaly, and some low, shrubby places, which they call glins." However, he states that the Irish "export

great quantities of wood to make barrels called pipe-
staves." In these woods he also noticed some fallow
deer, but in the time of the war he never saw any
venison served at the table, but only in the houses of
the Earls of Ormond and Kildare and of the English
commanders.

Another writer of that period, Sir John Davis, in
his *Discovery*, pays a remarkable tribute to the people
and country of Ireland. He has observed, he writes,
"in sundry journeys and circuits the good temperature of the air ; the fruitfulness of the soil ; the pleasant
and commodious seats for habitation ; the safe and
large ports and havens lying open for traffic into all
the west parts of the world ; the long inlets of many
navigable, and so many great lakes and fresh ponds
within the land, as the like are not to be seen in any
part of Europe ; the rich fishings and wild-fowl of all
kinds, and, lastly, the bodies and minds of the people
endowed with extraordinary abilities of nature." He
also gives the people credit for a desire to keep the
law. "I dare affirm," he writes, "that for the space
of five years past there have not been found so many
malefactors worthy of death in all the six circuits of
the realm, which is now divided into thirty-two shires
at large, as in one circuit of six shires, namely the
western circuit in England, and he adds that "in time
of peace the Irish are more fearful to offend the law
than the English, or any other nation whatsoever."

A great reformation had taken place in the character
of the people between the beginning of the sixteenth
and the first quarter of the seventeenth century. In
the beginning of the reign of Henry VIII. it was
reported that the king's laws were obeyed and

executed in four shires only, and Allen, Master of the Rolls, said that the "land of Ireland was so much decayed that the king's laws were not obeyed 20 miles in compass,"—hence the byword they dwelt "by west of the law, which dwell beyond the river Barrow." Many causes had helped to bring about this unhappy state of affairs. There were two customs, fosterage and gossipred, which encouraged the spirit of factiousness. "Fosterage or alterage," as Sir John Davis remarks, 'hath been a stronger alliance than blood.'" Of gossipred, or spiritual affinity, "no nation ever made so religious account thereof as the Irish"; and a juror "who was gossip to either of the parties might be challenged as not indifferent." It was with gossips as with Scotch shrimps—"look how they stick together." Among other things which lowered the people, Sir John Davis mentions "common repudiation of wives, promiscuous generation of children, neglect of lawful matrimony, uncleanness in apparel, diet and lodging." These Irish customs gradually contaminated the English colonists, who became worse than the natives themselves, as the verse in White Book of Exchequer hath it :—

> By graunting charters of peas
> To false English withouten leas
> This land shall be much undoo.
> But gossipred and alterage
> And leesing[1] of our language
> Have muckly holp thereto.

Something of the misrule and oppression of the Kildares has already been seen. But Maurice FitzThomas, the first Earl of Desmond, enjoys the

---

[1] *Leesing* means losing, cf. "Take heed you *leese* it not, Signior." B. Jonson, "Every Man out of his Humour," v. 1.

distinction, according to Davis, of being the first English lord that imposed coyne and livery upon the king's subjects, the first to reject English laws and government, the first to make a distinction between the English of blood and the English by birth. And as this Maurice, the first earl, raised the greatness of his house by Irish exactions, Gerald, the last earl, did at last ruin and reduce it to nothing by the like extortions. The first occasion of the rebellion was when he attempted to levy black rents and cosheries, after the Irish fashion, upon the Decies in the county of Waterford. In this he was opposed by Ormond. But the misconduct of the English nobility—the great territorial barons in Ireland—is sufficient to explain much of the lawnessness of the people. Sir Arthur Chichester, who was Lord Deputy, 1604-1616, attempted to carry out a great scheme of reform with some success. He established two other circuits for justices of assize in Connaught and Munster. The mountains and "glynnes" on the south side of Dublin were made shireland, and their people, who had been veritable thorns in the side of the Pale, were subjected to English law and reduced to quiet. The judges were increased "like good planets in their several spheres" to carry the light and influence of justice throughout the land. By these visitations of justice the people were taught that they were the subjects of the kings of England, and not the vassals of their lords, whose cosherings[1] and cesses were declared

---

[1] *Cosher* (Ir. cóιrιjι, a feast), to live at free quarters upon dependants or relations. See *The Irish Hudibras*, 1689:

> "A very fit and proper house, Sir,
> For such an idle guest to cosher."

"*Cosherings* were visitations and progresses made by the lord and his

to be illegal.   These assizes had considerable influence
upon the manners of the people, and caused them to
remove their glibbs, to convert their mantles into
cloaks, and to send their children to schools to be
taught the English language.   Sir John Davis, who
commends the judicious plantation of Ulster, where
the settler received more than 3,000 acres and was required to build and improve the country, had observed
of Poynings' laws that " they were like lessons set for
a lute that is broken and out of tune, of which lessons
little use can be made till the lute be made fit to be
played on."   The lute would seem to be made fit
now, for he observes of these reforms that " the clock
of the civil government is now well set and all the
wheels thereof do move in order.   The strings of this
Irish harp, which the civil magistrate doth finger, are
all in tune."   *The revenues*, at all events, were doubled,
by the giving of justice to all, and the people were
settled because they felt that their earthly possessions
were more secure, now that a tribunal of some kind
had been appointed.

followers among his tenants ; wherein he did eat them out of house and
home," writes Sir J. Davis in *State of Ireland.*   " Sometimes he contrived in defiance of the law to live by *coshering,* that is, by quartering
himself on the old tenants of his faimly " (Macaulay, *His. Eng.*)   The
same writer says,   " Commissioners were scattered profusely among idle
cosherers, who claimed to be descended from good Irish families."   In
the reign of Chas. I. (1672) an Act was passed for the suppression of
Cosherers and idle wanderers, threatening severe penalties " if any person or persons   .   .   .   shall cosher, lodge, or cesse themselves upon
the inhahitants"   Petty (*Pol. Anat.*, 1697) complains that " there are
yet to spare who are Cosherers and Fait-neauts, 220,000."   The *Times*
of March 11, 1865, defined a cosherer " as one who pretends to be an
Irish gentleman and will not work.   In Ireland the meanings of the
word are based upon the feudal custom of the lord of the soil to demand
lodging and entertainment for himself and his followers from his tenants.
But in England *cosher* meant to *chat,* e.g., "we coshered over the
events of the evening."   (Macaulay *Life and Lett.*, 1, 5, 339), and
caress, e.g., Trollope (*Barchester Towers*) speaks of coshering up people.

Sir John Davis comments on the neglect of Ireland
and the Irish by the English sovereigns. Here, indeed, he lays his finger on one of the causes of the
distress and unhappiness which our present gracious
sovereign is removing by his almost annual visits,
and points out that on every occasion when Ireland
was visited by a sovereign a general submission was
made. He also indicates the neglect of providing
the Irish and English of the Pale with equal laws.
But this atonement was made by Chichester's reform
in the reign of James I.

The state of Ireland on the whole cannot therefore be said to have been much improved by the first
362 years of English rule. The document in the
State Papers of Henry VIII's reign, known as " the
State of Ireland and the Plan of its Reformation,"
gives an eloquent but lurid description of the con-
dion of the country. This document asserts that
there were more than sixty counties called regions
in Ireland, some as large as a shire and others less,
occupied by the king's Irish enemies and governed by
sixty " chief captains," who rejoice in such high flown
titles as kings, princes, dukes, archdukes, who lived
by the sword, made war as they chose, held all their
property by the sword, and only obeyed those who
could subdue them with the sword. They had obtained their position by force of arms and were not
succeeded by their sons unless they were the strongest
of their nation—" for there shall be none chief captain
in any of the said regions by lawful succession, but
by fort mayne and election." The smaller chiefs,
called " petty captains," were described as making
war with the " chief captain " and one another.

The title "captain" may seem somewhat odd, but it was the usual English style of these gentry. For instance, Archbishop Alan when speaking of a certain part of Wicklow says—" ubi O'Byrne capitaneus." Spenser suggested an army of 10,000 foot and 1,000 horse, of whom 80,000 are "to lie in garrison upon the Earl of Tyrone, 1,000 upon MacHugh, the rest upon some parts of Connaught," and that the English colonists should be planted in strong numbers among the Irish septs, so that "they would not be able to stir or to murmur," and would establish the Lord Deputy at " Athie (Athy) or thereabouts, upon the skirt of that unquiet country, so that he might sit, as it were, at the very maine maste of the ship, whence he might easily overlooke and sometimes over-reach the Moores, the Dempsies, the Connors, O'Carroll, O'Molloy and all the heape of Irish nations which there lye hudled together without any to overawe them or containe them in duty." One of the most lawless of these captains was the above-mentioned Pheagh MacHugh of the O'Byrne sept, whose residence, or "fastness," was at Ballinacor, in Glenmalure, which appears to have been a camp of refuge for all the outlaws in the land, while their chief was " a base varlet, that being but of late grown out of the dunghill, beginneth now to over-crow those high mountaines." The time these people chose for their incursions into the Pale—their 'Castle season'—was winter, "for then the nights were longest and darkest, and the countries around about are most full of corn."

Besides these sixty captains of the Irish enemies there were thirty great captains of the degenerate English who had become absorbed by the native tribes and had adopted the Irish customs, and had neither English law nor sheriff. These had possession of Waterford, Cork, Kilkenny, Limerick, Kerry, Carlow, half the county of Meath, half the county of Kildare, half the county of Dublin and Wexford, the "county of Connaught," the "county of Ulster," and half the county of Uriel. All the English of these districts, except those dwelling in the walled towns and cities, had perforce to speak Irish, and to dress and live like the Irish, and as this Document pathetically remarks, all these English folk would "right glad to obey the king's laws if they might be defended by the king of the Irish enemies; and because they defend them not, and the King's Deputy may not defend them, therefore they are all turned from the obedience of the king's laws and liveth by the sword after the manner of the Irish enemies."

Furthermore, the loyal subjects of the king living in half the counties of Dublin, Kildare, Meath and Uriel (Louth) were grievously oppressed by the king's courts and justices, which were never reduced in number since the time when all the country was subject to the king's laws, and were so vexed by this unnecessary expense that they would gladly sell their freeholds rather than suffer their exactions. The freeholders of the marches where the king's law was not obeyed were in a worse plight, exposed as they were, both to the incursions of the king's enemies and the exactions of the king's officers. For "what with the extortion of coygne and livery daily, and with the wrongful exaction of posting money, of carriage and cartage daily," the king's yearly subsidy and tribute and black rent to the Irish enemies, the English folk of Dublin, Meath, Kildare

and Uriel were more oppressed than any other folk of
the land, English or Irish.

The document quotes a legend of S. Brigit in
Pandar's book, *Salus Populi*, where the holy woman
is represented as enquiring of an angel "of what
Christian land was the most souls damned," and the
angel showed her a land in the west part of the world.
Enquiring the reason why, she was informed
that "there the Christian folk dieth most out of
charity," owing to continual war, and that "without
charity no soul can be saved." The angel then
showed how "the Christian folk of that land "fell
down into hell as thick as any hail shower." For
"there is no land in the world of so long-continued
war within himself, *ne of so great shedding of Christian
blood*, ne of so great robbing, spoiling, praying
(preying) and burning, ne of so great wrongful extortion continually as Ireland." Campion, however,
told a different story. He writes that the Irish "are
in no ways outrageous against holy men." And he
mentions the argument between Giraldus Cambrensis
and the Archbishop of Cashel on the subject. The
former had declared that the Irish had not produced
a single martyr, to which the other replied that the
Irish people had ever spared the blood of the saints,
but that they have now been delivered to a nation that
is well used to making martyrs.

In answer to the question—"Why the Irish folk
be grown so strong and the king's subjects so feeble
and fallen in so great rebellion for the most part,"
the document proceeds to say:—"Some sayeth
that the prelates of the church and clergy is much
cause of all the misorder of the land; for there is ne

archbishop, ne bishop, abbot, ne prior, parson, ne vicar, ne any other person of the church, high or low, great or small, English or Irish, that wish to preach the word of God, saving the friars beggars: and where the word of God do cease, there can be no grace, and without the special grace of God the land may never be reformed."

CHAPTER XVI.

CLONMACNOISE AND DELVIN.

A BOOK on the Midland Septs of Ireland would be incomplete without some notice of the most famous of the midland monasteries—Clonmacnoise, generally known as the " Seven Churches," the chequered history of which is a mirror of Celtic life in the midlands. Seirkeiran, was founded by one Kiaran and Clonmacnoise by another. The latter was called Macantsaoir, or the son of a carpenter. Clonmacnoise, also known as Druim Tipraid (hill of the well), Clonensis Dunkeranensis, or the Dun of Kiaran, and Killoon, or the church of the graves, was for centuries an independent See. In 1568, however, it was united to Meath. When Meath was divided it was included in Westmeath. And in 1688 it was united to the King's County. For then " Clonmacnoise and 3,000 acres of land by the management and procurement of Mr. Thomas Coghlan, through the favour of Dr. Anthony Martin, Bishop of Meath, were taken from the barony of Clonlonan in Westmeath, and annexed to the barony of Garrycastle in the King's County."

Standing amid these splendid memorials of the ancient Celtic Church, the stone crosses, the groups of churches with their carved doorways, the graveyard with its monuments of departed kings, bishops and abbots, dominated by two noble round towers, the casual visitor cannot but be impressed, the initiated cannot fail to be inspired. Here is the Teampull

Cailleach, or " Church of the Nuns," finished by Dear-vorgail, the beautiful but fickle wife of O'Rourke, whose elopement with King Dermot of Leinster, in 1152, led to such irreparable disaster. In 1167 she found penitence and peace within these historic walls. There is the Reiliach Cailleach, or cemetery of the nuns. Here is the beautiful doorway made, as the Irish Chroniclers tell us, by the order of Odo, dean of Clonmacnoise in 1280. Here are interred the bones of Roderick O'Conor, King of Connaught and of all Ireland, in 1198, and with him an innumerable host of Irish kings and princes, O'Melaghlins, O'Kellys, MacDermotts, and others, who had been the public benefactors of the monastery in their lives and in their death were not divided from it. As Archdall in his *Monasticon Hibernicum* writes : " And what was a strong inducement and contributed much towards en-riching this house, it was believed that all persons who were interred in the holy ground belonging to it had insured themselves a sure and immediate ascent to heaven."

It is little to be wondered at, then, that Clonmac-noise was chosen with pious forethought, as their last resting place, by many who had evinced little piety and no religion in their lives. And we are not sur-prised to learn that " its landed property was so great, and the number of cells subjected to it so numerous, that almost half of Ireland was said to be within the bounds of Clonmacnoise." But the wealth and fame of the abbey proved to be the cause of its downfall. Its history is one long record of endowment and pillage, restoration and renewed burnings. The *Four Masters* and the *Annals of Clonmacnoise*, compiled

by one Tighernach, abbot of the monastery, who died
in 1088, and was reputed to be "a wise, learned, and
eloquent teacher and doctor," give us a full account of
its chequered career. The Ostmen generally have the
credit of the ruin of Clonmacnoise. But they only
followed the example of the Irish. We read that
Felim, king of Cashel, destroyed all Clonmacnoise by
fire, even to the door of the church, and slew many of
the clergy in 830. In 834 and 839 the Danes sailed
up the Shannon and plundered the abbey. Some
years later Turgesius, who had restored paganism in
Armagh and who desired to establish a pagan sanc-
tuary in the West, appointed his wife Ota as priestess
in Clonmacnoise to offer unspeakable sacrifices upon
its altars. But it is questionable if Turgesius was a
worse enemy of Clonmacnoise than Felim of Cashel,
who again, in 846, plundered the "tearmon lands and
houses of St. Kiaran," and brought upon himself the
malediction of the abbot from which he never recovered. During the years 930-960 the abbey was
plundered on several occasions by the Danes of Dublin and Limerick, as well as by the king of Cashel,
the Munstermen and the people of Ossory. In 1199
Cahall O'Connor plundered the "hospitals" of the
abbey, which probably refers to the "house of the
guests" erected 1106, and he was followed by the
English of Meelick, who plundered "the church, sanc-
tuary and town of Clonmacnoise, and carried away the
vestments, chalices and the books of the community,
and laid waste all the gardens and houses in the town."
In 1227, the town was set on fire three times by the
Irish, and in 1552 the garrison of Athlone plundered
both town and abbey and left "neither large nor small,

Q

bell, image, altarbook, gem, nor even glass in a window in the walls of the church." It is not surprising, then, that the once great school of Clonmacnoise, which received a letter from Alcuin, the learned secretary of Charlemagne, and a gift of two hundred sicli from his royal master, when Colchu, "master of all the Scots of Ireland," was its chief scribe (790 circ.), was, according to the report made to the Roman Pontiff in 1515, a neglected and ruined habitation, the see itself being valued at only thirty ducats a year.

On one occasion we read of a plunderer of this abbey being overtaken by a tardy justice. In 1108 the church was robbed of vestments presented by one king, the silver cup and gilt cross, the gift of another, and the silver cup which the Primate of Armagh had given. The perpetrator of the deed remained undiscovered until 1130 when Connor O'Brien found the jewels in the possession of a Dane of Limerick, one Gille Comhdhan, and delivered him up to the community for punishment. Before his execution the man is said to have confessed that he had tried to escape several times by sea from Ireland, but that on each occasion St. Kiaran with his staff turned the vessel back to land.

The cloictheach (round tower) of Clonmacnoise was finished by O'Malone in 1124, but we read that on Easter Day in 1135 lightning struck off the head of the cloictheach of Clonmacnoise, and pierced that of Roscrea. This is an important note regarding these mysterious buildings.

In the same barony of Garrycastle are some interesting ruins. These are at Clonoony, Moystown,

Liscloony, Fadden, and Tisaran, and are the remains
of what were once known as the "Fair Castles" of
MacCoghlan, lord of Delvin. The *Four Masters*
make mention of "a Coghlan of the Castles" so far
back as 1249, and when recording the death of John
MacCoghlan in 1590 say, "there was not a man of
his estate, of the race of Cormac Cas, whose mansions,
castles, and good dwelling-houses were better arranged,
or more comfortable than his. The castle of Clonoony,
some eight miles north of Birr, was probably built in
the reign of Henry VIII. The *Four Masters* describe
a conflict which took place in 1519 "between the tribe
of Fergal MacCoghlan and the tribe of Donal, in
which James MacCoghlan, Prior of Gallen, and heir-
presumptive of Delvin Eathra was killed by the *shot
of a ball* from the castle of *Cluain Damhna*. Cluain
Damhna, which means Damhan's or Davin's meadow,
was the original name of Clonoony, which is called
"Cluain-Nona" by the *Four Masters* at the year
1553. The expression *shot of a ball* is interesting
from the fact that the first muskets are said to have
been brought into Ireland from Germany in 1489. In
1553 we read of a bold enterprise on the part of a
"churl," who "acted treacherously towards the warders
of the castle, and slew three distinguished men of them
with a chopping-axe, tied a woman who was within,
and then took possession of the castle." Coins of the
Elizabethan period have been found at Clonoony, but
a far more remarkable find was the discovery made
by some workmen in 1803 in the vicinity of the castle.
In a cave they came across a heap of stones. Removing
these they found a large slab of limestone, eight feet
long by four wide and one foot thick. On the slab,

which covered the bones of two persons, was the inscription : —

> Here under leys Elizabeth and
> Mary Bullyn daughters of Thomas
> Bullyn son of George Bullyn the
> Son of George Bullyn Viscount
> Rochford son of Thomas Bullyn
> Erle of Ormond and Willsheere.

These persons must have been second cousins of Queen Elizabeth, their ancestor having most probably fled to Ireland to escape the wrath of Henry VIII., who seems to have attainted the whole Bullyn family, after the execution of the unfortunate Anne.

Another stronghold of the MacCoghlans was the Caislean-an-Fheadain or the Castle of Fadden, not far from Bellmount, the residence of Mr. Perry. This was built before 1520, when, as the *Four Masters* relate, " Torlogh, the son of Felim MacCoghlan, lord of Delvin Eathra, a man distinguished for wisdom and learning, a man of prosperity and great riches, who built the castles of Fadan and Cincoradh, died after a well-spent life." This castle of Fadden is also mentioned in the *Four Masters* under the year 1540, when " James Oge, the son of the prior MacCoghlan, was treacherously beheaded by Ceadach O'Melaghlin in his own castle, and great destruction befel the country on that account." In 1548 Edmond Fahy invaded the district of Delvin. For eight days he besieged this castle, and Cormac MacCoghlan, who was residing in it, was compelled to give him hostages, " after which he and Edmond made a gossipship with one another."

The castle had been attacked six years before by the sons of O'Madden, who plundered and burnt the town, but were beaten off and pursued to Tisaran. On a subsequent occasion the castle fell into the hands of the enemy, but was recovered in a remarkable manner by a prisoner who was confined in it, and handed it over again to the MacCoghlans, 1557. The MacCoghlans had other castles at Magh-Istean or Moystown, Lis-Cluaine or Liscloony, which was completed, according to the *Four Masters*, in 1556, and at Tisaran, which was plundered, and its churches plundered by the sons of O'Madden, for which act of sacrilege they were punished by Felim O'Melaghlin, who marched to Clonfert and plundered its church and monastery. Tisaran means Saran's house (*Teach-Sarain*). Saran was of the race of Dealbhna. His well, *Tobar-Sarain*, is near the church. Other castles were at Kincor and Gallen near Ferbane, and at Garrycastle, the garden of the castle, close to Banagher. The last gave its name to the barony.

In 1551 the MacCoghlan made his submission to the English Crown at Athlone, and obtained a pardon and a patent of his estate, and " Delvin Eathra was put under rent for the king." The MacCoghlans seem to have had some difficulty in keeping the peace. For we read that Art, the son of Cormac MacCoghlan, killed Robert Nugent, a foster-brother of the Earl of Kildare, in 1554. In retaliation the earl levied a *boroihme* or cattle tribute of three hundred and forty cows on the district as eric or fine. In 1585 John, the son of Art, son of Cormac MacCoghlan, attended Elizabeth's parliament in Dublin ; but shortly afterwards with 200 men he joined the O'Connors and O'Molloys in their rebellion. The most remarkable member of the clan was Thomas MacCoghlan, called the " Maw," who died in 1790. He is described by the Chevalier Montmorency as "a remarkably handsome man, gallant, eccentric, proud, satirical, hospitable in the extreme, and of expensive habits." The " Maw" maintained the old customs of the country, and the ancestral mode of living and law. His house was open to strangers. His tenants, who were his vassals, paid their rents, partly in kind, partly in money. When a tenant died he levied the fine of Mortmain and became heir to the deceased. No law save the Brehon code, occasionally enforced by the " Maw's " riding-whip, was allowed to be administered within his domain. He permitted no other member of the sept to use the " Mac." As he died without any lawful heir, his estates passed to the son of his sister, Denis Daly of Dalystown, and at his death were sold to different people. This MacCoghlan sat for the borough of Banagher in the Irish Parliament.

Delvin, which abounded in warlike castles, was not without its sanctuaries of religion. Banagher, *Beannchar* or pointed hill, is in the parish of Reynagh, called after St. Reynagh or Regnacia, sister of the St. Finian of Clonard, who died in 863, and founded a church called Kill-Rignaighe, the ruins of which are in the centre of the town. Near Ferbane are the ruins of the abbey described by Archdall as the " Monastery of Galinne in Delbhna, McCochlain " founded by Saint Canoc or Mocanoc about 492 and burnt by Felym McCroimhain in 820. The abbey seems to have been rebuilt by a colony of Welsh monks, who founded a school there and gave it the name it bears. In the vicinity of this abbey many fierce battles were waged between the MacCoghlans and the Fahys, O'Maddens and O'Melaghlins. The site of this abbey and its lands were granted to Sir Gerald Moore in 1612. The ruins thereof are in the demesne of Gallen Priory, the residence of Sir Andrew Armstrong, Bart. Not far from these ruins are the remains of another ancient house, the Abbey of Glin, founded by St. Diarmid, whose successor, St. Comgan, died in 563. It too went the way of all the Celtic foundations, being plundered in 1041 and destroyed by fire in 1077. At Killegally near Glin, where St. Trena was abbot in the sixth century, are also ruins. At Lemanaghan, or St. Manchan's grey land, are the ruins of another old establishment. In Archdall's time (1786) they were surrounded by a bog " at present impassable." Among the modern residences in the barony may be mentioned Ballylin, Doon, Mount Carteret, and Cloghan Castle. The last, in the parish of Lusmagh, was a stronghold of the O'Maddens, who ruled over Siol Anmchada, or Silancia. It was called " Cloghan O'Madden," and in 1595 it was besieged and taken by the Lord Deputy, Sir William Russell, who gave an interesting account of the incident in his journal. The roof of the castle being covered with thatch was set on fire. Then a fire was kindled at the door by the besiegers, who "burnd and kild in the castle fortie six persons, besides two women and a boye which were saved by my Lord's appointment." Cloghan Castle and its lands were granted to Garrett Moore in the reign of Charles II. It was the residence of the late Colonel Graves, who was High Sheriff in 1880, and whose son, Lieutenant Graves, R.N., lost his life doing his duty in the recent " Gladiator " disaster.

Of the warlike O'Maddens, space will only permit the notice of Eoghan (Owen) O'Madden, who defeated the clan Rickard Burke in 1336, and who died in 1346. A poet of his own day described him as "a man with the courage of a true lion, the Lion of Birra, with the venom of the serpent, the Hawk of the Shannon, a tower which defends the frontiers, a Griffin of the race of Conn of the Hundred Battles, a large man of slender body, with a skin like the blossom of the apple trees, with brown eyebrows, black curling hair, long fingers, and a cheek like the cherries." He appears to have married the daughter of MacWilliam, who is described as "of the fair hand and curling tresses." The O'Maddens had their own monastery at Meelick in the diocese of Clonfert and on the banks of the Shannon, founded by an O'Madden in 1479. The O'Madden, who died in 1566, is described as "learned in Latin and Irish, and the most inoffensive of the chiefs of Ireland in his time, the defender of his land, the pillar of protection of women, of the poor, of the weak and destitute." This panegyric proves that the warlike virtues were not the only qualities esteemed by the Irish of the Elizabethan period, and that while learning added the leaven of humanity it did not necessarily diminish their courage. Shannon Harbour, two miles north of Banagher, in the Delvin territory, was the scene of many a conflict between the septs who lived on the banks of the Shannon, principally the O'Maddens, Burkes and MacCoghlans Ath-Crochda, as the *Four Masters* call it, proved a veritable *ford of grief* to many a brave warrior in those days, as well as to many a lad and lass in more recent times. A terrible battle is said to have been fought here in

735 between the forces of Aodh Ollam, King of Ireland, and those of the King of Leinster. The *Four Masters* relate the complete defeat of the Lagenians, and an ancient poem sang with real pathos, " The great Shannon mourned that fight near the church of Kieran of Clonmacnoise."

The obituary notice of Tighernach, concerning whom the late Professor Eugene O'Curry in his *Manuscript Materials of Ancient Irish History*, said that "not one of the countries of northern Europe can exhibit an historian of equal antiquity, learning and judgment with Tighernach," is thus given in the *Chronicum Scotorum*, A.D. 1088. " Tigernach Ua Braoin of the Siol Muireadhaigh Comarba of Ciaran of Cluain-mic-nois and of Coman died." There are seven copies of these annals, two in the Bodleian, two in the Royal Irish Academy, one in Trinity College, and two inferior ones in the British Museum. Dr. O'Conor, who collected the MSS., held that "no good edition of Tighernach can be founded on any copy in the British isles ; for that of Dublin, and all those hitherto discovered, are founded on the Oxford MS. which is imperfect and corrupted by the ignorance of its transcriber." Tighernach dates Irish history from the time of Cimbaoth and the founding of Emania—"Omnia monumenta Scotorum usque Cimbaoth incerta erant." This was about 300 B.C. The annals were continued doubtless by other members of the fraternity down to the year 1407, more than three hundred years after his own death. Augustin MacGrady, "a canon of the canons of the Island of the Saints, a *Saoi* (Doctor) during his life, in divine and worldly wisdom, in literature, in history, and in various other sciences in like manner, and the *Ollamh* (professor) of good oratory, of western Europe, helped to compile this book until 1405, according to the entry for that year in the *Annals*. Some other member of the community carried it on to 1407. And our first great Irish historian Tigernach is not to be forgotten. Many critics, Stillingfleet, Innes and others, commend his historical judgment and wide scholarship. He cites Eusebius, Orosius, Africanus, Bede, Jerome, Josephus, and had a good knowledge of the Hebrew text, which he compared with the Septuagent version.

CHAPTER XVII.

MORE RECENT EVENTS IN THE COUNTY.

A short sketch of the more notable events that took place in the King's County after the subjugation of the Irish septs may prove interesting. On the 22nd of June, 1620, an order was made out by the Lord Chancellor giving Sir Laurence Parsons possession of "the castle and fort-village" and land of Birr, and converting the said land into the Manor of Parsonstown. On the 7th of July Sir Laurence was put into possession by the High Sheriff, Captain Francis Acland. In November of the same year he obtained a grant of a Tuesday market and two fairs to be held in Birr on the festivals of S. Mark and S. Andrew. This was doubtless done in emulation of Sir John MacCoghlan who had obtained a grant in 1612 to hold a market on Thursdays in Banagher. In those days a sheep cost three shillings and fourpence, and a quarter of beef, four shillings and sixpence. The O'Carrolls having tried in vain to be reinstated, Sir Laurence proceeded to give leases to about sixty persons, Irish and English. Some years afterwards the famous Bigo factory of glass was established in the Castle of Clonoghill, the ruins of which are at Syngefield, the residence of Sir Francis Synge, Bart. Molyneux, in his *Natural History of Ireland*, states that "from this place Dublin was furnished with all sorts of window and drinking glasses. One part of the materials, viz., the sand, they had out of

England ; the other, to wit, the ashes, they made in the place of ash tree, and used no other. The chiefest difficulty was to get the clay pots to melt the materials in. This they had out of the north." This factory did good work for some years. Remains of an ancient glass-house with broken crucibles and glass were found at Clonbrone, near Clonoghill, where St. Canice is said to have retired for meditation, and where in 1848 the skull of a bear was found at a depth of six feet among fallen trees of bog-oak by men making a new channel for the Camcor River. This discovery helps us to recreate the surroundings of those early saints, Kiaran and Canice, of Saigher, who lived in the centre of woods where deer and bear and wolf, as the townland of Breagmore or "great wolf" shows, abounded.

Sir Laurence Parsons made several ordinances for the improvement of the town of Birr. In 1626 he made a rule for the paving and cleaning of Birr in which he stated : "Since I am at great charges in digginge and bringinge of stones, which I intend to have layed in the middest of the streete onely, to serve for common passage, therefore it is the least that the inhabitants can doe to pave xii foote broade as well before theire houses as alsoe so longe and as farr as theire houses yards gardens or plotts doe reach and touch upon the streete, still carryinge the pavement twelve foote broade. This to bee done at the tenants charge both for stones gravell and workmanship."

The same ordinance forbade the casting of any " rubbidge filth or sweepings into the forestreete." For every such offence the constable was to levy four pence sterling. Another ordinance for the regulation

of drinking houses made in the same year shows the
very modern ideas of the new owner of Birr. It
commenced with a recital of the evils caused by allowing young women to "draw ale and beare," and
continued in these terms : "Therefore I do ordayne
that henceforwards noe single woman other than
hired servants for meate drinke and wages or clothes,
shall draw any ale or beare, or keepe vittling in this
towne, uppon payne to be sett in the stocks by the constable for 3 whole markett dayes, one after another,
and those which retaine suche in their houses to paie
xx d. sterling for each default; to be levied by the
constable and serjant Lewis Jones for repayring the
church and bridg of this towne." The repairs here
referred to consisted probably of the erecting of the
square tower or belfry of the old church. It would
be well, indeed, for the whole country if this ordinance concerning the sale of alcohol were the law of the
land.

This enlightened landlord also insisted on his
tenants having stone chimneys in their houses owing
to the fearefull experience that many townes and
villages have binn consumed by fire in divers parts of
this realme and occasioned thorowe fires made without
chimneys." Nor did he neglect the education of his
tenants. For in 1626 he presented a petition to the
Lord Deputy Falkland requesting that 200 acres of
unallotted land in Fearcall might be granted for the
use of the schoolmaster of the town of Birr, "who
teacheth the youth of that countrey to the great
good thereof."

In 1641 the town was attacked by the insurgents
under Colonel Moore. Mr. William Parsons, who

had been appointed Governor of Ely O'Carroll and of Birr Castle, defended it with the help of his own tenants and Captain Coote's infantry. The besieged were reduced to great distress, being compelled to eat cats and dogs and horseflesh. They were, however, relieved by Sir Thomas Lucas, Sir Charles Coote, and Sir Richard Grenville, with six troops of dragoons who had to make their way through the woods of Mountrath. The next year (1643) General Preston of the Roman Confederate Forces, who were sworn to bear allegiance to Charles I. and his successors, and to undo the work of the Reformation, attacked the town with a strong force. After a siege of two days the garrison, who were greatly outnumbered, surrendered, and were allowed to march out with their arms, half their plate, and money, all their books, papers, and manuscripts, and as much provisions as they could carry. This was on the 20th of January, 1642. The articles of agreement make mention of Captain Coote, Captain Oliver Darcy, and Lieutenant James Malone. One item is of interest: " It is agreed that the Lady Philips and the Lady Parsons shall have each of them two pair of sheets, and the Governor's lady and Captain Coote's lady shall have each of them two pair of sheets, a pair of pillow beers, and all their clothes of linen and woollen, with their trunk and chest to carry them in, and two feather beds for his children, and the red bed that is laced with willow-coloured lace, with its furniture."

In return for these honourable terms Mr. Parsons promised to use his interest with the Lord Justice and Council for the release of "Nicholas Egan and Catherine Preston, his wife, with her sister, a religious

woman." The latter were evidently relations of the
General. Lord Castlehaven in his *Memoirs* states that
he went into Birr to see the garrison march out, and
entered a large room full of men and women of
quality who besought him as an Englishman to bring
them safely to their friends, as they would have a
march of two days through the woods of Hy Regan
—the territory of the O'Dunnes still in the possession
of the Dunnes of Brittas—before they could reach
Athy, the nearest friendly garrison. "I went," he
says, "therefore to the general immediately, and got
to be commander of their convoy, and to make sure,
I called out three hundred foot and two hundred
horse, in whom I had much confidence, and carried
off the people, who were at least eight hundred, men,
women, and children, and though sometimes attacked,
I delivered them, with their luggage, safe to their friends."

After the surrender of Birr Preston marched
against Banagher, then called Fortfalkland—" a place
of strength enough to have held out against him,
longer than he could have staid in that season of the
year," as Dr. Warner wrote in his *History of the
Rebellion and Civil War in Ireland.*

But in consequence of the favourable terms granted
to the garrison of Birr, and to avoid falling into worse
hands, Lord Castlesteward, the Governor, capitulated
on the understanding that he and all his people
should be conveyed to the Fort of Galway. General
Preston, accordingly, sent two companies with them
as guard, but Colonel Burke, Lieutenant-General of
the Roman Catholic Confederates, made them return
to the Castle of Athlone, permitting the Governor
and a few attendants to pass.

Birr remained in the hands of the Confederates until 1650. General Preston, brother of Lord Gormanstown, one of the Lords of the Pale, and one of the moderate party of the Confederates, had occupied the town for some years as Commander of their forces in Leinster. Owing to a division created in these forces by the action of the Papal Nuncio, Rinuncini, who opposed the treaty between Ormonde, the head of the Protestant party in Ireland, and the Confederates signed on the 28th of March at Kilkenny, he had held aloof for some time. Rinuncini succeeded admirably in his purpose of sowing discord among the two political parties of Irishmen, who, if united, could have saved the country from the Cromwellian invasion. He was supported by Owen O'Neill, the rival of Preston, who attacked Birr in 1648, during Preston's absence, but was beaten off by one of the latter's officers. In 1650 Ireton, who had been appointed to command the Republican forces in Ireland by Cromwell, marched against Athlone, and leaving Sir Charles Coote to take it, advanced on Birr which the enemy had burned and abandoned on his approach. Ireton continued his marched on Limerick, leaving a garrison in Birr. But shortly afterwards the Marquis of Clanricarde attempted to relieve the town, and took the two castles, but was forced to raise the siege on the arrival of Colonel Axtell, the Governor of Kilkenny, who pursued him to Meelick, and defeated him with great loss.

The town of Birr had rest now from war's alarms for some years and prospered in trade and commerce. But in 1688 the country was infested by

robber bands called Rapparees, under one Fannin.
The Birr tenants sought safety within the walls of
the Castle. Colonel Oxburgh reported the matter
to Lord Tyrconnell, the Lord Lieutenant, making it
appear that Sir Laurence Parsons was garrisoning
the town against James II. Tyrconnell ordered the
officious officer to occupy the place in the name of
the king. Oxburgh set out forthwith against
Birr and demanded possession of the castle. This
was refused until a communication should be received
from Tyrconnell, and the siege began, to end in a
surrender after some days. On this occasion the
people in the castle were allowed to depart, with the
exception of Sir Laurence Parsons and five of his
tenants, who were thrown into prison and charged
with high treason in keeping the garrison against
the king. Mr. Jonathan Darby and his brother,
John, were also arrested and charged with the same
offence for their gallant rescue of Captain Coote.
The prisoners were tried at the Philipstown Assizes
on the 30th of March, 1689, before Sir Henry Lynch,
who sentenced Sir Laurence, Jonathan Darby, and
James Rasco to be " hanged, drawn, and quartered."
With great difficulty the convicted men obtained a
reprieve for a month. Sir Laurence was sent back
under military escort to Birr, and kept in prison
until the 2nd April, 1690, and was duly attainted by
the Dublin Parliament of James II. In the meantime Colonel Oxburgh, who was a member for King's
County, with two of his companies were quartered
in the castle, and the remaining twenty in the town of
Birr. The Roman priest, Rev. Thomas Kennedy,
was put in possession of the Glebe and tithes of the

parish by Garrett Trant, his Majesty's Receiver, in the absence of the Rector, the Rev. Richard Crump. In November 28th of the same year (1689) Colonel Oxburgh's officers took the key of the Church from the Clerk of the Parish and handed it over to the Roman Catholic clergyman, who held a service of reconsecration in the Church and celebrated Mass there until the Battle of the Boyne. Colonel Sarsfield, a gallant and kindly officer, having been sent to disband some of the soldiers of Oxburgh, who had become " Rapparees," held a review in the fields near Birr, and disbanded nine companies. He then proceeded to Portumna, where he disbanded forty-three companies of Lord Galway's army, who at once swelled the ranks of the Rapparees.

Oxburgh was then appointed Provost Marshall of the King's County, and signalized his appointment by the erection of a gallows, with three ropes in the market place of Birr, which was supposed to be intended for the three prisoners, Sir Laurence, Jonathan Darby, and James Roscoe. Having been erected on May-Day, 1689, it was called " Colonel Oxburgh's Maypole." On the 2nd of April an order came from James to Terence Coghlan, the High Sheriff, to bring these men to Dublin. This they reached after four day's travel, and were at once thrown into prison. But their release was at hand. For the news of the victory of William, brought to the Castle by no less a person than James himself, caused the doors to be thrown open for all the political prisoners in that city. Sir Laurence was appointed High Sheriff of the King's County by King William's Government, and also a Commissioner of Array; the

R

other Commisioners, many of whom have representatives still in the county, being John Baldwin, Daniel Gahan, William Purefoy, Samuel Rolls, Hector Vaughan, John Weaver, Jonathan, Darby, Humphrey Minchin, Archibald Adaire, Jeffrey Lyons, John Reading, and Richard Warburton.

After some months an attack was made upon Birr by Sarsfield, who was repulsed by General Douglas and fell back beyond the Shannon. After the battle of Aughrim the victorious army passed through Birr on its way to Limerick, leaving the sick and wounded in the Castle. The Birr garrison then sallied forth and took possession of the fort of Banagher and Cloghan Castle, Lieutenant Archibald Armstrong being left in charge of the latter place.

Towards the end of the eighteenth century the Volunteer Movement spread through Ireland which had been drained of its military forces by the American War. A volunteer corps was accordingly formed in the King's County. The *Parsonstown Loyal Independents* were raised in Birr and associated on the 15th of February, 1776. Their uniform was scarlet, faced with black, and their Colonel was Sir William Parsons, Bart., with Major L. Parsons, Captain B. B. Warburton, Lieutenants Treacy and Kearney. *Edenderry Union* was associated on May 1st, 1777. Their uniform was the same, and their officers, Captains Shaw Cartland and Digby Berkeley. The *Barony Rangers* were associated on March 17th, 1778 ; their uniform was the same ; and their officers were Colonel Andrew Armstrong and Captain Robert Shervington.

The *Tullamore True Blues* were raised in October

of the same year. Their uniform was scarlet faced with blue, and their colonel, Charles William Bury, afterwards Earl of Charleville. The *Mountain Rangers* were associated in August of 1779. They were raised in Kinnetty by Colonel Thomas Bernard, George Clarke being major, and John Drought captain, ancestor of Captain Drought, D.L., of Lettybrook. Their uniform was scarlet with black facings. The *Dunkerrin Volunteers* were associated in June of 1779. Their colonel was James Frank Rolleston, who is represented by Major Rolleston, D.L., of Franckfort Castle, Dunkerrin. The *Eglish Rangers* were associated in August, 1779. Their Major was Thomas Berry, their captain, John Drought, and their lieutenant, J. C. Clarke. The *Leap Independents* were raised in 1780 by their colonel, Jonathan Darby, ancestor of the present Mr. Jonathan Darby, D.L., of Leap Castle. The majority of these officers of the Volunteers have representatives among the gentry of the county, though some names have completely passed away. Meetings were held in Birr in 1781 and 1782, which were attended by the delegates of these corps, and on the 20th September, 1784, a general review was held by Sir William Parsons at Woodfield near Birr. The right wing consisted of the Offerlane Blues under Colonel Flood, the Lorrha Rangers under Captain Firman, and the Clanrickarde Chasseurs under Colonel O'Moore. The centre, commanded by Colonel Richard Croasdaile, was composed of the Mountmellick Infantry under Lord Carlow, the Eglish Rangers under Major Berry, the Maryborough Fusiliers under Sir John Parnell, and the Eyrecourt Buffs under Colonel Giles Eyre. While the left wing, commanded by Colonel Thomas Bernard, great-grandfather of Mrs. Caufield French of Castle Bernard, consisted of the Mountain Rangers, the Parsonstown Grenadiers, and artillery, and the Clanrickarde Brigade. This must have been a very gallant display, as the appointments and uniforms of the Volunteers left nothing to be desired.

The Volunteers were at this time some fifty thousand strong, and began to exert an irresistible influence upon the Government for the good of the country. In Dublin they held an imposing muster in College Green in support of Grattan's demand for free trade for Ireland, when two field-pieces were drawn up in front of King William's statue, labelled " Free trade or this." Lord North's Government, powerless to cope with such armed arguments, made the required concessions, and Ireland was permitted the free export of her wool and glass, the free importation of foreign hops, and trade with the "Levant Seas" and the English colonies upon the same terms as Great Britain. These concessions were wrested from the British Government by the Protestant nobility, gentry and yeomen of Ireland.

But the Volunteers had yet another work to do for Ireland. The Dublin Volunteer Corps opposed the perpetual Mutiny Act, which they declared was "an undermining of the constitution and an infringement of liberty." Other Volunteer Corps passed a similar resolution. On February 15th, 1782, 242 delegates representing 143 corps in Ulster, met in the church of Dungannon, under the presidency of Lord Charlemont, and passed thirteen resolutions in favour of legislative reform. On the 3rd of September, 1781, the delegates of the King's County Corps, under the presidency of

Colonel Rolleston, had passed several resolutions against the perpetual Mutiny Act, Poynings' Law, and other unconstitutional measures. In consequence of the determined attitude of the Volunteers Lord North resigned, and the new Ministry allowed the repeal of 6 George I., and Poynings' Law, limited the Mutiny Act to two years, granted a Habeas Corpus Act to Ireland, and other measures of reform. The Marriages of Protestant Dissenters—a measure only granted to England in 1836—were declared valid; various disabilities were removed from the Roman Catholics, and the penal laws were repealed.

As Grattan remarked in his great speech in the Irish Parliament on the 16th April, 1782 : " It was not the sword of the volunteer, nor his muster, nor his spirit, nor his promptitude to put down accidental disturbance or public disorder, nor his unblamed and distinguished deportment. This was much, but there was more than this. The upper orders, the property and the abilities of the country formed with the volunteer, and the volunteer had sense enough to obey them." The volunteer movement lost its prestige and influence in 1784. But it had asserted the claims of Ireland and prepared the way for Roman Catholic Emancipation in perhaps the most agitated times the country has known. And in this movement it is gratifying to learn that the Protestant gentry and yeomen of King's County played no mean part. And they maintained the same traditions in the militia [1] of

---

[1] The officers of the King's County Militia (19th) in 1809 were :— Col. H. P. L'Estrange (1798) ; Lt.-Cols. H. R. Stepney, J. W. Atkinson ; Majors C. F. L'Estrange, C. Baldwin ; Capts. G. Marsh, R. O'Connor, H. O'Connor, T. Hobbs, J. Fitzsimmons, James Drought, H. Croasdaile, D. Cuolahan ; Lieuts. R. Warburton, J Lancaster,

thé county which was presently formed. During the disturbances of 1798 the district around Birr was comparatively quiet.

One terrible murder was committed at Boveen near Sharavogue, the residence of the Earl of Huntingdon, when Mr. Thomas Doolan was done to death in a very callous manner. On Ash Wednesday, 1797, a number of men with blackened faces entered the room where the family were at dinner, and murdered the unfortunate man before the eyes of his wife and children, and decamped with the plate. Mr. Waller of Finnoe was murdered in the same way in more recent times. A pantry boy, however, witnessed the deed through a chink in the wall, and sixteen men were tried at Philipstown Assizes, with the result that two of them were executed at Newtown, near Birr, before their own doors

In 1800 a meeting of magistrates was convened in Birr to protest against the Union. They met in the old market house, but were compelled to return to

Bigoe Cuolahan, F. King, G. Sharpe, W. Dowling, J. Howard, J. L'Estrange, S. G. Pilkington, John Acres, W. Hodson, R. M'Clain, J. W. Watson, H. M. Ryves, John Falkner, John Abbot, Walter Strong, John Wetherall ; Ensigns T. B. Watson, H. Howard, D. Smith, Joseph Maxwell, Paymaster R. T. Fraser, Adjutant A. L'Estrange, Surgeon T. Waters, and T. McDonough, Quartermaster T. Howard. Of these officers there are still many representatives in the King's County. The regiment was called the 19th, but is now known as the 3rd Batt. Royal Canadians, Prince of Wales's Leinster Regiment. The 1st and 2nd battalions are the 100th and the 109th, and the 4th and 5th are the Queen's County and Meath Militia. In 1889 they were commanded by Lieut.-Col. R. G. Cosby ; in 1905 by Lieut. Col. Luttman-Johnson, and in 1908 by Col. Barry, D.S.O., with Lieut.-Col. Gamble, of Derrinboy, second in command. The present Earl of Huntingdon and his grandfather, Col. Westenra, were connected with the battalion for several years. The late Col. Thomas Bernard, of Castle Bernard, H.M.L. for King's County, was colonel for many years, and was succeeded in command by his brother, Richard Wellesley, Col. Thomas remaining full colonel.

their homes by Major Rogers, who was in command of the artillery, and Jonathan Darby, High Sheriff.

To shift the scene to Tullamore in 1808 we read of an exciting encounter that took place between the cavalry and infantry of the German legion quartered in that town and light brigade of Irish militia. The Irish charged the Germans with fixed bayonets and put them to a complete rout. A monument to Frederick Baron Oldenhausen, a German dragoon officer, in the graveyard of Kilcrutten, commemorates the conflict. In 1829 a duel was fought between John Doolan of Shinrone, and William Sadleir of Scalaheen, Tipperary, Doolan's second being William McDonough of Wilmount, County Galway. He was challenged on the ground by David Davis, who insisted that they should fight across a handkerchief. It appears that McDonough fired and killed Davis, for which he was duly tried at Philipstown Assizes, and was acquitted.

In 1846 the famous telescope was completed at Birr under the direction of the Earl of Rosse, and was improved by the late earl, a man of scientific and mechanical tastes. The King's County has since lived up to· the traditions thus created, the scientific work of the brothers Stoney, Johnstone and Bindon, both F.R.S., who were born in Oakley Park in Sierkieran Parish, and of the Hon. Clere Parsons, of turbine fame, being well known to all the world. In 1853, May 5th, the first public telegram from Birr was published in *Saunders' Newsletter* in Dublin. It was to the effect that the fair of that date was one of the best ever held in Birr. Banagher horse fair is too widely known to require mention. That such may ever be the character of our fairs and markets, and that our sons may worthily maintain the traditions of the past, in promoting the agricultural welfare of our country and the scientific interests of the world, is a prayer to which Irishmen of every religious creed and political faith will fervently say " Amen."

But that consummation can only be achieved by a complete reform of our system of economy. Even the casual observer must see that the weakness of Ireland is its contempt for industry on the one hand, and its distrust of industry on the other, whereby the labourer and the employer fail to effect such a combination as would render the land productive and enterprise successful. Our country is being steadily depleted of its most vigorous toilers, and nought is done to fill up the gap made by the exodus or to check that exodus. On the contrary, the young and ambitious, the industrious and intelligent, have every worldly inducement to abandon the homeland that will not support, employ, or educate them in such a way that they can earn a living therein, and to seek new fields of industry in the far west. Sectarian differences and mutual distrust impede education and economy at every point. The natural result is that the nation is slowly dying; its energies are decaying, its children are departing, its trade is depressed, its labour is degraded and its tillage is declining, while the disabilities of the employer, the farmer, and the labourer, are increasing every year owing to the mismanagement of our material resources, the inefficient control of the work, and the unreliable character of the workman. Labour requires to be reorganised on an ethical basis; education must be made more practical in its aims; capital must become more disinterested in its investments. The national decay is a proof of the unwisdom of spending one's life in the pursuit of political ideals and of the necessity of facing the facts of actual life. An Act of Parliament is not the panacea for a state of things created by too much eloquence and too little diligence, but a regeneration of the national spirit is. An exchange of landlords will not raise the national credit unless it is followed by a change of character. The work of reform is no longer hampered by the inter-tribal warfare or oppressive statutes described in the preceding pages. The Irish people have their national destiny in their own hands; they must work out their own salvation themselves without the assistance of Parliament. There are no longer grievances to be redressed, but there is character to be reformed. And if the national life is to be renewed, the principles of economy must be studied and a new spirit of enterprise infused.

Is it sound economy to have a premium on idleness and endeavour at a discount, to banish the employer and to abolish sport; to allow foreign produce and manufactures to compete on equal terms with our own in every market; to fill our baronies with unemployed labourers struggling with starvation on half an acre of ground; and to imagine that all the ills our country has inherited can be removed by the creation of so-called "economic" holdings for men, who have no capital to buy stock or intention to till the soil? The result is as evident, as it is inevitable, namely, that the thrifty, the temperate and well-to-do will gradually acquire the farms of the dilatory, the impecunious and the intemperate.

It does not pay in the long run to allow the land to

become impoverished, to take hay crop after hay crop from the same field, to purchase second-rate farming implements and machines made in America because cheaper, to buy the stuff dumped down by foreign countries in our markets, to use inferior seed and manures, to live on credit, and to trust that Providence will correct our mistakes and pay our debts. Change of ownership can not of itself improve the land—the only security of our national life—unless the new landlords prove industrious themselves, and capable of employing and controlling labour. Our economic efficiency depending on the co-operation of land, labour and capital, the three agents of production, peasant ownership can lead to no lasting benefit so long as agricultural produce is unprotected, the capitalist discouraged and the labourer dismissed.

On the one hand, we have stately asylums for the insane, all too small for the increasing demand, and spacious unions for the inane, maintained by a ruinous tax on the land for the accommodation of casuals, too lazy to dig but not ashamed to beg, and children who become demoralised by their surroundings—for the really deserving poor prefer " out-door relief," and the aged poor are to receive pensions nominally from the State, in reality from another iniquitous tax on the land—while, on the other hand, we see universal signs of decay and decline. Over every village a ruined mill, gaunt spectre of a crushed enterprise, throws its dark shadow, and makes its mute appeal to Ireland to protect its industry and to defend its trade against the ruthless invader—not the Saxon this time—and every unjust attempt to undersell and monopolise. One may well ask—Is it sanity to allow foreign potatoes and bacon to compete on equal terms with our own even in pig-producing and potato-growing districts ? Is it sanity to allow the parasites, the drones and the weak-minded to multiply, and to permit the able-bodied and industrious to be diminished if they will not migrate ? It seems, indeed, to be the fate of Irish industry to be starved out by its " Cosherers and Fait-neants "—of whom Petty complained in 1691— men who demand support, but despise work ? Is it sanity to imagine that we can live by the land alone, and that the State must manage everything—railways, factories, and co-operative stores ? The improvement effected in the early part of the seventeenth century by Sir Lawrence Parsons, described in this chapter, is a proof that reform of industry is possible if the men be found capable of initiating, capitalizing and controlling it. A social regeneration would follow the resuscitation of some of those industries mentioned in these pages, in which we were once the dreaded rival of England. When those ruined mills, which once gave employment to the country-side, hum once more with the sound of machinery ; when those expensive workhouses are converted into homes for workers ; when one quarter of the area of the country is tilled ; when the raised character of the labourer encourages capitalists to invest in home securities and to combine to develop national industries, and when the national produce receives State protection, then industrial inefficiency and agricultural depression will no longer act as a double brake upon the wheels of progress, and our economic salvation shall be accomplished.

CHAPTER XVIII.

IRISH CUSTOMS AND CURIOSITIES.

IRELAND was ever in an unsettled state. This was due in a large measure to the number of warlike septs who regarded each other with feelings of mutual hatred and distrust, and had seldom an *entente cordiale* with one another for any length of time. This is not to be ascribed altogether to the inbred love of fighting in the Irish, but also to the unsettled state of life and property within the borders of the various septs. There were two customs connected with the inheritance of land which were answerable for this unrest. In the first place, when the chieftain died it did not follow as a matter of course that his eldest son or the next-of-kin succeeded; but the tanist was often selected who could secure his election by force of arms. And by the law of gavelkind the other tenantries were divided among all his sons, legitimate and illegitimate. Then came in the other custom, often acting contrary to this and causing grievous complications, of the chief claiming to inherit the land of his tenant who died during his office. It is little more than a hundred years since one of the old chieftains of King's County died who used to insist on this right. He was Thomas Coghlan, M.P. Banagher, and the last of the MacCoghlans "of the Fair Castles" of Delvin Ahra, commonly known as "the Maw" who has already been described. He levied the fines of Mortmain when a vassal died, become heir of the defunct farmer, settled points of law—the Brehon Code—with his whip, and received his rents partly in kind and partly in money. He died so recently as 1790. These two customs made life and property uncertain and are probably answerable for the fact that "though the Irishry," as Sir John Davis writes (*Ireland before* 1603, p. 291), " be a nation of great antiquity and wanted neither wit nor valour, and though they had received the Christian faith above 1,200 years since and were lovers of music, poetry and all kinds of learning, and possessed a law abounding with all things necessary for the civil life. . . . They did never build houses of brick or stone, some poor religious houses excepted, before the reign of Henry II." He continues : " Neither did they plant gardens or orchards or inclose or improve their lands or live together in settled villages or towns or make any provision for posterity."

The same writer also condemns severely the custom of coyne and livery or the practice of enforcing food and fodder for one's soldiers. " This most wicked and most mischievous extortion was originally Irish ; for the chiefs used to lay bonaght upon their people and never gave their soldiers any other pay. But when the English lords had learned it they used it with more insolency and made it more intolerable ; for the oppression was not temporary or limited either to place or time, but because there was everywhere a continual war either offensive or defensive, and every lord of a country and every marcher made war and peace at pleasure ; it became universal and perpetual, and indeed was the most heavy oppression that was ever used in any Christian country." The Irish custom to which Sir John Davis, who advocates a strong English Government, refers was called *Bonaght*, and was of two kinds—the greater and the less, the greater being free quarters at discretion or in specie, while the less was commutation for it in money or food. The Irish gentry were rather inclined to live upon their tenants and to enjoy the *dolce far niente* of country life and produce. By the law of gavelkind every son of a landed proprietor was to inherit a portion of the estate ; and their portion was to be divided between their sons in their turn, so that many of the large estates would be reduced in time to the proverbial "three acres and a cow." These people considered trade or occupation of any kind degrading to any gentleman. Accordingly, they did no work, but lived by their evils and on their people. Sir John Davis refers to this practise of *coshering* in the passage—"They chose rather to live by theft, extortion, or *coshering* than seek any better fortune abroad, which increased their septs and surnames into such numbers that there are not found in any kingdom of Europe so many gentlemen of one blood, family, and surname, as the O'Neills in Ulster, the Burkes, in Connaught and the Geraldines in Munster and Leinster."

By this incessant coshering upon the tenants the lords did literally eat them out of hearth and home, so that the saying, "Devour me but defend me" passed into a proverb, and owing to the oppressions of the Desmonds, the Irish proverb, "quod me alit extinguit" was used.

While his other cessings of the kern called

Kernety, and his privileges, "cuttings, tallages, or spendings, high or low at pleasure," made him a veritable tyrant and his tenant a very slave. This incessant billeting of half-savage kerne and gallowglasses on farmers, which was practised by English and Irish alike in Ireland, caused many freeholders to sell their property and betake themselves to a better ordered realm. While those who remained had lost all heart for work and interest in labour, for the fruit of a year's toil might be consumed by these unwelcome visitors in one night, and consequently "became idle and lookers-on, expecting the event of those miseries and evil times," that is, waiting like Micawber for something to turn up. Such a state of affairs made them a distinctly crafty people.

It was probably from this oppressed class, as well as from the wild sons of decayed gentry that the three kinds of *neer-do-weel*, "the Horseboys, Carrows and Jesters," of whom Spenser writes were recruited. The horseboys were the predecessors of the hostlers, the carrows were "a kind of people who wander up and down to gentlemen's houses, living upon cards and dice, the which, though they have little or nothing of their own, yet they will play for much money, which if they win, they waste most lightly, and if they lose, they pay as slenderly, but make recompense with one stealth or another;" while the jesters were "notable rogues, not only partakers of many stealths, but privy to many traitorous practices, and common news-carriers, with desire whereof you would wonder how much the Irish are fed, for they used commonly to send up and down for news, and if any meet with another, his second word is—what news?" Sir John Davis also comments upon this trait which he ascribes to indolence. "This idleness," he writes, "make the Irish the most inquisitive people after news of any nation in the world." Like the Athenians of old the Irish spent "their time in nothing else but either to tell or hear some new thing." The news-carriers, "Skelaghs" (which connected with Scelaidhe, historian) who then performed the office of the *Morning Post* and the *Evening Telegraph*, were condemned by the Statute of Kilkenny because they were thought to raise trouble among the people, but they still continued to exist.

The poets of Spenser's time were also degraded by the prevailing spirit of licence and cunning so that they ceased to sing of themes that inspired feelings of virtue and honour, but rather praised the deeds of the lawless and the desperate and incited the young and foolish like Silken Thomas to similar acts of outrage and folly. Spenser (*View of the State of Ireland*, p. 123) describes the hero of one of these political outbursts. He was no milksop, but spent his days in arms and valiant enterprises. He never ate his meat until his sword had won it. He did not spend his nights under his mantle in a cabin, but kept others awake to defend their lives, while the flames of their burning dwellings were his light by night. His music was not the harp or the soft lays of love, but the clash of arms and the cries of the terrified. At last he died, not bewailed of many, but causing many to wail, who had at great cost procured his death. In such terms which were thought commendatory by the Irish, this swash-buckler is described.

The mantle[1] was the favourite garment among the
Irish, as the *toga* was among the Romans. It served
as a covering both by day and by night. When
Grace O'Malley went to Elizabeth's Court she wore
a loose mantle which completely enveloped her handsome person, covered her head and concealed her
yellow petticoat. Such a garment when gracefully
folded make a picturesque figure. But the English
Government regarded it askance. For, as Spenser
writes—" Any man disposed to mischief or villainy
may under his mantle which is close-hooded over
his head, go privily armed, without suspicion of any
cover (his head concealed, he is unknown), neither is
his pistol or skein (knife) seen, which he holds in
readiness." The mantle was also a protection against
the gnats which " doe more annoy the naked rebels,
whilst they keep the woodes and doe more sharply
wound them than all their enemies' swords or spears,"
and also formed an effective defence when wrapped
several times around the left arm against a sword
cut. Spenser, however, thought the law against the
wearing of the Irish apparel a hardship. " And were
there better to be had," he writes ; " yet these were
fittest to be used—as namely the mantle in travelling,
because there be no inns where meet bedding may be

---

[1] On one historic occasion the mantle served as the protecting *aegis* of
Ireland. It was when Turgesius the brutal Norse conqueror, demanded
the daughter of O'Melaghlin, the King of Meath, and she was sent to
the palace of the tyrant, accompanied by sixteen beautiful youths, dis-
guised as women, and armed with the Irish skean. As the foreigner
hastened to embrace the princess, her companions threw aside their loose
gowns, and having put the attendants of Turgesius to the sword, made
him prisoner and bound him, and a few days after the villain was thrown
by command of the king, bound as he was into the waters of Loch
Annin, where he embraced death. The whole story is well told in
Keating's *History of Ireland,* under the date 879.

had, so that his mantle then serves him for his bed.
Then the leather jacket, in journeying and camping,
for that is fittest to be under his shirt of mail and to
cover his trouse (trousers) on horseback."

Although he seems to have admired the saffron-
coloured skirts and mantles which the Irishmen wore,
and which has been duly proscribed by Act of Parliament, Spenser had no weakness whatever for the
glibbs or hideous bush of hair often dragged down
over the brow and serving effectually to conceal his
features ; and which was so " monstrously disguising "
that a man's thievish face would hardly be discovered.
The glibbs was not only cultivated for the purpose of
disguise, but also for the sake of defence. Spenser
remarks that the Irish went " to battle encased with
armour, trusting to their thick glibbs which they say
will sometimes bear off a good stroke."

The same writer in his *View of the State of Ireland*
describes the Irish horseman comparing his armour
and array with that of Sir Topas, knight and slayer
of giants. whose complexion was like scarlet and
whose hair was like saffron.

The passage in the *Canterbury Tales* is worthy of
citation :

> He worthe[1] upon his steede gray,
> And in his hand a launcegay —
> A long sword by his side.
>
> He didde[3] next his white lere
> Of cloth of lake[4] fine and clear,
> A breech and eke a shirt ;
> And next his shirt an haketon,[5]
> And over that an habergeon,[6]

[1] Was mounted.   [2] lance.   [3] donned.   [4] lawn.   [5] a quilted
jacket.   [6] breastplate (hauberk),

For [1] piercing of his heart :
And over that a fine hauberk,[2]
Was all y-wrought of Jewes' werk,
Full strong it was of plate.
And over that his coat-armour.[3]

With reference to this description, Spenser writes : "You may see the very fashion and manner of the Irish horseman most truly set forth in his long hose, his riding shoes of costly cord waine, his hacqueton (or doublet), and his habergeon (coat of mail), with all the rest thereunto belonging." And "the furniture of his horse, his strong brass bit, his sliding reins, his shank-pillion (or saddle-pad) without stirrups, his manner of mounting, his fashion of riding, his charging of his spear aloft above his head, and the form of his spear"—all these Spenser declares were introduced by Englishmen into Ireland. There is, however, one point of resemblance between the Irish horseman and the gallant Sir Topas of Chaucer which escapes the keen eye of Spenser :—

The colour of the knight's hair—
His hair, his beard were like saffron.

Saffron was the colour of the Irish horseman's shirt. This deep yellow colour seems to have been the national colour of the Emerald Isle.

Spenser also seems rather partial to the Irish woman's dress ; and among other portions of feminine millinery speaks of "their long-slieved smocks, their half-slieved coats and their silken fillets," for which "they will devise some colour either of necessity or of antiquity or of comeliness." He also alludes to a peculiar kind of head-dress—"the great

[1] to prevent.   [2] coat of mail.   [3] knight's tunic, bearing his coat of arms.

linen roll which they wore round their head," which may have been the predecessor of the white lace-frilled caps much affected by our great-grandmothers, and worn even in our times. It is not so long ago that two ancient dames in the King's County had a small argument which was concluded by one seizing the white cap of the other, dragging it from off her grey hairs and tearing the ruffles, of which there were many yards, in pieces!

Campion (1571) gives an interesting description of the dress and appearance of the people. "Clean men they are or skin, a red hue," he writes, "but of themselves careless. The women are well-favoured, clean-coloured, fair-handed, big and large, suffered from their infancy to grow at will." He goes on to say that "Linen shirts the rich do wear for wantonness and bravery, with wide-hanging sleeves, plaited, thirty yards are little enough for one of them. They have now left their saffron and learned to wash their shirts." "Proud are they," he remarks, "of long-crisped glibbes and do nourish the same, with all their cunning, to crop the front thereof they take it for a notable piece of villainy." In another passage he says "Some of them be richly plated, their ladies are trimmed rather with massive jewels than with garish apparel and it is considered a beauty in them to be tall, round and fat."

In the tale of Etain, preserved in an eleventh century MS. we have a fair representation of the Irish ideal of beauty in the early times. The maiden's arms were "as white as the snow of a single night, and each of her cheeks were as rosy as the foxglove. Even and small were the teeth in her head, and they shone like pearls. Her eyes were as blue as a hyacinth, her lips delicate and crimson; very high, soft, and white were her shoulders. Tender, polished, and white were her wrists, her fingers long and of great whiteness; her nails were beautiful and pink. White as snow, or as the foam of the wave was her side; long was it, slender, and soft as silk. Smooth and white were her thighs; her knees were round and firm and white; her ankles were as straight as the rule of a carpenter. Her feet were slim and as white as the ocean's foam; evenly set were her eyes; her eyebrows were of a bluish black, such as ye see upon the shell of a beetle. Never a maid fairer than she or more worthy of love till then seen by the eyes of men." It would be difficult to find a more beautiful description of a beautiful woman than this description of Etain in Dr. Leahy's *Romance of Ireland.* There is a delicate and subtle refinement, an aloofness from the sensual which makes one think of a classic statue in pure and polished alabaster.

The ladies and gentlemen of the olden time gave much attention to their nails. Crimson-coloured nails were affected. " I shall not crimson my nails," wails the unhappy Deirdre. While they dyed their eyebrows black, and carefully combed out their long tresses which were often elaborately curled. Their garments were of many bright colours—and their girdles richly ornamented. The people seemed thus to be most careful of their persons and appearance. The gentle courtesy of Cuchullin and Ferdia at the Ford of Ferdia (Ardee) when these mortal foes kissed each other before fighting, spoke words of kindness and gentleness to each other during the intervals of the fight, and exchanged healing ointments for their wounds, is also a proof that the sentiment of chivalry was as purely expressed in the noblest Irish life as it was at the court of King Arthur. It is a great shock to one's feelings to pass from these high, refined standards of life to the pages of Fynes Moryson (1600) and to read his charges of barbarity, indecency, drunkenness and uncleanness against the Irish.

He tells us the Irish " eat no flesh but that which dies of disease or otherwise of itself." He says "even the lords and their wives drink at home till they be drunk as beggars," and speaks of the "nasty filthiness of the nation in general." The only word of praise for ought Irish to be found in his pages is for Irish whiskey—"The Irish *aqua vitae*, vulgarly called usquebaugh, is held the best in the world of that kind, which is made also in England, but nothing so good as that which is brought out of Ireland." He seems to have been a connoisseur in this subject, for he says the usquebaugh is preferred before our *aque vitae*, " because the mingling of raisins, fennel-seed, and other things mitigating the heat and making the teeth pleasant makes it less aflame." And the only touch of humour in his description of filth and foulness, in which he revels *ad nauseam*, is his picture of some Irish, who had obtained possession of some sumpter horses, and found in the baggage " soap and starch carried for our laundresses, but they thinking them some dainty meats did eat them greedily, and when they stuck in their teeth bitterly cursed the gluttony of us English churls, for so they term us." We do not go to Whitechapel to see how the English live; we cannot believe that these pictures are a fair representation of Irish life in those days.

But to pass on to more agreeable topics, Spenser had much to say in praise of the skill and courage of these wild Irish troops—the martial predecessors of the Dublin Fusiliers. " I have heard," he says, " some great warriors say that in all the services which they had seen abroad in foreign countries, they never saw a more comely man than the Irishman, nor that cometh on more bravely in his charge ; neither is his manner of mounting unseemly though he lacks stirrups, but more ready than with stirrups, for in his getting up his horse is still going whereby he gaineth way."

With regard to their vigour and endurance he says —" Yet sure they are very valiant and hardy, for the most part great endurers of cold, labour, hunger and all hardness ; very active and strong of hand ; very swift of foot ; very vigilant and circumspect in their enterprises ; very present in perils ; very great scorners of death." It is remarkable that the greatest compliment an Irishman can be paid in our day is to be assured that he is " a very hardy fellow," hardy implying vigour, build, as well as courage, and that the characteristic of the northern nations of Europe, especially noticed by Lucan in the first century of our era, was this scorn of death, which helped the Irishman to bear himself with courage and to make " as worthy a soldier as any nation he meeteth with." Gainsford's *Glory of England*, published in 1618, informs us that "the name of galliglas is in a manner extinct, but that of kern is in great reputation, as serving them in their revolts and proving sufficient souldiers but excellent for skirmish," and that they the Irish are desperate in revenge, "and their kerne thinke no man dead untill his head be off."

Those who are interested in the revival of the Irish language—which Campion says he finds it solemnly avouched in some of their pamphlets that Gathelus, and after him Simon Brecke, devised it out of all other tongues then extant in the world!—will find much to commend in Spenser's remarks on the subject. It is well known that his royal mistress, Elizabeth, was keen on the study of the language, and the translation of the Scriptures into Celtic for which she actually provided the type, much to the disgust of Lord Cecil, her adviser, who asked if she considered a language worthy of preservation in which such an expression as " Di dav duv uv ooh " [1] could be found. As a set-off against this story, there is that recorded by Camdem of the Irish chieftain who refused to learn English because it made them make wry mouths when trying to speak it. "It is unnatural," wrote Spenser, "that any people should love another's language than their own," and quotes the Scripture "for out of the abundance of the heart the mouth speaketh," which he applies to the case of the Irish tongue speaking the things in the Irish heart, for words are the "image of the mind."

Should any carp at Spenser's short and easy method with the rebels and his occupation of the then charmingly situated demesne of Kilcolman in the county of Cork, let them not forget this plea for the Irish language which was unpopular in his time with his

---

[1] ᴅıċ ᴅᴀḃ, ᴅuḃ, uḃ, oṁ (sounds dih dav duv uv ovh)—a black ox ate a raw egg.

set, and let them remember that one of the most glorious and high-souled poems the literary world has ever read—" The Faerie Queen "—" the wild fruit which salvage soil hath bred," was written on Irish soil, " far from Parnassus Mount," in full view of the grand old mountains of Kerry and in the breezes of the Galty More—" the Mountains of Mole " —and in the inspiring vicinity of the modern town of Buttevant, then known as Kilnamullagh, or the church of the hills. This Spenser, however, explained as the church of the Mulla, his name for the little river Arobeg that flowed murmuringly past his castle walls and by whose waters the poet was wont to court the Muse. To it he alludes in the lines—

> It giveth name unto that ancient cittie,
> Which Kilnemulla clepped is of old.

From his house at Kilcolman the poem containing these lines, " Colin Clout's Come Home Again," was sent to Sir Walter Raleigh on December 27th, 1591. From his affectionate allusions we see that the poet loved the Irish hills—" Old Father Mole " among them, and woods and rivers—of which he gives a list in *Faerie Queen*, Book IV., Canto XI., and in *Colin Clout*. And from his pathetic description of the natives, we learn how he pitied them. He tells us that after a short campaign, the inhabitants of Munster were brought to such wretchedness that any stony heart would rue the same ; "out of every corner of the woods and glens they came, creeping forth upon their hands, for their legs could not bear them. They looked like anatomies of death ; they spoke like ghosts crying out of the graves. They did eat the dead carrions where they did find them, yea and one another soon after, in as much as the very carcases they spared not to scrape out of their graves ; and if they found a plot of watercresses or shamrocks, there they thronged to a feast for a time, yet not able to continue there withall ; that in a short space there were none almost left."

Such a picture, pitiful and revolting, reminds us of what we have read ourselves, and our fathers have told us, of the terrible potato famine of last century, when the "ruthless Saxon" sought to alleviate the miseries of those who could not help themselves. This picture must not, however, be regarded as representative, but as local. We are not surprised to learn that Spenser never recovered from the shock of that fatal day in October, 1598, when the Munster hillsmen plundered and burned his castle to the ground, and with it a beloved child and many a precious manuscript. It was his death-blow dealt by the people he pitied, and in the land he loved, and from which he drew the imagery of his poetical landscapes.

Spenser often throws an interesting light upon some old-standing custom of the natives. For instance, when writing of their manner of moving about with their cattle from one mountain pasture to another, he says—" There is one use among them to keepe their cattle, and to live themselves the most part of the yeare in boolies, pasturing upon the mountains and waste, wilde places, and removing still to fresh land as they have depastured the former." The word *booley* is evidently the Irish *buaile*, a place where a cow (bo) is kept or milked. He sees in this custom a trace of Scythian origin, for the Scythians used to live with their herds, and, like the Irish, on the milk of their flocks ; but he disapproves of it for the reason that they who lived among cattle could never rise above a state of barbarism, and their boolies often became the refugees of outlaws and the receptacles of stolen kine.

Spenser also compares the Irish style of weapons and mode of warfare, marriage, dancing, singing and burying with the Scythian, With regard to their mode of burying, Campion in his *History of Ireland* says—"They follow the dead corpses to the grave with howlings and outcryes, pitifull in apparence, whereof grew (as I suppose) the proverbe 'to weepe Irish.'" It is not improbable that the Irish *caoinan*, or lamentation for the dead, was derived from the East. The Jews, we know, practised this custom to increase the sadness of their funeral solemnities. The funeral cortèges of the Greeks were preceded or followed by women called *Threnodoi*, playing mournful strains on the flute ; while the *praeficae*, or mourning women, who sang the Naenia, were a prominent feature of the Roman obsequies. David's lament over Saul, the Persian chorus in the *Persae*, the Carthaginian wail for Dido, and the Scotch Coronach, "He is gone on the mountain," remind one of the Irish caoinan ; while the *Ulooloo*, the burden of the chorus, is identical with the Latin *ululo*, and the Greek *ololuzo*. In an account of a caoine in Ireland written many years ago, the dirge was described as beginning with the words "Ulooloo, why did you die ? It was not for want of good living. You had plenty of potatoes and meal . . ." The refrain of all these caoines seem to have been—"Ulooloo, why did you die ? "

Camden tells us that even before death "certain women, hired to lament, stand at the joining of the cross-roads, and spreading out their hands, call on the dying man with certain outcries fitted for the nonce; and as if they would stay the soul as it laboured to free itself from the body, recount all his wordly wealth and enjoyment. They tell him of his wife, of his personal beauty, of his fame, of his kinsfolks, his friends and his horses. They then demand of him why he will depart; and whither; and to where he is going? They expostulate wlth the soul, accusing it of unthankfulness; and tell it with piteous wailing, that it is now about to leave the body to go to haggish women, who appear by night and in darkness."

Spenser refers to these wailings for the dead in an interesting passage in which he attempts to establish the Scythian origin of the custom. " There are other sorts of cryes," he writes, " also used among the Irish, which savour greatly of the Scythian barbarisme. as their lamentations at their buryals, with dispairfull out-cryes, and immoderate waylings, the which M. Stanihurst might also have used for an argument to prove them Egyptians. For so in Scripture it is mentioned that the Egyptians lamented for the death of Joseph. Others think this custome to come from the Spaniards, for that they do immeasurably likewise bewayle their dead. But the same is not proper Spanish, but altogether heathenism, brought in thither first either by the Scythians or the Moores that were Africans, and long possessed that country. For it is the manner of all pagans and infidels to be intemperate in their waylings of their dead, for that they had no faith nor hope of salvation. And this ill custome also is especially noted by Diodorus Siculus, to have been in the Scythians and is yet among the Northerne Scots at this day, as you may reade in their chronicles."

This "ill custome" and "the wake" must be regarded as present survivals of Paganism, for Christianity has taught us "not to sorrow as those who have no hope for those who sleep in Christ." The Celtic heart clings to old customs for fear of giving offence to something invisible, and of meeting with bad luck in consequence.

The *caoinan* can, however, not be said to be altogether rhyme without reason, if we may judge from the elaborate account given of it by Miss Beaufort in "The Transactions of the Royal Irish Academy," in which she describes the relations and the *caoiniers* ranging themselves in two divisions, one semi-chorus at the head and the other at the feet of the corpse, and the two choruses chanting to the accompaniment of the harp their doleful verses in answer to each other, and at the conclusion of each stanza uniting in a general chorus. The verses were of four lines, consisting of four feet each, and the subject of the song was the greatness and many virtues of the deceased who was often addressed. Some of these rhyming women were skilful and much sought after, and made quite a good thing out of their gloomy profession. And as the funeral procession moved forth to the distant cemetery it was joined by every passer by, who also lifted up his voice and wept, even though he had no acquaintance with the deceased, in order to show his sympathy with those who were weeping. This custom has not altogether died out, but though it is considered correct form in the country to turn back and follow any funeral one meets for some distance, the habit of howling has fortunately been abandoned. It was indeed rather strange, as octogenarians relate, to see people howling to their hearts' content, and then indifferently inquiring who was being buried.

Arrived at the cemetery the procession of relatives and criers, whose spirits all through these doleful proceedings have been sustained with spirituous liquors, walked three times round it chanting the Creed. But during the interment the caoine with its mournful cadences and clapping of hands was resumed. After this fashion the Irish for many centuries used to bury their dead. The last occasion on which the writer knows of such a caoine was that raised in Valentia by the Irish women in honour of the beloved rector of that island. Very solemn and weird indeed must the voices of lamentation have sounded as the procession of boats moved slowly over the waters. The same custom prevails to this day in Palestine where, as Thompson says, "they weep, howl, beat their breasts, and tear their hair according to contract. But fluteplayers varied the monotous dirge in several households." [1]

Spenser, in his desire to establish a connection between the Irish and the Scythians, falls back on such authorities as Olaus Magnus, Solinus, and Io Bohemus! He rejects the Spanish origin of the Irish as an absurd theory, partly, we think, from conviction and partly because of the Elizabethan Englishman's hatred of Spain; and declares that the Irish act foolishly in

---

[1] Cantabat moestis tibia funeribus, Ov., Fast VI.

trying "to ennoble themselves by wresting their auncientry (ancestry) from the Spaniard, as of all nations under heaven, the Spaniard is most mingled and most uncertain."

He also waxes indignant with M. Stanihurst for endeavouring to derive the Irish from the Egyptians who came into our island under the leadership of Scota, and who in all their battles used to call upon the name of Pharaoh, crying "Ferragh, Ferragh." What an interesting discussion M. Stanihurst would have carried on with the holders, if there were any in his day, of the British-Israel theory! He and they might possibly have lost themselves in an "Egyptian darkness." With regard to this battle cry—"Ferragh Ferragh," Spenser declares that many Irishmen were called by the name of Ferragh, which he derived from the Scotch Fergus. And in his *Faerie Queen*, iv. 2, he immortalized the name which may be preserved in the Irish *Forrach* or *Farrach* or meeting-place as in *Forrach-mach n Amhalgaidh* (the assembly place of Awley's tribe) by introducing a knight, "Sir Ferraugh" who had carried off the false Florimell from Braggadocio and who lost her to Sir Blandamour, who unhorsed him in a sudden onset.

Among the Scythian customs adopted by the Irish he mentions the "loose jiggs;" so that to please Spenser we should have in future to speak of Scythian jigs instead of Irish reels. He also derived from Scythia the Irish custom of calling on their captain's name in battle, for example, the O'Neills shouting "Laundarg-abo," that is the bloody hand, the O'Briens "Laund-laider," or the strong hand, as they came to close quarters with their foes.

And describing the Irish mode of fighting, he writes : " Their confused kinde of march in heapes, without any order or array, their clashing of swords together, their fierce running upon their enemies, and their manner of fight, resembleth altogether that which is read in histories to have been used by the Scythians."

He then passes on to another sphere—the superstitious practices of both nations—to establish their connexion. He says that the common oath of the Scythians was by the sword and by fire,[1] and that the Irish were accustomed when going to battle to " say certain prayers or chants to their swords, making a cross there with upon the earth and thrusting the points of the blades into the ground ; thinking thereby to have the better successe in fight." He also says that the Irish use commonly to swear by their swords and at the kindling of fire and lighting of lamps to say certain prayers and use superstitious rites which prove that they venerate the fire and the light like the northern nations. The Scythians concluded solemn compacts by drinking a bowl of blood together, and the Northern Irish did the same.

But while insisting on the Scythian origin of the great mass of the people, he acknowledges that some of Spanish descent were found on the Southern and Western coasts of Ireland, which were frequently visited by strangers "repayring thither for trafficke and for fishing, which is very plentifull upon these coasts." And among the Spanish customs he mentions the wearing of the moustache. " This," he says, " was the auncient manner of the Spaniard, as yet it is of

[1] Lucian hath ' by the sword and by the wind.'

all the Mahometans to cut off all their beards close save onelie their moustachios which they wear long." This custom, he says, was due to the fact that hair on the face was found unpleasant in warm countries; while on the contrary the northern nations wore all their hair on head and face, and therefore "the Scythians and Scottes wore glibbes to keep their heads warm and long beards to defend their faces from cold. And as amongst the old Spaniards the Irish women have the management of all household affairs both at home and abroad, ride on the wrong side of the horse, and wear a deep smock sleeve.

While from the Gauls he would derive the custom of drinking blood and smearing the face therewith. But while the Gauls drank the blood of their enemies, the Irish drank the blood of their friends. At the execution of one Morrogh O'Brien he saw, he tells us, an old woman who was his foster mother taking up his head and sucking the blood that flowed therefrom, saying that the earth was not worthy of it; and also steeping her face and breast in the blood, and tore her hair crying out and shrieking most terribly. Campion remarks that Solinus said that the Irish were wont to embrue their faces in the blood of their slain enemies in order to seem terrible and martial.

Spenser also alludes to the Irish custom of holding assemblies upon a rath or hill, which he says they held in order to discuss wrongs between township and township and one private person and another. He alleges that "these round hills and square bawnes which you see so strongly trenched and thrown up" —which we know as raths and forts—were folkmotes or meeting places for the people, and that many

T

villainous deeds have been wrought, and many Englishmen and good Irish subjects murdered at the
same meeting-places. " For the Irish never come to
those raths but armed, whether on horse or foot, which
the English nothing suspecting are there commonly
taken at advantage like sheep in the pen-fold." We
presume the long mantle was a complete concealment
for their weapons and the long glibbs hanging over
the eyes afforded a perfect cover for their evil
intentions.

Spenser suggests that the round hills were cast up
by the Danes as forts for their protection in each
quarter of the cantred so that in case of any sudden
alarm they might betake themselves thereto, and that
the other bawns which were "foure square, well-
entrenched," were built by the Saxons for parley and
discussion. Other mounds, cairns and stone monuments, according to him, mark the scene of some
battle or burial; and with regard to the gigantic
dolmens and cromlechs which in his time were called
" Giants' Trevetts," because it was thought that no
one but giants could have raised them into their
present position, it is interesting to note that even
in his day there was much discussion over these then
remains of prehistoric man, and that some went so
far as to deny that they had been placed there by
man's hand or art, "but only remained there so since
the beginning and were afterwards discovered by the
deluge and laide open as then by the washing of the
waters or other like casuality." The latter suggestion
quoted by Spenser is not very remote from the theories
of inland sea and glacier, which are said to explain
certain strange marks of men's hands and animals'

feet which have been found imprinted on many of the stones in Ireland.

But these and kindred subjects have been discussed in *Celtic Types of Life and Art*, and I shall not, therefore, weary my readers further than to invite them to make personal researches in the history of Irish life and customs which will indubitably prove as instructive as interesting.

NOTE TO CHAPTERS XIII. AND XIV., Etc.

THE following is a short glossary of difficult legal terms in these and other chapters, most of which are Irish :—

Bieng (Irish), a bribe given to the Brehon for his favour in settling disputes, in the State Papers of the period means money, cattle or horses given to the lords marchers or their followers to secure favour ; *Black-rent*, a bribe paid by English to Irish neighbours to abstain from plunder (Black-mail in Scotland) ; Bonacht also *bonogh*, Irish *buana*, billeted soldier, and bunadh, a soldier ; O'Reilly gives *buanacht*, free quarters for soldiers ; *Bonneh* or *Boyne*, the same as coin in *coyne and livery*, bonn is Irish for groat, exaction for maintenance of the lords, gallowglasses or kerne, also bonagium ; *Byerahe*, a quarterly exaction by the lord on persons living under his jurisdiction ; *caanes* (Ir. *cain*, tribute), ransom for murder, theft or felony, also a fine for not giving he lord the pre-emption ; *Coyne* (Ir. coinnimh entertainment) generally *coyne and livery*, free quarters for man and horse, livery is the English word for *deliver* ; also *coyne and foy* ; also *coine bon* ; *Cuddee* (Ir. cudoich, night's portion) ; also cody, night's supper taken by the lord for himself and retinue ; *kyntroisk*, a forfeiture of a beef or animal for refusing coin and livery, probably from Irish cain, fine and truscad, fasting, a fine for having made the soldiers fast ; *mertyeght*, exaction of meat, drink and candles upon a visit of a great man. The following words refer to crime :—*Alterages*, one of the amends for offences less than murder ; also meant nourishing (*alo* Latin, nourish) of a child ; *garty*, ransom for felony ; *sault*, ransom for murder or manslaughter ; *slauntiagh*, surety or bail ; *srahe*, means a tax ; *urragh* from Ir. oireacht, a clan or family ; *oireachtas*, meeting of the clans ; *Regrating* means buying and selling in the same fair or market.

APPENDIX.

SOME KING'S COUNTY FAMILIES IN THE EIGHTEENTH CENTURY.

THE plan followed in compiling these notes has been to deal only with those families who were actually resident in the county, and whose names appear, either as members of Parliament, High Sheriffs, or Grand Jurors. Owing to lack of space, it is inevitable that many names must be passed over; and since Mr. Hitchcock has written fully on families of native origin, we have dealt principally with those who, from time to time, have settled in the county. Most of the landowners, at the beginning of the eighteenth century, held their estates under patents of Elizabeth or James I., while some represented families which had been established from a period anterior to the formation of the county in 1558. The presence of French names may be ascribed to the fact that the Huguenot settlement of Portarlington is situated on the borders of the county. With few exceptions, the families of Dutch descent, such as Westenra, Bor, Grave, etc., derived from merchants who had settled in Dublin after the persecutions of Alva, and not, as might have been expected, from the adherents of King William.

In cases where families are still represented in the county, we have endeavoured to outline the descent;

and we may be pardoned for giving rather fuller information about those, of whom particulars could only be obtained from wills and other unpublished documents. Though no order has been adopted in enumerating the different families, we have chosen the style of a narrative, in the hope that it may lend some interest to a subject, which must necessarily be little more than a mere recitation of names and dates.

In the eighteenth century, as at present, the largest estate in the King's County, was in the possession of the Digby family. This great property, comprising the entire barony of Geashill, belonged to the FitzGeralds, from whom it came to Sir Robert Digby, of Coleshill, Warwick, on his marriage in 1600 with Lettice, only child of Gerald FitzGerald, Lord Offaly, and granddaughter of Gerald, eleventh Earl of Kildare. This lady, who had been created by James I. Baroness Offaly for life, gallantly held Geashill Castle against the insurgents in 1641. Her son, Robert Digby, was elevated to the peerage of Ireland in 1620 as Baron Digby, of Geashill, with remainder to his brothers. He was the ancestor of the present peer. In 1765 an earldom was conferred on the seventh baron, but this title has since become extinct. The Lords Digby, having much finer seats in England, have seldom resided at Geashill Castle, which during the greater part of the eighteenth century, was occupied by the agent of the estate. The Right Rev. Essex Digby, Bishop of Dromore, a younger brother of the first lord, was father of the Right Rev. Simon Digby,[1] Bishop of Elphin, from whom the Digbys of Landenstown, Ballincurra, and other Irish branches are derived.

Unlike the owners of Geashill, who have usually resided on their English estates, the Parsons family have always made Parsonstown their home. It was Sir Laurence Parsons, younger brother of Sir William Parsons, Bart., Lord Justice of Ireland, who first settled at Birr. The

---

[1] He was better known as an artist than a divine (Lecky : Ireland in the Eighteenth Century, Vol. I., p. 205). Some of his work in water-colour is in the possession of his descendant, Col. Digby, of Ballinacurra, Co. Westmeath.

two brothers came to Ireland about 1590, but the male
descendants of Sir William, who was of Bellamount,
Co. Dublin, came to an end on the death of Richard,
second Earl of Rosse, in 1764.

In 1677 Sir Laurence Parsons, of Birr Castle, grandson
of the first settler, was created a baronet. His son, Sir
William Parsons, many years M.P. for King's County, died
in 1740, and was succeeded by his grandson, Sir Laurence
Parsons, third baronet, who augmented the family fortunes
by his marriage with Mary, elder daughter and co-heiress
of William Sprigge, of Cloonivoe, King's Co. (by Catherine,
daughter of Edward Denny, of Tralee, Co. Kerry, M.P.).
Sir William Parsons, fourth baronet, M.P. for the King's
County, who succeeded his father, Sir Laurence, in 1749,
was High Sheriff, 1779, and long foreman of the Grand Jury.
He took a prominent part in the Volunteer movement,
and held a great review at Woodfield, near Birr, besides
raising a corps called the Parsonstown Loyal Independents.
In 1792 Laurence Parsons-Harman, M.P. for Longford,
Sir William's half-brother, who had inherited Newcastle,
Co. Longford, from his mother's family, the Harmans,
was raised to the peerage of Ireland as Baron Oxmantown,
being advanced in 1806 to the Earldom of Rosse, with
remainder, in default of male issue, to his nephew, Sir
Laurence Parsons, fifth baronet, of Birr Castle. Lord Rosse
died in 1807, when the earldom devolved on his nephew
according to the limitation, while the Newcastle estates
were inherited by his only child Frances, wife of Robert
King, first Viscount Lorton, grandfather of Colonel
Wentworth King-Harman, now of Newcastle. Laurence,
second Earl of Rosse, who represented King's County and
the University in Parliament, was father of William, third
earl, the celebrated astronomer, and great-grandfather of
the present peer.

Charleville Forest, now the seat of the Lady Emily Bury,
was at the beginning of the eighteenth century the residence
of the Forth family. It was then called Redwood, and
James Forth, who had succeeded to the estate at the
decease of his father, John Forth, in 1680, was High Sheriff
in 1711, and represented the county in Parliament, 1713-14.
James Forth left no male issue, and soon after his death,
Charles Moore, second Lord Moore, and proprietor of the

town of Tullamore, removed from Croghan in this county
to Redwood, which he named after himself, Charleville.
He was Muster Master-General in Ireland, and was elevated
to the Earldom of Charleville in 1758, but dying without issue in February, 1764, his titles became extinct.
His estates devolved on his widow for life, and at her death
in 1779 came to his grand-nephew, Charles William Bury,
then a minor, the only child of John Bury, of Shannon
Grove, Co. Limerick, whose mother had been the earl's
only sister. Charles William Bury, of Charleville, sometime
M.P. for Kilmallock, was created in 1797 Baron Tullamore,
in the peerage of Ireland, and subsequently advanced to
the dignities of Viscount and Earl of Charleville. These
titles became extinct on the death of the fifth earl in 1875,
when the estates devolved on the present owner, the Lady
Emily Howard-Bury, a daughter of the third earl.

After the death of Charles Moore, Earl of Charleville,
in 1764, his widow removed to Dublin, while Charleville
was occupied by Capt. Thomas Johnston, whose name is
found on the Grand Jury for several years subsequently.
It was while on a visit to the Johnstons at Charleville that
Dr. Pocock, Bishop of Meath, who attained some eminence
as an author and traveller, died of apoplexy in September,
1765. Johnston's sister, Eliza, married in 1745 George
Stoney, of Greyfort, Co. Tipperary, and through this
marriage Emell Castle, which had been purchased by the
Johnstons from Richard Carroll in 1782, has at length
devolved on its present possessor, Johnston Thomas Stoney,
now of Emell Castle.

Though the name is now unknown the family of Lyons
held for over 150 years a prominent position in the county.
Captain William Lyons was one of the settlers of James I's.
time, and his possessions comprised Killeen and part of
the great wood of Fercall. The estate of Clonarrow, afterwards called River Lyons, had been the seat of Geoffrey
Philips, who died in 1601, leaving, with other issue, two
sons, Henry and Colley. As the names Colley, Geoffrey,
Philips and Henry are found in the pedigree of the Lyons
family, we may presume that they acquired that estate by
marriage with a Philips.

Charles Lyons, of Killeen, High Sheriff, 1663, married
Margaret, daughter of Thomas Moore, of Croghan, M.P

and died, 1694. John Lyons, who purchased Ledeston,
Co. Westmeath, in 1715, and was ancestor of the family
seated there, was, apparently, his younger son; Geoffrey,
the elder, born 1654, succeeded to Killeen, was High
Sheriff, 1693 and 1702, and married his cousin, Jane
Moore, of Croghan. This Geoffrey had issue, three sons
and four daughters, viz., Colley, Thomas, Philips, Anne,
Mary, Elizabeth, and Susan, who married Thomas Nesbitt
in 1701.

Colley Lyons, of River Lyons, the eldest son, was sometime M.P. for King's County and High Sheriff, 1715. He
married, 1706, Susanna, daughter of Elnathan Lumm, and
died 1741, leaving a daughter, Anne, wife of Richard Cane,
of Larabrian, Co. Kildare (by whom she had a son, Lyons
Cane), and an only son, Henry, who succeeded his father.

Henry Lyons, of River Lyons, many years M.P. for
King's County and foreman of the Grand Jury, was High
Sheriff in 1744. In the previous year he had married
Anne, daughter of the Right Hon. George Rochfort, M.P.,
and sister of Robert, first Earl of Belvedere, by whom he
had issue three daughters and co-heiresses: Elizabeth,
married in 1762 Robert Barry, M.P. for Charleville; Anne,
married John Nixon; and Henrietta, who married in 1780
Robert Garden. Henry Lyons died at Bath in 1782, his
wife surviving till the following year. After his death the
house at River Lyons, which is near Philipstown, remained
unoccupied, and has since become a ruin. Through his
youngest daughter the property came to the Gardens, from
whom it passed by marriage to Arthur Champagne, Esq.

The family of Wakely, who still retain their ancestral
home, was seated at Ballyburley as far back as 1550. Its
representative at the beginning of the eighteenth century
was John Wakely, M.P. for Kilbeggan, who built Ballyburley Church in 1686, and was High Sheriff of the King's
County, 1695. He married Elizabeth Lambert, niece of
the Earl of Cavan, and was succeeded by his eldest son,
Thomas, who was High Sheriff, 1726. This Thomas
Wakely, of Ballyburley, who died 1751, had three sons:
John, of Ballyburley, High Sheriff, 1763, whose male
descendants expired in 1842; James, who d. unm.; and
Francis, great-grandfather of His Honour Judge Wakely,
the present owner of Ballyburley.

With ramifications endless and residences innumerable, the Armstrong family, though still represented in the county, cannot be followed in detail. Their original ancestor came from the Scottish border, and settled in Fermanagh. Several of his sons established themselves in the King's County, Edmund at Stonestown; Thomas, the third son, at Ballycumber, and Archibald, the eighth, at Ballylin. Edmund's heir male and representative, Andrew Armstrong, of Gallen Priory, many years M.P. for the county, and twice High Sheriff, was created a baronet in 1841, and the title is now enjoyed by his grandson, Sir Andrew Armstrong, third baronet; while Archibald was ancestor of Sir George Armstrong, Bart., the well-known proprietor of the "Globe" newspaper, who obtained a similar honour in 1892. General Armstrong, who founded Woolwich Arsenal, was also a member of this family.

At the Summer Assizes, 1779, no less than four Armstrongs were on the Grand Jury, three of them being named Andrew.

Besides these branches of the one family, there were also the Armstrongs of Mount Heaton, who came of a different stock.

Mount Heaton, near Roscrea, now Mount St. Joseph's Monastery, received its name from the Heatons, who were of Yorkshire ancestry. The Rev. Richard Heaton, of Mount Heaton, otherwise Balliskannagh, died in 1666, leaving three sons and three daughters. Edward, the eldest son, succeeded, but on his death in 1703, the estate came to his next surviving brother, Francis, who was High Sheriff of the King's County in 1705. Francis Heaton, of Mount Heaton, married, 1704, Elizabeth, daughter of Robert Curtis, of Inane, Co. Tipperary, M.P., and had four daughters, of whom Mary, married, 1731, William Armstrong, of Farney Castle, Co. Tipperary. Through this marriage Mount Heaton came to the Armstrongs, who were not, however, related to the other families of that name in King's County, being derived from a Captain William Armstrong, who had settled in Co. Tipperary about 1660. The Rt. Hon. John Armstrong, of Mount Heaton, M.P. died 1791, leaving a son, William Henry Armstrong, of Mount Heaton, M.P., who sold that estate to the Hutchinsons in 1817.

Corolanty, now the seat of Edward Francis Saunders,
Esq., who represents the male line of that ancient family,
formerly of Saunder's Court, Co. Wexford, and Newtown
Saunders, Co. Wicklow, was built about 1698 by John
Baldwin. His father, Captain John Baldwin, who belonged
to a Warwickshire family, got a grant of lands at Shinrone,
and was High Sheriff of King's County in 1672. John
Baldwin, junr., High Sheriff, 1697, survived his father less
than a year, and died in 1699, leaving, with other children,
Thomas, his heir; Mary married, 1700, Edward Crow, of
Spruce Hall, Co. Galway; and Catherine married, 1704,
Thomas Meredyth, of Newtown, Co. Meath, M.P.

Thomas Baldwin, who succeeded to Corolanty, was born,
1679, and died, 1732, leaving by his wife, Mary Eyre, of
Eyrecourt, two sons and two daughters, viz., John;
Thomas, who became Attorney-General of Jamaica;
Margery, married, 1718, Charles Sadleir, of Castletown
Co. Tipperary; and Lucy, who died, unm., in 1768.
John Baldwin, the elder son, was of Corolanty, but, being
extravagant, dissipated the estates, and died without issue
in 1754. His widow soon afterwards married Hervey,
Lord Mountmorres.

Part of the Corolanty property came into the possession
of Dr. Richard Baldwin, Provost of Trinity College, who
died in 1758, leaving the whole of his large fortune to the
University. Though his parentage has been the subject of
some dispute, he was not in any way related either to the
Corolanty family, the Queen's County Baldwins, or to the
Baldwins of Dublin, who subsequently settled at Boveen,
near Shinrone. Sir Brydges Baldwin, of Dublin, Knight,
who died in 1765, was nephew of Richard Baldwin, of Dublin
(died 1768), from whom the Baldwin-Hamiltons derive.
This Richard Baldwin had an only son, Richard, of The
Four Crosses, Co. Wicklow, High Sheriff, 1756, who was
father of Colonel Charles Baldwin, of Boveen, High Sheriff
of King's County, 1802. By his wife, Miss Barry (whose
taste for acting Sir Jonah Barrington has so severely
criticised), the only daughter of Sir Nathaniel Barry,
Bart., the celebrated Dublin doctor, Colonel Charles
Baldwin left an only son, Charles Barry Baldwin, of
Boveen, M.P. grandfather of the present representative.

The Warburtons of Garryhinch have held that estate

since the reign of Charles II., when their ancestor, the
original grantee, was Clerk-Assistant to the Irish House of
Commons.   His eldest son, Richard Warburton, of
Garryhinch, was M.P. for Portarlington, 1692-1713.
George Warburton, third son of Richard, eventually
succeeded to the estates, and was ancestor of the present
possessor ; while the fifth son, William, married Barbara,
daughter of Lytton Lytton, of Knebworth, Herts, by whom
he had a son, Richard Warburton-Lytton, of Knebworth,
grandfather of Edward George, first Lord Lytton, the distinguished novelist and statesman.

Moystown, near Banagher, now the seat of Bolton
Waller, Esq., was for nearly two hundred years the home
of the L'Estrange family.   Thomas L'Estrange, first of
Moystown, who was included in the Act of Attainder,
1689, represented Banagher 1692-93, 1695-99 and 1703-13.
He married Miss Peisley, and had a son Henry, of Moys-
town, M.P., ancestor of Colonel Henry Peisley L'Estrange,
of Moystown, D.L., fourth of his name in lineal succession,
who sold the estate about the middle of the last century.
Through the marriage of Henry L'Estrange, eldest son of
Thomas, of Moystown, with Frances Malone, of Litter,
King's County, the Malone property came to the
L'Estranges, and eventually descended to the late Revd.
Savile L'Estrange-Malone.   Henry Malone, of Litter, High
Sheriff, 1720, belonged to the same family as Richard
Malone, Lord Sunderlin, whose brother Edmond was the
celebrated commentator on Shakespeare.   Another branch
resided at Pallas Park, in this county, once the seat of
James Tilson, who married, in 1750, Gertrude, Dowager
Countess of Kerry.

The Vaughans of Golden Grove descend from Hector
Vaughan, who hailed from Pembrokeshire.   By patent,
30th December, 1668, he obtained a grant of part of the
estate in King's County of Terence Coghlan, Attainted ;
and acquired, by marriage with Mary, only daughter and
heiress of Captain William Peisley, the estate of Golden
Grove, otherwise Knocknamese, which has ever since remained in the possession of his descendants.   William
Peisley Vaughan,[1] who lived to a very advanced age, was

[1] His two sons, Hector and Billy Vaughan, were at Athy School in
1718. See the " Autobiography of Pole Cosby," (recently published in
the Journal of the Co. Kildare Archaeological Society, vol. II., p. 90).

High Sheriff, 1738; he was succeeded by his grandson, William Peisley Vaughan, who served the same office in 1766. The male line of Vaughan became extinct in 1842, when the property devolved on Mary, wife of Samuel Dawson Hutchinson, of Mount Heaton, she being the only child and heiress of John Lloyd (a younger son of the Gloster family), by his wife, Martha Vaughan, of Golden Grove, and the property is now enjoyed by her son, William Peisley Hutchinson-Lloyd-Vaughan. Through his mother, Mr. Vaughan also represents the family of Lloyd, of Gloster, settled there for over two hundred years. For three generations, ending with the late Colonel Hardress Lloyd, members of the family represented the county in parliament. John Lloyd, of Gloster, Barrister-at-Law, was also returned in two parliaments as member for Innistiogue. He was Colonel of the Shinrone Volunteers, and through his mother, Henrietta Waller, of Castletown, county Limerick, descended from the Parliamentarian General, Sir Hardress Waller.

The family of Nesbitt is of long standing in the county, descending from Albert Nesbitt, of Tubberdaly, High Sheriff, 1710, who was a scion of the family of Woodhill, county Donegal. Gifford Nesbitt, of Tubberdaly, died in 1773, having devised the estates to his nephew, John Downing, who assumed the name of Nesbitt, and died in 1847. On the death of the latter's daughter in 1886, they passed to her cousin, Edward John Beaumont, now Beaumont Nesbitt, the present possessor.

Humphrey Minchin, of Ballynakill, county Tipperary, M.P. for that county, succeeded in 1686, on the death of his elder brother Thomas,[1] to the estate of Busherstown, formerly Butcherstown, where his descendants have since resided. On Friday, 23rd March, 1764, as recorded in the "London Magazine" for that year:—"The house of Humphrey Minchin, of Bushestown, King's County, Esq., was broke open and robbed of cash, with several Bank Notes, and was afterwards set on fire, by which his Library and Books of account were consumed, with several papers of Value, and with them some Examinations of Felony, which were next day to have been forwarded to Clonmel Assizes;

---

[1] One of his daughters married Dr. Thomas Parnell, the poet.

and suspecting this mischief was purposely contrived to destroy the said Examinations, has offered a reward of £50 for the discovery of the first Person, and £10 for each of the others." George John Minchin, D.L., with whom the male line terminated, died in 1897, when the estates came to his nephew Captain Richard Welch, now of Busherstown, who has assumed the surname and arms of Minchin.

Cangort, originally Camgart, *i.e.*, the marshy field, has been the seat of the Atkinsons since the time of James I. Anthony Atkinson, of Cangort, married, 1709, Mary, daughter of Admiral John Guy, who is said to have been instrumental in breaking the boom at the siege of Derry; he was M.P. for St. Johnstown, 1711-13, and for Belfast, 1713-14, and died in 1743, leaving numerous issue. His eldest son having died in his lifetime, he was succeeded by Guy, the second, but he, being a beneficed clergyman in the north of Ireland, Cangort was long occupied by Charles, a younger son, who acted as agent for his brother. This Charles was ancestor of the branch now settled at Ashley Park, Co. Tipperary, while the present owner of Cangort is descended from the Rev. Guy. One of their sisters married Francis Sanderson, ancestor of the late Colonel Edward James Saunderson, of Castle Saunderson, M.P.

The Bernards were a Carlow family, and the Castle Bernard branch descended from a Thomas Bernard, who settled in Birr about the middle of the eighteenth century. His name first appears on the Grand Jury in 1766, and his son, Thomas Bernard, of Castletown, now Castle Bernard, High Sheriff, 1785, took a prominent part in the Volunteer movement, raising and maintaining a corps known as the "Mountain Rangers." Thomas Bernard, junr., Colonel of the King's County Militia, who succeeded his father in 1815, was High Sheriff in the year of the Irish rebellion, and long M.P. for the county. Mrs. Caulfield French, his granddaughter, at present owns the property, and the male line of Bernard is extinct.

Like the Bernards, the Drought family came from Carlow, settling in the King's County towards the close of the seventeenth century. They resided first at Cappagowlan, otherwise Songstown, near Ballyboy. John Drought, of Cappagowlan, married Mary, daughter of

Eusebius Beasley, of Ricketstown, Co. Carlow (who was nearly allied to the Earls of Aldborough), and had, with other issue, two sons, Thomas, of the Heath, otherwise Droughtville, ancestor of the Lettybrook family ; and John, who settled at Whigsborough, which had previously belonged to Captain James Sterling, now represented by the Sterling Berry family. John Drought, junr., of Whigsborough, was High Sheriff in 1780, and Thomas Drought, of Droughtville, Colonel of Volunteers, in 1789.

The history of Leap Castle has been dealt with in another part of this book. Jonathan Darby, of Leap, great-grandson of Jonathan Darby, High Sheriff, 1674, married in 1745 Susanna Lovett, and had issue seven sons, and a daughter Sarah, wife of Sir Jonathan Lovett, Bart. Several of the sons distinguished themselves. Admiral Sir Henry D'Esterre Darby, K.C.B., who succeeded to Leap on the death of his elder brother in 1802, commanded the "Bellerphon" at the Nile ; Verney Lovett Darby, Barrister-at-Law, was sometime M.P. for Gowran, while Christopher, the youngest son, attained the rank of General in the army. The present proprietor of Leap descends from John Darby, who succeeded to the estate on the death of his brother, Admiral Darby, in 1823.

Rathrobin, the seat of Col. M. W Biddulph, was originally a castle of the Molloys, and doubtless owes its name to one Robin Molloy, The present mansion was built by the Biddulphs, about 1694, but greatly altered and enlarged by its present owner. In a Deed of 1st March, 1722, between "Francis Bidolph" and others, and Charles Sadleir, of Castletown, Co. Tipperary, the name is spelt "Rath Robin." This Francis Biddulph changed his residence to Fortal, near Birr, and his son, Nicholas Biddulph, of Fortal and Rath-robin, was High Sheriff of King's County in 1741. On the latter's death in 1762, the estates devolved on his two daughters and co-heiresses, but in 1811, by will of the survivor, Mrs. Bernard, of Castle Bernard, who died without issue, Rathrobin and Fortal came to her cousin Margaret, Lady Waller. Francis Harrison Biddulph, of Vicarstown, Queen's Co., as heir of entail immediately took proceedings against Sir Robert and Lady Waller, as a result of which he eventually succeeded to Rathrobin, while Fortal passed to his cousin, Nicholas Biddulph, of Congor,

Co. Tipperary.   Francis Harrison Biddulph, who married
1797, Mary Marsh, a descendant of the saintly Jeremy
Taylor, Bishop of Down and Connor, was grandfather of
the present representative.

The family of Wetherelt, now unknown in this country,
long resided at Castletown Clonkeen, otherwise Castle
Wetherelt.   William Wetherelt, of Castletown, married
Miss Hurd, of Lisdowney, Co. Kilkenny, and dying in
1703, was succeeded by his eldest son, Hurd Wetherelt,
High Sheriff, 1736.   Hurd Wetherelt, of Castle Wetherelt,
married, 1717, Frances Heighington, of Donard, Co.
Wicklow, and had issue an only son, Vans Wetherelt, of
Castle Wetherelt, High Sheriff, 1757, who died unmarried,
1764, and seven daughters.   Of these, Emilia, married in
1767 John Dames, of Rathmoyle, King's County, who is
now represented by the family of Longworth-Dames ; while
Frances, the youngest, became the wife of the Revd. John
Mulock, of Bellair, King's County, from whom descend the
Homan-Mulocks, and the Hon. Sir William Mulock,
K.C.M.G., Chief Justice of Ontario.   With the close of the
century the Wetherelts (or Wetheralls, as the name came
to be written) sank in importance, and appear to have lost
much of their property.   Sewell Wetherelt, of Castletown,
who married Miss Bird, of Bally-cumber, in 1779, was the
last of the family to reside there.

The Tarletons have resided at Killeigh for seven genera-
tions, and are descended from Gilbert Tarleton, a native of
Lancashire, who died at Killeigh in 1656.   Sir Banastre
Tarleton, Bart., who won such reputation during the
American War, also came from Lancashire, and was
doubtless one of the same stock.   Digby Tarleton, of
Killeigh, grandson of the original settler, married in 1705,
Arabella, daughter of William Weldon, of Rahinderry,
Queen's County, and had, with other issue, John Tarleton,
of Killeigh, whose son, John Weldon Tarleton, was on the
Grand Jury in 1778, and from him the present representative
is lineally descended.

In 1768 the name of Bor is first found on the Grand
Jury.   Cornelius Bor, of Utrecht, who settled in Dublin in
1600, was the ancestor of the Ballindoolan family, other
branches being settled at Bor Court, Co. Dublin, and Bor-
mount Manor, in Wexford.   Christopher Bor came from

Meath and settled at Ballindoolan, still the property of the descendants, about the middle of the eighteenth century ; he was High Sheriff of King's County in 1777, and married same year, Anne, daughter of Edward Loftus, of Grange, Co. Westmeath, by whom he had a son, Humphrey, of Ballindoolan, D.L., grandfather of the present proprietor. Christopher's brother Edward, who married Jane, daughter and heiress of William Peacock, of Tinny Park, otherwise Tinnemuck, King's County, was the Grand Juror of 1768.

. Like the Bors the family of Grave was of Dutch origin, and possibly derived its name from the town of Grave in Holland. It was the Revd. Joseph Grave who founded the fortunes of the family in the King's County by acquiring the Ballycommon property. A man of ability, he had been a Scholar of Trinity College ; and, in consequence of his marriage with Abigail, daughter of Right Revd. Simon Digby, Bishop of Elphin, obtained the important living of Geashill, which was in Lord Digby's gift. He died, Vicar-General of the Diocese, in 1743, leaving, with four daughters, three sons, of whom, Joseph, the youngest, was sometime Chaplain, 93rd Foot, and many years Rector of Ballycommon.

Simon Grave, of Ballycommon, the eldest son, succeeded his father, and was on roll for High Sheriff in 1747 and 1748. He died suddenly in 1750, a young man and unmarried, when the property came to his next brother, William, of Ballynagar. This William Grave, who was fond of hunting and thriftless, married twice, and died, leaving several children, of whom the survivor, Letitia, married in 1801, Revd. Franc Sadleir, D.D., Provost of Trinity College ; he had previously sold Ballycommon to Daniel Chenevix, Lt.-Colonel of the Royal Regiment of Artillery, in 1760. Like his wife, Miss Arabin, Colonel Chenevix, was of Huguenot descent ; he is at present represented by Henry Chenevix, J.P., King's County. Daniel Chenevix, of Ballycommon, was High Sheriff, 1764, and died in Dublin, 1776.

The Kings of Ballylin are a branch of the Roscommon family of King, now represented by Sir Gilbert King, Bart., and appear to have settled in the King's County about 1765. John King, who purchased Ballylin from the Armstrongs, was father of John King, M.P., High Sheriff of

U

King's County in 1782, who devised Ballylin to his nephew,
Revd. Henry King. John Gilbert King, of Ballylin, only
son of the Revd. Henry, was some time M.P., King's
County, and died unmarried in 1901, when he was suc-
ceeded by his nephew, Henry Louis Mahon, now of
Ballylin, who has assumed the surname and arms of
King.

The family of Holmes, once resident in this county at
Belmont, Liscloony, and Derryholmes, frequently repre-
presented the borough of Banagher in Parliament. Peter
Holmes, of Johnstown, Co. Tipperary, M.P. for Athlone,
1727-31, was High Sheriff of King's County 1707, and
grandfather of Peter Holmes, of Peterfield (Johnstown)
some time M.P. for Banagher. George Holmes, of Liscloony, King's Co., High Sheriff, 1713, brother of the first-
named Peter, was also M.P. for Banagher. He died in
1731, and was succeeded in the representation of Banagher
by his eldest son, Galbraith Holmes, High Sheriff, Co.
Longford, 1731, and Cavan, 1737, who does not appear
to have had a residence in King's County.

Gilbert Holmes, of Belmont, High Sheriff, 1771, married
in 1752, Mary Sanderson, of Castle Sanderson, and died,
1810, leaving issue. His eldest son, Peter Holmes, was
of Peterfield, Co. Tipperary, having inherited that estate
by will of his kinsman, Peter Holmes, of Peterfield,
M.P., who died in 1802 ; the third son, Revd. Gilbert
Holmes, afterwards Dean of Killaloe, was grandfather of
Major Hardress Holmes, now of St. David's, Co. Tipperary.

Readingstown, now Rahan, long perpetuated the family
of Reading, who seem to have settled there about the
middle of the seventeenth century. John Reading, of
Readingstown, High Sheriff, 1671, married Phoebe,
daughter of Colonel John Otway, of Cloghonan (Castle
Otway), Co. Tipperary, and died, 1690. Two of his sons,
Otway and Nicholas, settled near their mother's relatives
at Borrisoleigh, Co. Tipperary, while John, the eldest son,
succeeded to the King's County estates. This John
Reading, of Readingstown, was High Sheriff in 1703, but
subsequently removed his residence to Clonegown, in this
county, having sold his Readingstown property to the
Judge family. Exshaw's Magazine for 1757, thus notices

the death of his widow, who survived him some ten years :
" Died the widow of John Reading, late of Readingstown,
King's County, sister of the Brigadier Borr."

Arthur Judge, of Readingstown, High Sheriff, 1750, was
the eldest son of Peter Judge, of Ballysheil, King's County,
by his wife Mary, daughter of Nicholas Toler, of Graige
(now Beechwood), Co. Tipperary. Peter's youngest son,
Samuel, who succeeded his father at Ballyshiel, died in
1813, leaving three daughters and co-heiresses, viz. : Mary,
married, 1782, John Percy, of Ballintemple, King's County ;
Martha married, 1783, Very Rev. Edmund Burton, Dean
of Killaloe ; and Frances, married, 1790, Thomas Mulock,
of Kilnagarna, King's County.

Another branch of this family resided at Gageborough
(originally Gaichborough), and derived from John Judge,
an elder brother of Peter, of Ballyshiel, who married, 1703,
Elizabeth, daughter of Colonel Robert Poyntz, by Rebecca,
daughter and heiress of John Gaich, of Gaichborough, M.D.

FAMILIES REFERRED TO IN THE ABOVE.

Armstrong, of Gallen.
Atkinson, of Cangort.
Baldwin, of Corolanty.
Baldwin, of Boveen.
Bernard, of Castle Bernard.
Biddulph, of Rathrobin.
Bor, of Ballindoolan.
Bury, of Charleville.
Champagné, of River Lyons.
Chenevix, of Ballycommon.
Dames, of Rathmoyle.
Darby, of Leap.
Digby, of Geashill.
Drought, of Droughtvi"le.
Drought, of Whigsborough.
Forth, of Redwood.
Gaich, of Gaichborough.
Grave, of Ballycommon.
Heaton, of Mount Heaton.
Holmes, of Belmont.
Holmes, of Liscloony.
Hutchinson, of Mount Heaton.
Johnston, of Emell Castle.
Judge, of Ballysheil.

King, of Ballylin.
L'Estrange, of Moystown.
Lloyd, of Gloster.
Lyons, of River Lyons.
Malone, of Litter.
Minchin, of Busherstown.
Moore, of Croghan.
Mulock, of Bellair.
Nesbitt, of Tubberdaly.
Parsons, of Parsonstown.
Peacock, of Tinnemuck.
Peisley, of Golden Grove.
Percy, of Ballintemple.
Philips, of Clonarrow.
Poyntz, of Gaichborough.
Reading, of Readingstown.
Sprigge, of Cloonivoe.
Sterling, of Whigsborough.
Tarleton, of Killeigh.
Tilson, of Pallas.
Vaughan, of Golden Grove,
Wakely, of Ballyburley.
Warburton, of Garryhinch.
Wetherelt, of Castletown.

GENERAL INDEX.

www.ingramcontent.com/pod-product-compliance
Lightning Source LLC
Chambersburg PA
CBHW071640270326
41928CB00010B/1990